THE
CRACKED CORNUCOPIA
or
SCOTLAND'S PATTERN OF HISTORY

Essays towards a cultural history

by

Robert H.S. Robertson

Resource Use Institute Ltd.,
Dunmore, Pitlochry, PH16 5ED, Perthshire,
Scotland

1993

By the same author
MINERAL USE GUIDE
or Robertson's Spiders' Webs
(Cleaver-Hume Press, London 1960, 1961)

with A.G. Clement
SCOTLAND'S SCIENTIFIC HERITAGE
(Oliver and Boyd, Edinburgh, 1961)

FULLER'S EARTH: A HISTORY
of calcium montmorillonite
(Volturna Press, Hythe, Kent, 1986)

HISTORY OF CLAY RESEARCH
IN GREAT BRITAIN
(The Mineralogical Society, London, 1989)

"It is the perpetual struggles of man to acquire abilities, to hold back disorder, to frame a firm civilisation, to climb out of selfish passions into reasonable civic life; that is the theme of our search into these dim ages which have many lessons to teach us in search of the betterment of the world"

Written in a shaky hand by Petrie in hospital in his 89th year.
M.S. Drower, p.422

R H S Robertson © 1993
ISBN 1 872579 03 5
Typeset by Wordwright
Communications, Aberfeldy
Printed by Milne, Tannahill
& Methven, Ltd., Perth

in Baskerville,

Contents

Appendixes

NOTE:

When quoting authors, I use their spelling; thus Ramessu II and Rameses II were the same person.

Following T.E. Lawrence's *The Seven Pillars of Wisdom,* (1935 ed.) p.25, I admit lack of consistency.

Illustrations

Figure

Tables

Acknowledgments

Twenty days before I was born, my parents attended a Friday Evening Discourse by Professor W.M.Flinders Petrie at the Royal Institution on 28th April 1911. The subject, *The Revolutions of Civilisation,* was later expanded to a small book, which became the most consulted one at home. My grandfather Hugh Hutton Stannus was Petrie's architectural photographer at Abydos in 1902-3. I am grateful to my father, Sir Robert Robertson, for taking me to meet Petrie, impressive in his old age.

I wish to thank Dr I Eiddon S Edwards for providing dates from the Cambridge Ancient History, of which he had been one of the editors for the previous fifteen years, and from later work; Dr Gayre of Gayre; Dr Edward C Kirby; and Dr Jacques Martin of Nice, France, for helpful criticism; Mr Ron B Greer of the Resource Use Institute and Robbie the Pict for the loan of books and other help; Mr Robin L.C.Lorimer for directing me to tragic events in the reign of Nero; Mr Michael E Walker, editor of *The Scorpion* (see Bibliography) for permission to reproduce parts of several articles which I wrote for him; the University of St Andrews for letting me use the library and their Mr Kenneth Fraser for guiding me to the literature on the Ligurians; and I also wish to thank Mr Murray G Dickson for reminding me "that the best is the enemy of the good" - that I should not decline to go ahead with these studies because I do not know the answer to all the problems I encounter.

I am most grateful to Miss Jenny Nevile, who specially prepared for this book Figs 14a,b and 15a,b, showing the first three notes of European, Scottish, North American and Australian Aboriginal songs, and to Dr Graham Pont, senior lecturer in the Centre for Liberal and General Studies at the University of New South Wales, Australia. And to Mrs Janet Wilkie for calling my attention to some aspects of life among the Hopi Indians.

I also thank Professor Mariya Gimbutas for allowing me to reproduce ceramic designs which suggest the meaning and antiquity of round dances; and Peter Berresford Ellis for letting me quote his words on the Coligny Calendar; and, very gratefully, Dr R. Stuart Haszeldine, for finding many valuable works in biosocial science, and for his sound advice and encouragement, when it was badly needed.

Father Rupert Loughlin, Pitlochry very kindly gave me a commentary on the subject of predestination.

I nearly forgot to thank the Royal Bank of Scotland for asking the Bank of Santander to send me a copy of Henri Guiter's translations of the Pictish ogham inscriptions. For the story of Troy I am indebted to Ian Wood and the BBC, and the map of 7th century trading cities in Europe to Dr Richard Hodges, Director of The British School of Rome. My special thanks go to Derek Pretswell whose criticism of the text has led to many improvements. In answer to him I should explain that I use the word 'I' where I am the author or discoverer; and the word 'we' where I mean you, the reader, and myself travelling together on this unconventional quest for knowledge about the past.

Finally, for a good biography of Sir William Matthew Flinders Petrie, KBE, FRS, FBA, see *Flinders Petrie, A Life in Archaeology* by Margaret S. Drower from which I have made a few quotations. The present book is the development and updating of only one of Petrie's discoveries, the structure or pattern of history.

Introduction

The cultural history of a country is a history not of great leaders, revolutionaries, kings or queens but of the arts such as sculpture, literature and music. Yet this book is not a history of art in a full sense, but only a way of throwing light on the periodic rise and fall of civilisation in Europe and neighbouring areas during the last 9000 years or so. Civilisation itself is hard to define; Kenneth Clark in his famous series of talks on BBC television (1969) admitted that he couldn't define it in abstract terms. He followed John Ruskin in believing, on the whole, that "Great nations write their autobiographies in three manuscripts, the book of their deeds, the book of their words and the book of their art. Not one of these books can be understood unless we read the two others; but of the three the only trustworthy one is the last." Clark could not bring himself to dwell on the decline and fall of a period of civilisation, preferring to bring to the public in his inimitable style the greatest works of the 'high summer' of civilisation during the last 1000 years.

Other authors also restrict their time-scale with loss of clarity. Jean-François Revel (1985) for example says, correctly, that "democracy is a relative newcomer on the historical scene. In certain areas, it is only approximately 200 years old: in other areas, it is of very much more recent origin. Characterised by participation, self-criticism, debate, tolerance and consent, it is a fragile system of government; and who is to say that it is not a historical accident, a brief parenthesis, that is closing before our eyes?"

This book will seek to find answers to the question "what must Democracy do to be saved?" I do not believe that the question can be answered in the light of experience in the years 1791-1991 alone. A much longer perspective is required, millenia perhaps rather than centuries. Then if we can see how we stand in the course of European history and study its great cultural peaks and its Dark Ages, we should perhaps be able to decide upon an acceptable course of action.

Failing to take a long view of history our political leaders also fail to take a long projection into the future. At best all planning is short-term and based on anachronistic ideologies; at the worst it scarcely exists; crisis follows crisis. If a crisis is resolved in a spectacular manner, as in the Falklands war, other impending crises remain unattended. It does not matter whether the aggrieved parties win or lose, the disruption and cost to society is enormous; and when the crisis is ended, innumerable protestors sink back spiritually exhausted. Desirable reforms are weakened because of this debilitating procedure. What is it that makes democracy so vulnerable? Power in the wrong hands, especially in the hands of special interest groups, such as business or labour, is one answer. The interpretation of the word 'democracy' is a reflection of the current culture. Can democracy become more advanced than 'radical' without resorting to discredited ideas of the right and of the left?

Our starting point is a review of the Flinders Petrie book *Revolutions of Civilisation*. His early dates were wildly incorrect; these have now been corrected by reference to more recent sources (see Chapter 10), which are based on written and astronomical evidence.

Petrie, (1853-1942), was a scientist with a sensitive, critical and artistic eye to the contemplation of works of art. The Committee of the Egyptian Exploration Fund did wisely to appoint him to begin scientific archaeological work in Egypt in 1883. One of the reasons was that he was ideally suited for putting into chronological order objects which showed gradual changes in design - typology (Chapter 1).

In his little book Petrie showed that the decline and fall of Rome was not an isolated, monstrous and inexplicable fact, as chronicled by Gibbon (1776), but was part of a recurrent phenomenon. A civilisation by his definition could persist for thousands of years but always showed rises and falls, which he called **periods** (see Chapter 2, figure 6). I have followed his convention because it avoids isolating the Greco-Roman culture from its pre-Indo-European-speaking forerunners or from the European culture, sometimes called 'Medieval', which followed. The convention shows how a civilisation developed from prehistoric times and reminds us that some prehistoric arts have survived for millenia and affect our culture today.

Petrie's methods of studying the progress of cultural history led him to enunciate eight significant discoveries - they might even be called laws - which are given in Table I; and these eight laws are summarised in the first eight chapters of this book (Figs 6 and 7).

Petrie's Eight Laws of Cultural History

1. Individual arts develop from an archaic stage, often suddenly reach a peak of near perfection and then gradually decline in taste and execution.

2. The arts follow each other in the same order: sculpture, architecture, drawing and painting, literature, music, and mechanics. These are following by wealth and then rapid decline.

3. The spread in time between the individual 'peaks' in successive periods has been widening.

4. The rise and fall of a civilisation is genetically caused.

5. *All periods begin with the infusion of new blood, with the arrival of more vigorous stock.

6. In the Classical Period of Greece and Rome it took six to eight hundred years from the Homeric Dark Age to the peak of sculpture and as long again to the Fall of Rome.

7. The rises and falls of cultural civilisation do not correlate well with religious belief and not very well with the history of philosophy or of the codification of laws.

8. Politics is not a cause of cultural change but is a consequence.

In the light of more recent knowledge this could be changed to
5. All periods begin with the infusion of new memes and genes, with the arrival of more gifted or vigorous people.

In the discussion of each law I bring in some new methods of study. The behaviour of a people is only to a limited extent controlled by its genetic composition. Petrie's analysis, however, becomes much more convincing when one bears in mind the memetic changes which occur in a population (Chapter 19). There are in history examples of true migrations of people; but there are also probably even more examples of memes being transmitted by comparatively few bearers of new ideas, of a religious , technical, linguistic or artistic nature. In Petrie's day these very different modes of transmission of qualities that spread and diffuse were not known and historians have been wise to avoid the strictly genetic analysis of history. The distinction between genetics and memetics could bring archaeologists and historical linguists together where now they are divided. Europe has been occupied by much the same people for thousands of years, but influences, of such diversity as farming and Indo-European languages have been absorbed by the ancient people. Scots are an example of an aboriginal people who have accepted many different memes, as these influences are called, and fashioned new arts from them. Scots are part of the foundation of Europe, and may have a special role to play in European affairs in the future. The Swiss, who are not unlike the Scots in this respect, are discussed in Chapter 15.

The third new method of study is mathematical. Catastrophe theory (Chapter 24) is brought in as a model of the mechanism of the periodic decline. The treatment may be more pictorial than rigorously mathematical; yet it gives some clues to desirable changes, for changes are clearly needed.

No one knows what drives civilisation forward. The pattern of history is mysterious. We pause to look at some other so far totally unexplained phenomena in the hope of finding ways of understanding them.

Finally a summary is given of some areas of work in the Resource Use Institute which encourages long term research and studies which could lead to future reforms thought to be necessary or desirable so as to avoid the unpleasant prospect of a decline towards another Dark Age or a very long haul up for those who have had a Dark Age within the last few centuries. We also look at the impact on each other of peoples who are in different phases of history.

Not all the lines in the pattern of history are related to the arts. Petrie found that there was a line through peaks of wealth and one for what I call 'civilisational wars'. I have added a wedge-like phenomenon, called 'mindless wars', as well as, in appendixes, 'calendrical reforms' and 'long sea journeys', which also have lines of their own.

Of the fourteen linear arrangements recognised in the pattern of history, one is ominously different from the others, the wedge of 'mindless wars', which, if not understood and brought under control, could prematurely destroy European civilisation. Perhaps it has. Hence the title *The Cracked Cornucopia*.

I owe much to Sir Gavin de Beer's Rede Lecture (1965). He had "attempted to sketch a picture with a very broad brush on a very large canvas" and was aware that nearly everything he had said might be controverted. What he had been principally concerned to do was to show how natural science, in his case genetics, anatomy, and physiology, can be applied to problems of history and prehistory. I have added typology of artefacts, some features of music and dancing, memetics, and catastrophe theory and other observations, bringing together many apparently unrelated parameters in an attempt to visualise the multi-dimensional complex of cultural history.

Sir Gavin finished his lecture with the words "Our unique cultural heritage is so rich that it has become split into many streams, and if only some of them could be knitted together again, knowledge and pleasure would be greatly enriched. The present book is my own effort to make the history of culture a happy hunting-ground for many.

This is a book of discovery. My main function is to bring to the attention of the reader what at first appears to be a wonderful collection of unconnected facts and to show that there are unsuspected but meaningful connections. We become aware of new faculties in our minds and of new ways of looking at the world. Our teacher in this process could be J. B.S. Haldane (Dronamraju, 1985).

Haldane abandoned the selfish culture of England and identified himself in his last years with India. Another Nobel prizewinner, Sir James Black has recently been installed as Chancellor of Dundee University. Just before moving north he told *The Courier and Advertiser's* Medical Reporter that he was very happy to be going home (he comes from Fife) and was very flattered to be asked. Dundee has a lot of areas of excellence, work of international standing ... (it is) in a position to do things which here in London we find quite hard.

"It's possible to be more independent when you're away from the centre of things where there's tremendous pressure of space, budget and organisation.

"Scotland has a very good reputation for independence in scholarship, for coming up with great new ideas which run at variance to the standard things and partly this may have something to do with the people who live there. I dare say it is a cultural question."

Chapter 1
Law No 1 The Typology of Sequences of Designs

Individual arts develop from an archaic stage, often suddenly reach a peak of near perfection, and then gradually decline in taste and execution.

Petrie was interested in the history of ordinary people and not just in their rulers or upper class. He focussed therefore on everyday objects and diverted archaeology from the hunting for art treasures in palaces and temples. His method of exploring a whole site, throwing light on the whole population, was crucial to his understanding of what life was like from earliest times.

Even in the first, prehistoric period of Egypt, patterns on **white slip bowls** showed the rise and fall in this art (Fig. 1). In the archaic stage the basketwork lines are carefully imitated. In the middle stage the design "has almost freed itself from the basket origin and has become a clear and independent design, a Maltese cross with sprigs between the arms. In the late stage only an unintelligent degradation of the basket pattern has survived."

EGYPT. I<small>ST</small> PERIOD.

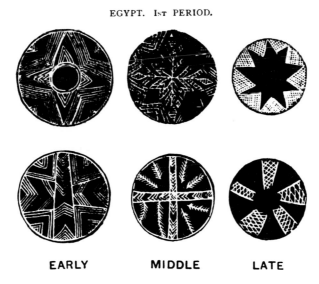

EARLY   MIDDLE   LATE

Fig. 1
Growth and decay of patterns on white slip bowls

Petrie's second period showed even more distinctly the growth and decay of **flintwork**. Fig. 2 shows the early, middle and late stages in the art of working flint. The intricate scalloping of flintwork at its peak makes one marvel at the skill of these prehistoric craftsmen. Also in Fig. 2, **animal figures** engraved on slate are shown to degrade from a neat clear drawing to a senseless outline. Contemporary pottery had become rough, without any artistic feeling.

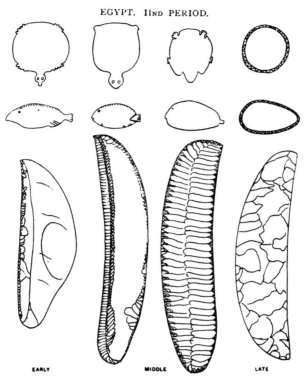

EGYPT. IInd PERIOD.

EARLY   MIDDLE   LATE

Fig 2.
Growth and decay of slate animal figures and of flintwork

Another example of Petrie's first law is given by the growth and decay of representation of **the Royal Hawks**, emblems of the king's soul. In Fig 3, the eight pictures at the beginning are of the kings of the Ist dynasty, the other four are of the IInd and IIIrd dynasty. The first figure, of the time of Mena, hardly attempts the characteristics of a hawk. In the second figure the form of the wings and the shape of the head have been designed. The third figure shows us the type at its best, the points of the bird having been fully grasped, as in the detail of the marking near the eye and on the neck, the feathering of the legs and the gripping claws. The fourth observes these points, but in the artificial style of the copyist. The fifth and sixth rapidly deteriorate; later figures even lose the form of the head; the type is copied as a matter of mere routine. It was no coincidence that the largest and finest tombs come from the time of the third figure and that the best stone vases also come from this time.

Fig.3.
Growth and decay of Hawk figures.

The development of cultural peaks was best illustrated by Petrie's many photographs of **sculpture** from the literate period of ancient Egypt (periods IV to VI) to the Classical period (VII).

Some of the archaic work is vigorous and appealing but recognisable as being before the prime by being only "good in parts". When sculpture reaches its peak, there is bold handling of the stone masses, delicacy and sureness of touch, good balance, good use of the material in proportion and artistic simplicity. In the continuous decline that follows there may be overelaboration for a while, then dull and tasteless copying; finally very poor craftmanship.

About 450 B.C. Greek sculpture reached its peak. He noted the perfect freedom of work in the famous figure of the piping maiden upon the end of the Ludovisi throne (Petrie's fig 40) and the stele of Hegeso (his fig. 1). "The great mass of Greek sculpture gradually fell off from this standard during several centuries. Then next came the still lower Roman copies of Greek work, of wearying banality, until we reach the stumpy, clumsy figures of the age of Constantine, or the still coarser outlines from the catacomb tombs, such as that of Bellicia."

For period VIII Petrie gives as an example of the most perfect medieval sculpture the head of Emperor Henry VI at Bamberg about 1245 AD. European sculpture from then on deteriorated as may be seen in some dreadful alabaster figures in 16th and 17th century churches.

Fig. 4
Anonymous, after 1258. Statue of ADAM, detail, in limestone.
Musée des Thermes et de l'Hôtel de Cluny, Paris (1989)

In his table showing the date when archaism was finally abandoned in sculpture, Petrie had narrowed the time down to 1240. Aiming to check Petrie's judgment I visited an exhibition covering hundreds of years of ivory figurines at the Victoria and Albert Museum. There were two carvings which sprang to the eye as being the first to be free of archaic traits: they were dated 1230 and 1240AD on labels so small that they could not be read when the search for the 'sculpture peak' was being made.

Petrie's dating was also confirmed by the editor of the Musée de Cluny guide (1990) who writes of "a group of work which features roundish faces, often with almond-shaped eyes, drapery with deep folds ending with "tear-drop" or pointed beak shapes, which reflect the "stylistic revolution" that occurred in Paris around 1240, an example being the Last Supper. Certainly what remains of the twelve apostles, sculpted for the Saint-Chapelle de Paris before 1248 are very fine in the handling of drapery. The head of an anonymous Adam (fig. 4) carved in limestone after 1258, though perhaps too slavishly classical Greek in the portraiture, has a brilliantly executed hairstyle.

Even as late as 1283 the funeral effigy of Blanche de Champagne shows a most characterful lady with a whimsical smile in the difficult medium of beaten brass supported on a wooden core. I have found that I agree closely with Petrie's judgment in typological dating of artifacts of the present millenium.

These studies also show that size is no object in the pattern of cultural history. A sculptor is a sculptor whether he produces a colossus or a hand-held object.

A steady decline in execution is notable in **English church brasses**, Fig 5, some of the best work in this medium having been done on the Continent in the 13th century. Certainly the archaic stage is not to be seen in England. As Petrie describes them "Perhaps the most perfect in design is that of Joan de Cobham in 1320, and for the grace of attitude and flow of the drapery this is unsurpassed. Descending a century, we meet the stiff lines, bad anatomy of the arms, and formal expression of Lady Bagot in 1407. In 1512, the style has become stiff and wooden, as in the brass of Anne Astley, with the swaddled twins in her arms. Another century on, by 1605, we have passed out of all the traditions, and reach an age of trivial externals in the figure of Aphra Hawkins".

49. JOAN DE COBHAM.
1320.

50. LADY BAGOT.
1407.

51. ANNE ASTLEY.
1512.

52. APHRA HAWKINS.
1605.

Fig. 5.
The decline of engraving on English church brasses
(*Petrie's Figs. 49 to 52*)

Degradation in style can also be seen in the **seals** of monarchs and others. "Perhaps the most perfect artistic feeling on any seal is seen in that of Simon de Montford, engraved about 1240." "By the 15th century the designs had become heavy, formal, and badly proportioned."

Chapter 2
Law No 2 The Arts' Consistent Order

The arts follow each other in the same order; sculpture, architecture, drawing and painting, literature, music and mechanics. These are followed by wealth and rapid decline.

Petrie, as we have seen, reckoned that in Period VIII **sculpture** reached its peak in 1240 AD. He used the same criteria for **painting**; and saw that there was no work of Giotto that is beyond the archaic stage, down to 1330. "The chapel of S Felice at Padua shows that as early as 1379 complete freedom was attained by Altichiero and Jacopo d'Avanza;" they were not fully surpassed by other masters till about 1450. The date 1400 was taken by Petrie for the peak of this art.

For **literature** Petrie took 1600 as the peak. Perhaps the date can be given more accurately. Sir Edmund Chambers (1929), an authority on the dating of Shakespeare's works, wrote that "in Richard III (1592-93), [autumn to autumn] he begins to come to his own with the subtle study of the actor's temperament which betrays the workings of a profound interest in the technique of his chosen profession. The style of the earliest plays is essentially *rhetorical*; the blank verse is stiff and little varied in rhythm; and the periods are built up of parallel and antithetic sentences [a formalist trait of archaism] and punctuated with devices of iterations, plays upon words, and other methods of securing emphasis, that derive from the bad tradition of a popular stage, upon which the players are bound to rant and force the note in order to hold the attention of a dull-witted audience." Freedom from these archaic devices came with *The Taming of the Shrew* ('93-'94), *Love's Labour's Lost* ('94-'95), *A Midsummer Night's Dream* ('95-'96), *Romeo and Juliet* ('94-'95), *Richard II* ('95-'96) and *Two Gentlemen of Verona* ('94-'95). The peak of literature as defined by Petrie could be said to be 1594±1, rather than 1600-01, the year of Twelfth Night and Hamlet, which are more highly developed works.

He admits that **music** is more difficult to estimate impartially. "Perhaps we may say that Haydn was still archaic in most of his life, but steps freely for the first time in his great symphonies of 1790; while Beethoven shows some memories of archaism only in his earlier symphonies, from 1796 onward. Hence, perhaps, 1790 may be accepted as the turning point." This agrees with Mozart's best period between *Le Nozze di Figaro*, 1786, to *Cosi fan Tutte*, 1790 and *Die Zauberflöte*, 1791, in the year of his death, two centuries ago.

This is a suitable place to say again that identifying the peak of an art has nothing to do with aesthetic judgment. In any archaic stage there is formalism; in the development after the peak, when freedom is attained, there is elaboration and later the most patent decadence. In music successive composers in a given period could 'improve' on earlier work only by the introduction of dissonance, unusual tempi, a greater richness in the choice of instruments, and finally the use of the 12 tone scale or complete atonality.

The peak of **mechanics** in the 19th century was taken as Fowler and Baker's Forth Railway Bridge, which was opened in 1890. This daring and awe-inspiring cantilever structure was roughly contemporary with Eiffel's famous, frivolous tower in Paris, built in 1889 for purely ornamental purposes, but greatly exceeded it in size, usefulness and beauty. It was made of steel rather than of cast or wrought iron.

It was when he compared the peak dates for the Greco-Roman period VII that Petrie noticed that the arts were achieving freedom in the same order, sculpture 450 BC, painting 350 BC, literature 200 BC, mechanics 0, science 150 AD, and wealth 200 AD. Since Period VII is bimodal with respect to literature, he took the mean date between Thucidides and Xenophon (380 BC) in Greece and Cicero (50 BC) in Italy. There is little evidence concerning the development of music in this period; or to allow one to judge when mechanics was at its peak. Science was greatly advanced by Ptolemy AD 150 in geography and by Galen 180 AD in medicine.

Earlier periods were handled in the same way and the peaks were plotted in his extremely interesting Fig. 57, reproduced here as Fig. 6. The graph was constructed by arranging the peaks of literature vertically to represent the 'high summer' of each period. The peaks of sculpture are the easiest to date by 'typology'. They can be traced to earlier times than literature and appear along a straight line on the left of literature. The other arts appear on the right; Petrie did not comment on their curvature, though it is obvious that the peak of wealth in his diagram will never meet the line of Period VIII. He did however recognise that there would be a peak of science and a peak of wealth some time after 1911.

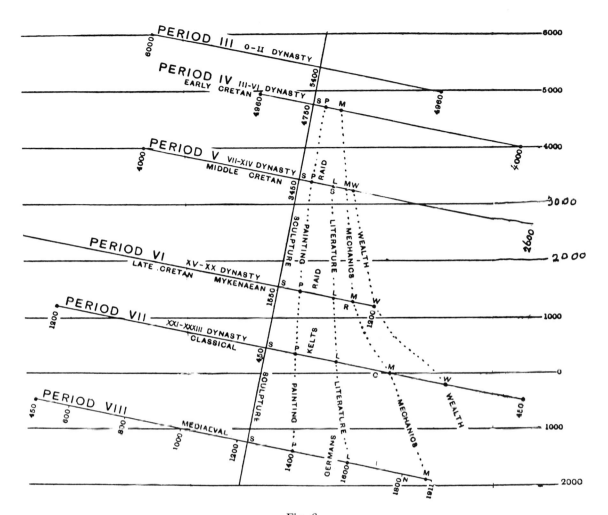

Fig. 6.
The periods of mediterranean civilisation III to VIII
(*Petrie's famous Fig. 57*)

Chapter 3

Law No 3 The Lengthening Period

The spread in time between the individual peaks in successive periods has been widening.

The most remarkable feature of this graphical representation of cultural history is the lengthening of the time between the peaks in successive periods. The lengthening period, even more clearly shown in Fig. 9, is discussed again in Chapter 23.

Chapter 4

Law No 4 The Geographical Boundaries of a Civilisation and its Genetic Origins

The rise and fall of a civilisation is genetically caused.

The ups and downs of a civilisation belong to a people or a group of peoples and are not restricted to a clearly defined geographical area. People living in a different civilisation are very likely to be in a different phase. The phasing is therefore kept by a people when it migrates to a land of a different time-phase; thus the Etruscans had their greatest power about 600 BC, not very long after Ashurbanipal, and many centuries before the Romans flourished. The Moors in Spain were akin to the Berbers and were Atlantics, whereas the Spaniards were Gothic in the upper classes at least, and there was also a Dinaric or Dinaric-Armenoid element. The Moors did not involve a markedly 'alien' racial invasion, but they did introduce some degree of genetic vigour. Their early architecture and then their scholarly activity in Spain from the 10th to the 12th century were in phase with the Mesopotamians.

So also did the Greeks retain their phase in Bactria; and Petrie thought that the phase clinging to a people could be discerned in subsequent ages, - "certainly the most flourishing period of medieval Tuscany was earlier than the rest of Italy by a few centuries, just as it had been in earlier centuries."

Now that European civilisation has spread to North America, South Africa and Australasia, the present state of culture affects them all, for they must fall and rise in one body.

Chapter 5
Law No 5 Conquest the Precursor of a Periodic Rise

All periods begin with the infusion of new blood, with the arrival of more vigorous stock.

In any Dark Age an effete or played out people can be easily conquered or taken over by a more vigorous stock or culture. It should not be understood that this kind of conquest must always be carried out by a large invasion of incomers, nor that miscegenation on a large scale occurs during a Dark Age. A new language can be imposed by a relatively small number of an élite class. Petrie says little about language as a cultural feature; many nations like the Welsh rate it highly; others like the people of Sarawak have had foreign languages forced upon them. At one time in the last century several dozen languages were spoken in that country. English then became the language of government and now it is Malaysian, all within a single lifetime. Nevertheless the forcible *replacement* of one language by another has been classified as cultural genocide (Chapter 19).

In trying to find an analogy for this type of conquest, I first thought of the subduction of a geological plate beneath the edge of a neighbouring plate it is moving towards, but an overwhelmed people is not drawn down into the depths but is covered over by outside forces, people or ideas, and by those which rise from within the mass to form a crust. I shall therefore use the word **obduction** in the Latin and English sense of covering over. Thus one may say that a people are obducted by a foreign or immiscible ruling (obducting) class. In geology, obduction means the overriding or overthrusting of oceanic crust on to the leading edges of continental plates (Coleman, 1971). It is a pity that in German *Obduktion* has come to mean a post-mortem examination!

Obduction of a population does not mean that an ancient people have completely disappeared; indeed where intermarriage between the ruling class and the aboriginals is rare and where the ruling class are not numerous, the older population may survive for millenia and parts of their culture also.

Parallel cultures can co-exist, though not always comfortably. The Ligurians may not have mixed much with the early Celts. The Irish catholics do not readily marry protestants. Nor do Guanche families in the Canary Islands join the Spanish incomers. The French Swiss are to some extent kept apart from the German Swiss though they show civilised tolerance for each other!

Chapter 6
Law No 6 The Length of Period

In the Classical Period of Greece and Rome it took six to eight hundred years from the Homeric Dark Age to the peak of sculpture and as long again to the Fall of Rome.

Petrie's diagram gives the impression that in modern periods of civilisation it takes six to eight hundred years from a Dark Age to the peak of sculpture and as long again to reach the end of a decline. On the other hand the most civilised and cultured part of the periods has greatly lengthened over six millenia. Petrie, by showing that the 'high summer' in the periods (sculpture to wealth) was lengthening, was unable to explain why cultural history is apparently slowing down, - why, for example, the peaks of sculpture and music are separated by as much as 550 years. Jacques Martin (1986) has suggested that there is in any culture an ever-increasing flow of information with intricate patterns of feedback loops. People know more about events, so they think that more is happening. As time elapses, a civilisation takes longer and longer to reach its various cultural peaks, spends more time on elaborations and on introducing new arts or sciences. Therefore one is led to a conclusion in contradiction with the common assumption. In fact there is a slowing down of history.

Today, the information flow is so great that it is full of 'noise' and is difficult to master, making decision-making more complex and very often erratic. Decision-makers have willy-nilly to take into account too many elements; a rapid increase in the flow of information can lead to stale-mate in the decision-making process, - to nothing effective being done because the leaders of society are afraid of not mastering the consequences of their decisions.

Chapter 7
Law No 7 Civilisation and Religion

The rises and falls of cultural civilisation do not correlate well with religious belief and not very well with the history of philosophy or of the codification of laws.

That a civilisation's rises and falls do not correlate well with religious belief may be illustrated by the transcendance and persistence of Christianity right through the last European Dark Age. It was founded before the Fall of Rome in 410 AD; it survived in Byzantium and elsewhere; and sustained people in their long haul upwards. The church was a great patron but not directly the creator of the succession of arts. The creativeness resided in the people.

Chapter 8
Law No 8 Government and Politics

Politics is not a cause of cultural change but is a consequence.

In Petrie's words "government is of great concern but of little import. Constitutional History is a barren figment compared with the permanent value of Art, Literature, Science or Economics". I agree, except that I would omit the discipline of economics. Petrie continues "What man *does* is essential in each civilisation, how he advances in capacities, and what he bequeathes to future ages; the relations between the different classes of a country are merely subsidiary" - or so it seemed in 1911.

After an invasion in a Dark Age, thought Petrie, there must be strong personal rule. "The holding together of the invaders, the decisive subjection [obduction] of the invaded, the strife of the fusion of peoples, all require an autocracy of greater or lesser scope - This last stage lasts during four to six centuries".

The next stage is an oligarchy, when leadership is still necessary but the unity of the country can be maintained by law instead of by autocracy. In Greece and Rome this stage lasted about four centuries; in Medieval Europe about five or six centuries.

"Then gradually the transformation to a democracy takes place, beginning about the great phase of literature in Greece, Rome and Modern Europe. During this time of about four centuries wealth - that is the accumulated capital of facilities - continues to increase," though not without setbacks through wars, as we shall see elsewhere. "When democracy has attained full power, the majority without capital necessarily eats up the capital of the minority, until the weaker population is swept away to make room for a stronger people. The consumption of all the resources of the Roman empire, from the second century when democracy was dominant until the Gothic Kingdom arose on its ruin, is the best-known example in detail.," Hence it can be said that politics is not a cause of cultural expression but a consequence.

As Oswald Spengler put it (1917), "the more formless and feckless the electoral mass, the more completely is it delivered into the hands of the new powers, the party leaders, who dictate their will to the people through all the machinery of intellectual compulsion; fence with each other for primacy by methods which in the end the multitude can neither perceive nor comprehend; and treat public opinion merely as a weapon to be forged and used for blows at each other.... But this very process, viewed from another angle, is seen as an irresistible tendency driving every democracy further and further on the road to suicide."

Or, as Jonathan Swift wrote, "whoever could make two ears of corn or two blades of grass grow upon a spot of ground where only one grew before would deserve better of mankind than the whole race of politicians put together." This is our justification for focussing on creative achievements and for thinking about how to invent a more stable and acceptable form of democracy in which all the talents of a people are pooled and given a chance to be expressed for the common need and for the special needs of individuals.

Chapter 9
How Petrie's book was received

C.E. Kenneth Mees, D.Sc., F.R.S., Vice-President in charge of Research, Eastman Kodak Company, Rochester, New York, developed his idea of the Helix of History on the basis of Petrie's *Revolutions of Civilisation* (1911) in his valuable book *The Path of Science* (1946) and gave a summary of previous views about Petrie's book, not having noticed that Bernard Shaw had quoted it with approval in his Presidential Address to the British Academy (*Proceedings*, 1919, p.3 ff) Petrie himself thought that *Revolutions of Civilisation* was his most important book and that it had been for this that he had received his knighthood in 1923. (MS Drower, p303)

R.G. Collingwood (1927), for example, questioned the value of his standards of artistic achievement, pointing out that what Petrie calls decadent another critic of art might consider beautiful. "Beauty is in the eye of the beholder" he claimed, and there are no dark ages except in the sense in which every age is dark, and there are no decadences. Yet he failed to realise that Petrie's assessment of a work of art was technical and had nothing to do with the enjoyment the work gave at any time. Schönberg's music is only technically overelaborate, having moved so far from the breakaway from archaic features in music in Mozart's time; yet it is greatly admired by many musical people in the 20th century. "Modern Art" is likewise classified as decadent by Petrie's precise definitions, yet its exhibitions draw many admirers.

Also, writing in *Antiquity* (1931), O.G.S. Crawford started with Petrie's idea that the development of a new phase of civilisation depends upon the crossing of two stocks having their own cultures and concluded that each phase has a life of its own and may be regarded as if it were a species composed of living creatures. "Thus the life of each phase corresponds to the life of a species as a whole; the units composing the phases at any moment of history correspond to the individuals composing the species; and a phase, therefore, is born and passes through maturity to decline and extinction, just as does an individual", an idea he admitted was not new since Sir Arthur Keith (1928) had written "The resemblance between the body physiological and the body politic is more than an analogy; it is a reality".

Mees dismissed Collingwood's views, as I do, on the grounds that Petrie's cycles are not based on any view of beauty by the onlooker; they are based on the technical skill shown in execution. He accepted Petrie's general thesis of periods in the history of civilisation but redrew his chart in the light of J.H. Bearsted's new (but still pre-14 Carbon) dating of 3000 BC as the beginning of the Egyptian Third Dynasty and 1800 BC as the end of the Twelfth Dynasty. He found it was no longer possible to draw a straight line for sculpture and the cycles clearly differed in length, the early ones lasting only about 500 years, while the classical and medieval cycles lasted 1650 and 1500 years, respectively. This he felt was wrong, so, in a second revision of the chart three periods of history were omitted, the Hyksos invasion of Egypt 1800-1600 BC, the Dark Age in Greece 1200-1000 BC, and the "Dark Ages" 450-1000 AD. No reason was given for these changes but, by dividing the Greco-Roman and the Medieval periods into two, periods were made to look as if they lasted for 500 years. In this way he managed to show the beginning of a Modern Period not at a Dark Age like all the other periods but at a time of high culture when experimental science began to be effective. Modern science, in Petrie's treatment of this theme is a series of cultural peaks between Mechanics and Wealth; and I see no reason to change the rules for plotting cultural history simply to disguise Europe's unfortunate position on a declining slope. It took Mees two unjustified revisions to make it appear that European civilisation has been on the up and up since 1700 AD. It is only science that has had its rapidly succeeding peaks in the last three centuries. My more strict revision of Petrie's diagram in the light of recently accepted dating shows that in Europe only those in the North Western countries and probably Switzerland can be in the happy state of moving upwards from a Dark Age about 1720 AD.

By 1989 one was less assured that a Dark Age was always accompanied by massive conquest and miscegenation; but could accept that a people declining in vigour would always be a prey to takeover by an aggressive class of foreigners, such as armies or businessmen. The conquerors may not always have married into the older population.

There is little doubt that the genetic element in human history, much neglected by historians before Petrie, had no chance of being seriously studied after Hitler. Political teaching of the Left supported nurture to the exclusion of nature in the rather sterile argument about which was the more important in the development if human beings. The Eugenics Society wisely changed its name to the Galton Society and the growing, more scientific interest in heredity led to the formation of the Biosocial Society as well. The time has come then to reconsider the *Revolutions of Civilisation* in a more enlightened way.

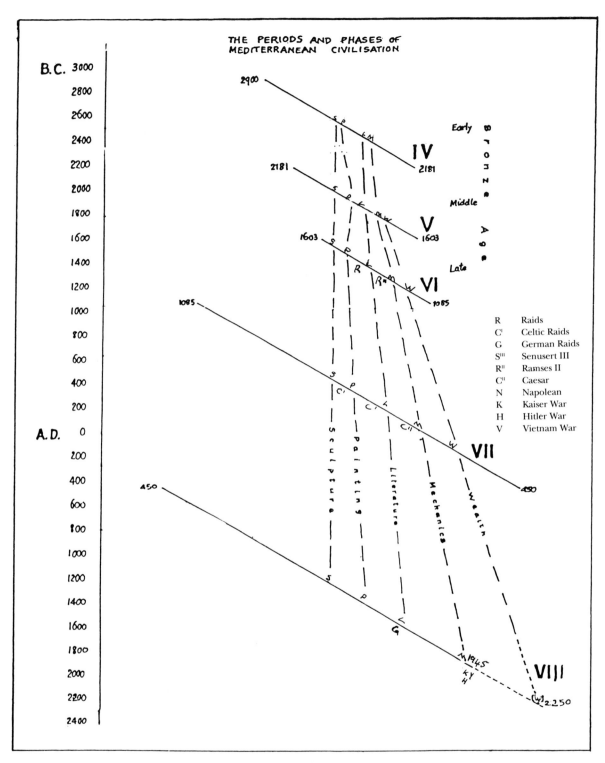

Fig. 7
The periods and phases of Mediterranean civilisation. Periods IV to VIII revised.

16

Chapter 10
PETRIE UNPETRIFIED
The date corrections

When it became known that Petrie's early dates were erroneous *Revolutions of Civilisation* was discredited and, in the end, almost forgotten. On the advice of Dr. I. Eiddon S. Edwards, one-time keeper of the Egyptian and Assyrian collections in the British Museum, I adopted dates drawn from the Cambridge Ancient History and, later, from J. von Beckerath's *Abriss der Geschichte des alten Ägypten* (1971)). These are shown, alongside Petrie's in Table 1.

Corrections to dates given by Petrie
Table 1 – Egyptian Dates

Period	Peak			Petrie B.C.		Accepted here B.C.
IV	S		Sneferu	4750	c.	2590
	P		Nefermaat	4700?	c.	2540
	M		Assa	4650?	c.	2490
V	S		Rise of the XIIth dynasty	3450		1980
	P		Senusert II's death	3396		1929
	L		Hymn of Senusert III	3320	c.	1860
	M		Amenemhat III's tomb	3270		1797
	W		End of dynasty	3250		1788
VI	S		Early in Amenhotep I	1550	c.	1525
	P		Tahutmes III	1470		1470
	L		Akhenaten's Hymn to the Aten	1380		1365
	M		Colossi of Ramessu II	1280		1280
	W		Ramessu III	1180		1180

S=sculpture   P=painting   L=literature   M=mechanics   W=wealth

The revised diagram (fig 7, having the benefit of modern dating from written and astronomical evidence) shows that the cultural lines are practically straight, and we can see for the first time how structured and precise is the rise and fall of periods of **civilisation**.

Kenneth Clark (1969) was right in saying that the enemies of (high) civilisation are fear of war, plague and famine - and of the supernatural. He knew that in the most civilised times in history there was confidence in one's own mental powers. Vigour, energy, vitality made a civilisation as conceived by him. By restricting his idea of civilisation to what Petrie called its 'high summer', Clark had no idea of where we are going, and commented that "sweeping, confident articles on the future seem to me, intellectually, the most disreputable of all forms of public utterance. The scientists who are best qualified to talk have kept their mouths shut". More profoundly J.B.S. Haldane summed up the situation when he said "my own suspicion is that the universe is not only queerer than we suppose, but queerer than we can suppose".

The only alterations I have made in the construction of the diagram are to plot the sculpture peaks vertically and to add K, H and V to indicate the Kaiser, Hitler and Vietnam wars as these were very serious checks in the course of European (and Western) history.

Of course, many features of Petrie's diagram are preserved in the redated version. Of interest are the recurrence of raids, usually from the north, between the cultural peaks of Painting and Literature in Periods V, VI and VII; and shortly before the Mechanics peak were the wars of Senusert III, Rameses II, Julius Caesar and Napoleon. All of these may be described (not very aptly maybe) as 'civilising' wars because the conquerors brought laws, roads, trade or units of measurement in their wake. The pattern of history in this respect has been quite extraordinarily regular.

But how can one explain the terrible and apparently 'mindless' wars which disgraced the first half of this century? I submit that the murder of six million Jews and the atrocities of the three wars named are not in any way features of a high culture. On first reflection one could say that a Dark Age had begun in 1916, the battle of the Somme, or in 1945, when the two bombs were dropped on Japanese cities. It looks as if civilisation had collapsed prematurely, since a true Dark Age would not be expected before about 2430 AD. If a Dark Age had indeed begun prematurely it was strangely illumined by the cultural momentum of some very striking peaks of attainment, such as in polymers, communications, data processing, computer control in industry. Eagerly awaited are benign results of biotechnology. Possibly within 20 or 30 years the greatest peak of all may come, an acceptable form of family planning and population control. To account for these brilliant developments in a time of decline one would have to postulate a series of "ivory castles" in which the research workers were to a large extent protected from the nastiness of a decaying social culture around them. Indeed about 50 per cent of all scientists are working in the 'defence' industries and are somewhat protected and isolated. An explanation for this strange state of affairs was not apparent until later in these investigations into history (chapter 38 on Human Progress, a Present Review)

Chapter 11
The Geographical Boundaries of a Civilisation and Time's Spiral.

In spite of inaccurate, early dating Petrie clearly showed that Mesopotamian civilisation was never in phase with the Mediterranean (Egypt and Europe). The Mesopotamian periods were always some centuries before the West's. This was often a misfortune for the middle East because when they were at a low ebb they became subordinate to Europe. The opposite is also true.

The probability arises that somewhere in the world there may be some peoples who will be at or near a high stage of civilisation. Further study is needed to determine whether Japan, for example, is in this happy position, or how China and the eastern parts of Russia lie. The massacre at Beijing in 1989 indicates a low point in a period.

Petrie's Mesopotamian dates also had to be corrected - Table 2.

Table 2
Mesopotamian Times of High Culture

	Petrie's dating	Recent dating
Enneatum	4450BC	~2500 BC
Naramsin	3750	~2291-2255
Khammurabi	2100	~1792-1750
Ashurbanipal	640	640
El Mamun	820AD	820AD

The amended dates not only failed to fit Fig 6, depicting Mediterranean civilisation, but were similar to some dates in Scottish history and prehistory. By combining Mesopotamian dates with events in the north and northwest of Europe we can see (Fig 8) that neither of these areas have European affinities. However, at this stage of the study the time-phase relationship between these countries beyond the borders of European civilisation was not clear. Our interest was aroused by Renfrew, Thom and Gayre.

According to Renfrew (1977) the impressive stone buildings of Maes Howe in Orkney date from 2300 BC about the time of Naramsin, selected by Petrie as being a distinguished figure contributing to a high state of culture. The dates of the Neolithic observatories, described by Alexander Thom (1971), cluster around 1700BC and are only a little later than Khammurabi, the lawmaker (about 1792-1750 BC). Indeed lawmakers like Khammurabi and Solon, who flourished in Athens in 594BC, laid the foundations for a state of high culture; so the East and Northwest are fairly closely in phase. R Gayre of Gayre commented that the builders of megalithic works may have been Atlanto-Mediterraneans, whose monuments are found all the way from Malta to Scotland.

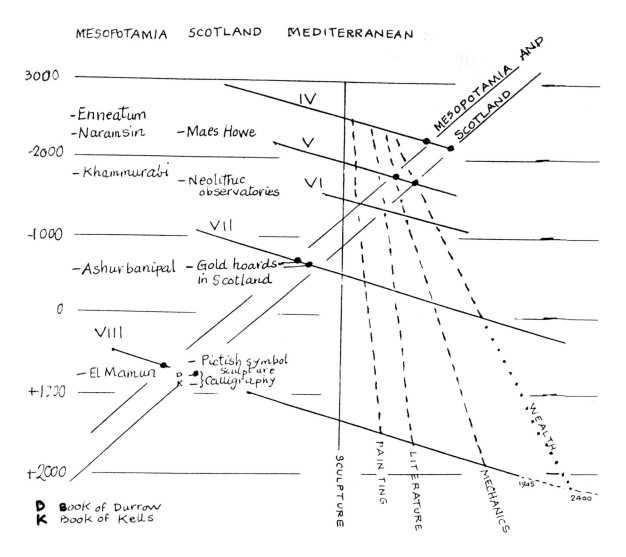

MESOPOTAMIA   SCOTLAND   MEDITERRANEAN

3000

-Enneatum
-Naramsin   -Maes Howe

-2000

- Khammurabi
            - Neolithic
              observatories

-1000   VII

-Ashurbanipal   - Gold hoards
                  in Scotland

0

VIII

- El Mamun   - Pictish symbol
                    sculpture
              }Calligraphy

+1000

+2000

D Book of Durrow
K Book of Keils

MESOPOTAMIA AND SCOTLAND

IV
V
VI

SCULPTURE PAINTING LITERATURE MECHANICS WEALTH

1945   2400

Fig. 8   Phase difference between Mesopotamia - and - Scotland's
          and Mediterranean Culture

(Petrie 1911 and Robertson 1980)

Fig. 8.
Phase difference between Mesopotamia - and - Scotland's and Mediterranean Culture.
(Petrie 1911 and Robertson 1980).

In a later period several hoards of gold objects found in Scotland have been dated at about 700 BC, not long before the time of Ashurbanipal. Were these gold pieces votive offerings of an ancient people who had been genetically enriched by the Beaker Folk who settled about 1500 BC in the northeast of Scotland and eventually produced a series of banking families (Coutts, Arbuthnott, Barclay and others)? This would not be surprising since the Dinaric people (although partly Nordic) seem to be distantly related to the Armenoid. The other great region of settlement was in Yorkshire where one finds the same attachment to "brass" (=money). (Gayre 11 Jan 1978)

Fig 8 was therefore redrawn so as to enable one to calculate the beginning of European civilisation (Fig 9) and this final construction - takes Picto-Scottish cultural history on its own. Some other cultures in the same time - phase, such as the Phoenicians', the Provencal and the Swiss, are examined in later chapters.

Time's Spiral

The path of cultural history is more like a spiral than a helix as Mees saw it. Each sculpture peak occurs at an increased, not an equal, length of time, except between Periods V and VI which are anomalous. According to John Michell (1973 p.15) the movement of time was considered by ancient astronomers to move not in a circle but in a spiral! J.D. Unwin (1940) was another writer who liked to stress the spiral and undulatory nature of human history, according to Aldous Huxley's introduction to *Hopousia* (p.15).

History, seen as a spiral impressed upon a cone, is a cornucopia, the symbol of abundance. The "quarterly journal of the new economics", *Abundance*, unfortunately ceased publication in the third quarter of 1987 - a portent that thinking in this field was being discouraged. No successor was found for the learned but aged editor, V.R. Hadkins.

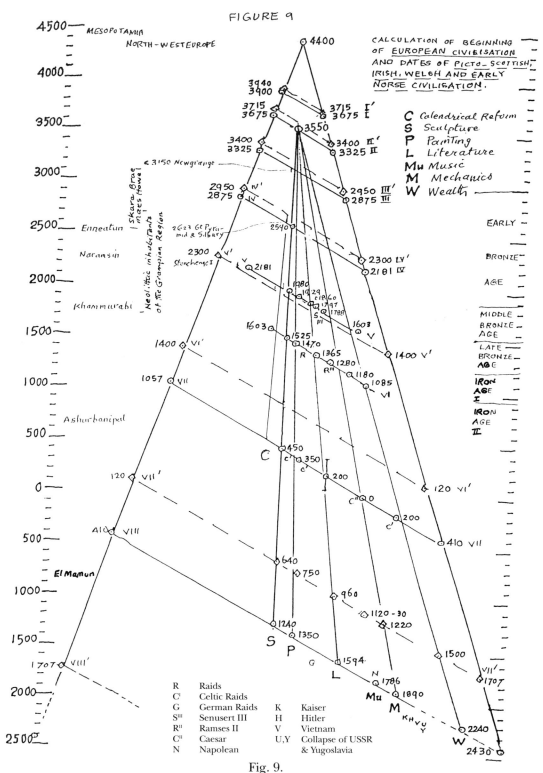

Fig. 9.
Petrie's whole diagram (Periods I to VIII) with the periods of different phase (V′ to VIII′).
© R.H.S. Robertson

Chapter 12
When did European Civilisation begin?

The triangular diagram (Fig 9) which represents the ever-lengthening periods from IV to VII can be traced backwards from 24 August 410 AD, the sacking of Rome by Alaric, the Christian chief of the Visigoths (end of period VII), through 2181 BC (end of period IV), to where that line of Dark Ages meets the continuation of the sculpture line - the baseline of the diagram. The meeting point is about 4400 BC. The cultural history of the Northwest of Europe appears to have 'begun' at the same time as that of the rest of Europe, for, about 4500 BC, when a cluster of houses was built at Quanterness in Orkney, the social life was still relatively egalitarian.

Petrie's first three, prehistoric periods by this construction would be about 3800-3600 BC for period I, 3600-3300 BC for period II and 3300-2900 BC or a little later, for period III.

The individual cultural peaks point to the year 3550 BC where they apparently meet, though it is probable that numeracy preceded literacy and that the beginnings of socially-structured, though not yet urban, life required some kind of numerical tally of traded goods. Poetry and songs would have been committed to memory, long before writing was invented or introduced.

Excavations at Balbridie Farm on Deeside, Aberdeenshire, have shown that Neolithic farmers could construct about 3500 BC a huge architecturally advanced timber building earlier than anywhere in the world for the period and on a par with the royal feasting halls of the Anglian Kings of Northumbria who lived thousands of years later. Ian Ralston, who first excavated the site with Nicholas Reynolds in 1980, said that their botanical colleague, Alan Fairweather, had examined some 15,000 charred cereal grains, which had trickled down into the post holes formed when the building was burned down 5500 years ago. About 11,000 of the grains proved to be three-quarters emmer and a fifth barley; but a separate sample collected from these post holes consisted of three quarters breadwheat and only 10 per cent emmer and 6 percent barley. The breadwheat and flaxseed, 76 of which were counted, prove that these Neolithic inhabitants of what is now Buchan, were a bright and innovative lot. Breadwheat and flax were not grown, for example, in Fife, until the Bronze Age.

It was in this period II, about 3500 BC, that hunter gatherers introduced farming methods and produced a surplus of food and wealth. This change was accompanied by division of labour and a stratification of society. Among the emerging élite class were those mathematically gifted specialists who could design astronomical devices capable of setting a calendar in order that barley and wheat could be planted at the right time. Before then observations of animal behaviour gave a clue to planting times; and even today some people in South India make calendrical calculations with no elaborate observatories.

In Northwest Europe the megalithic astro-architects built the famous summer solstice measurer at Newgrange in about 3150 BC, some thousand years before the

Stonehenge structure was used for the same purpose. In Appendix l calendrical reform is discussed as another series of cultural peaks falling on a straight line on our diagram; it is in fact the first of the arts. Lawgiving also occurs before sculpture, e.g Solon and Justinian, since a legal system was needed to be in place before the final rise to a higher style of culture could proceed.

Triskele

Chapter 13
THE BOUNDARIES OF EUROPE

Europe's eastern boundary

No one has clearly defined the eastern boundary of Europe. We have seen (Fig. 9) that the first four periods of cultural history were common to Egypt, the Continent of Europe, the northwestern countries, the northern strip of Africa as far as the Canary Islands, Mesopotamia and the Phoenicians' coastal homes in the eastern Mediterranean.

In **Egypt** between 2181 and 2160 BC there were many kings with short reigns: dissolution of royal power; and social and political chaos. The ancient artistic tradition was disrupted during this time (dynasties VII and VIII); pyramids were ransacked and statues destroyed. These violent times were part of the Intermediate Period, between the Old and Middle Kingdoms, and are shown as a break in the civilisation line between periods IV and V. The even longer break in this line, between periods V and VI corresponds with the Second Intermediate Period of Egypt between Dynasties XIII and XVII, 1786-1567 BC. Until 1603 BC Egypt suffered decay of central authority and seizure of power by the Hyksos Kings, who infiltrated from Asia. The result was a decline in artistic standards and ideas, traditional culture being replaced by Hyksos ideas and techniques down to 1567 BC. Not that all was bad. The lyre, oboe and tambourine had been introduced to the Egyptians who were ready for them as their peak of music would have been ca 1750 BC. Improvements in cloth-making were also welcome. But when Egyptians grew exasperated by their foreign rulers they turned the horse-drawn chariots and bronze weapons against the Hyksos army and administration and the Egyptian Pharaoh Ahmose I began the splendid XVIIIth dynasty (1567-1320 BC).

Table 3 is a potted history of **Troy** adapted from Michael Wood's *In Search of the Trojan War* (1985). It confirms the shortened periods V and VI, previously noticed in Egypt, and the interaction of the cultures of the ancient peoples and the Indo-European-speaking people. Wood's map of the Near East and the Aegean in the 13th century BC suggests that the eastern edge of Old Europe is a strip of country running along the south coast of the Black Sea where the Kaska tribes used to live, westwards to Troy, then south via Smyrna and Ephesus to Miletus to Halicarnassos; and on to Cyprus and that part of Turkey which is immediately north of Cyprus - that was western Cilicia as far eastwards as Tarsus. Within this tract lay the Hittite empire.

Table 3

TROY

	Founded by Neolithic settlers from Kum Tepe by the Dardanelles 3600 BC.	Beginning of period II and of settled, organised life.
I	Settlement on a sea-girt promontary, 2500 BC	Calendrical point on IV´
II	A royal citadel (Priam's treasure) until is was sacked by fire in 2200 BC	Wealth point, ca 2320 on IV´ Dark age ending period IV´
III	2200-2000 BC	Beginning of period V´
IV	2000-1900 BC	Up to calendrical point of V´
V	1900-1800 BC	Sculpture on V' [Hammurabi]
VI	ca 1760 BC Arrival of Indo-Europeans and the horse 1500 BC Contacts with Mycnean World begin ca 1250 BC Destruction of Troy VI, the 'Trojan War'	Wealth point of V´ Dark age, protracted end of period V´
VIIa	ca 1250-1180 BC Sack by 'Sea People'	the same
VIIb 1	1180-1100 BC	
VIIb 2	ca 1100-1000 BC Site abandoned soon afterwards	Destruction so complete that VI´ did not begin
VIII	700-300 BC - Greek Ilion, archaic and classical. 'A small market town'	Period VI, calendrical to sculpture, as in Greece itself. A short-lived recovery.
IX	ca 300 Hellenistic Ilion. City walks of Lysimachus. Population 3 or 4 thousand. 190 BC 'no tiles left on the roofs' 85 BC city sacked in Mithriditic war 4th-5th century AD economic life declining 6th century, city life ends 9th century, impoverished bishopric still on site 1309 AD Troad falls to Turks Founding of village of Ciplak Site finally deserted.	End of very thin period VI´ Again a feeble rise in period VII´ and Church presides over cultural disappearance of the 'Old People', as with the Picts

From Michael Wood (1985)

Development of Civilisation in Northwest Europe

As we saw in Chapter 12 the Picto-Scottish period VII´ was constructed from a time-line drawn through the peak of sculpture at 640 AD. Previous periods were simply drawn from the Dark Age of period VII´ backwards, eg 120 BC - 1400 BC for period VI´ and 1400 - 2200 BC for period V´. Periods IV´, III´, II´ and I´ appear to coincide with the Mediterranean periods IV to I. Fig. 9 shows very well the apparent anomaly of periods V and VI. Since those breaks the Picto-Scottish and related cultures have been centuries ahead of the Mediterranean.

We are now ready to 'predict' the course of Scottish cultural history from the peak of sculpture 640; we read the intercepts with the other peak-lines; these give us painting 750, literature 960, music 1120, mechanics 1220, wealth 1500 and the lowest point of a Dark Age 1720. These dates will be discussed *seriatim*.

Chapter 14
Sculpture

Working in bronze in the first millenium BC is best known in the Celtic work of Hallstatt, Austria, and continuing into the Iron Age designs of La Tène, north Switzerland. The designs of La Tène are instantly recognisable, usually because of the use of compasses in their construction. Some beautiful examples of this style, on shields and scabbards especially, may have been presents imported for tribal leaders in Britain. They and other fine work on the Continent belong to the Mediterranean period Vll. The La Tène style was attempted by a few bronze-workers in Britain during the last few centuries BC (Megaw and Megaw 1989), but this truly Celtic art form should not be confused with the native Pictish which came to a peak of perfection about 640 AD.

For the masterpieces of 'Celtic' metalwork in the 6th to 9th centuries AD, see 'The Work of Angels' as Giraldus Cambrensis called it (Susan Young 1989).

Dillon and Chadwick (1967) echoed Petrie unconsciously when they asked what are the basic qualities which we recognise in 'Celtic' or Pictish art wherever it is found; they wrote "Perhaps the most fundamental is its originality, the choice of and combination of motifs, chiefly from the world of nature, the animal and vegetable world, with only occasional and incidental human elements, the whole forming a fantastic creation of the imagination, remote from reality. An invariable element in these creations is the refinement of mind which inspires the compositions. There is a total absence of coarseness of conception or of treatment. This refinement expresses itself everywhere in delicacy of line, an unerring artistic taste in the use of flowing curves and their purpose in a given design. Some of these 'class l Pictish symbols' are represented in Fig.10.

Fig 10
Pictish animal symbols from Class I stones. *(Henderson, p.13)*

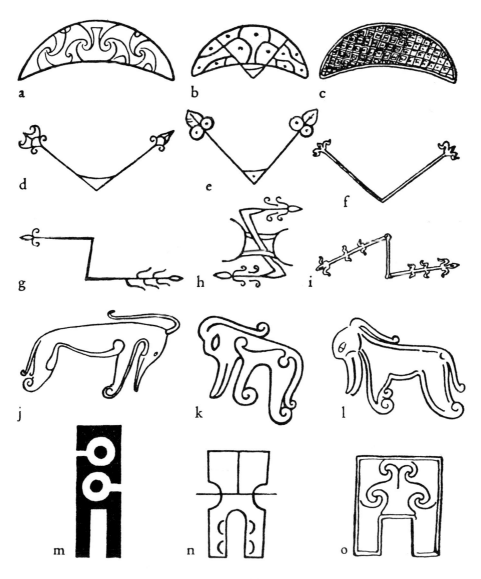

Fig 11
The declining symbol in Pictish art.   *(Henderson, p. 113)*

Not now surprisingly to us we find that by 700 AD the Class 1 symbol stones show evidence of copying and transition to 'Class ll symbol stones' (with the symbol of the cross in addition) which are ornate and not so free. Indeed, it was R.B.K. Stevenson, one time keeper of the National Museum of Antiquities of Scotland, who first pointed out decadence in the infilling of the Pictish crescent symbol; and Isobel Henderson (1967) has found other series of what she calls the declining symbol (Fig.11.). Here we have Petrie's typological law No. 1 well illustrated.

As we might expect, the peak of geometrical book design is found in the Book of Durrow, variously thought to be late 7th century or even as early as 600 AD; and the greatest Pictish work of calligraphy and illumination, the Book of Kells, was made in the 8th to 9th century. The Anglo-Saxon calligraphers were also in this phase though they introduced some elements of European La Tène art. The Pictish animal designs are not unlike Scythian art from north of the Black Sea. Certainly the Pictish deer is very like a Scythian depiction.

Petrie was the first to attempt a historical account of the *Decorative Patterns of the Ancient World* (1930). The continuous interwoven lines of late Pictish crosses come from a widely disseminated tradition. Examples can be found in Scandinavia, Tuscany, Lombardy, as well as Ireland, Scotland and England. The artists, who required an ingenious geometric construction to draw them (Bain, 1951,1977) could have belonged to the 'old people' in any of these countries. This special art appears not to be Celtic; some of its square and diagonal key patterns were first produced in the Ukraine and Yugoslavia in 20,000 to 15,000 BC (Bain, p.71)

Contemporary with Pictish art, that is from the 7th to 9th century, there was great commercial activity in the recently rediscovered towns of Dorestad on the Rhine (Denmark), Quantevic (near Montreuil, ESE of Le Touquet, France) and four Anglo-Saxon ports in England - York, Ipswich, Lundenwic (Aldwych, London) and Hamwic (Southampton). Though all of these were important large towns in the time of Charlemagne (Hodges 1987) they were abandoned by the 10th century, as if they belonged to period VII´ rather than to period VIII. Perhaps the inhabitants were relics of the Old People. See Fig. 12.

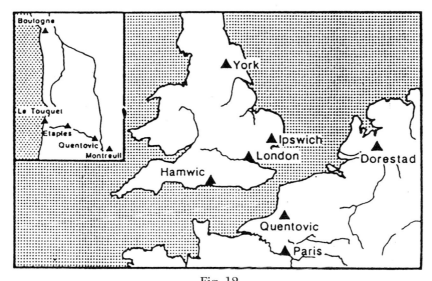

Fig. 12
Trading areas of seventh-century Europe. The inset shows the location of Quentovic.
From R. Hodges 1987.

A GLANCE AT VIKING ART

Since Pictish sculpture did not long survive the culture shock of the loss of the native languages, one must look elsewhere in Northwest Europe to see the final stages of decline in sculpture. During the years from 789 to 1085 AD, the Vikings were much given to decoration applied to stone (least successfully), wood, jewellery or martial and civil appliances. It is characterised by vigour and vitality, a direct reflection of the people's character, but by the end of these three hundred years, their art is almost decadent in its refinement, at a time when the outward energy of the Vikings seems to have been spent.

Viking art is based on animal forms, a decorative art in a tradition that can be traced back to the art of the late Roman Empire (Graham-Campbell and Kidd, 1980); but again a simple art form was transformed when it reached Scandinavia. Successive art-styles are defined by a continuous development in the treatment of contorted and convoluted bodies of the animals; such increase in complexity is a sign of decadence in the Petrie sense, though the resulting impression of chaos is often brilliant and dramatic. The schemes of ornament were standardised, self-assured and owed little to the art of the rest of Europe until the end of the 11th century when it finally succumbed to the Romanesque art of western Europe. In Viking art the phasing is Pictish and Eastern not European.

Chapter 15
Literature

Whatever languages were spoken in Pictland in the first millenium AD, the pressures of invaders and of the Church against them were so great that little survives of them today; yet it is reasonable to suppose that the Picts would have reached a literary peak about 960 AD according to the diagram. However a peak of literature does occur at this time in other parts of Europe. The fine nature poetry of the Irish poets and the Welsh works of Taliesin and Aneurin are in the Pictish or pre-Celtic phase; and splendid Welsh verse was composed as late as the 13th century, long before the time of 'European' Shakespeare. One can see in the earlier Welsh and Irish poems archaic features such as their strict rules of alliteration though it is hard to date the time when a freer style had been adopted.

The events of one of the finest of the Norse sagas, the Njálssaga, were from about 975 to about 1015 AD, but the work was not written until 1230 to 1280. The calculated peak of literature lies in the time of the Norse rhapsodists, who kept the stories alive for up to 400 years by recitation, equalling the feat of the Homeric rhapsodists (those who 'stick together'). Freemasons have preserved over an even longer period their ancient lore, which must be committed to memory and faultlessly recited.

When Margaret, later the Saint, married as his second wife, Malcolm III Canmore, King of Scotland in ca 1070 AD, she found the country ready for literary education, as well she might since Pictish had been eliminated. Even if she "laid the way open for continental and English influences of every kind to pour into the land", the native population, of course, continued to exist. She died in 1093.

A remarkable peak of literature, however, did occur in Provence; this deserves closer study because what Pictland and Provence had in common was a Stone Age genetic heritage, which determined their cultural history.

Provence

In *The Literary History of the Troubadours*, Mrs Dobson (1807) made an abridgement of a French study by Monsieur de Saint-Palaye of the lives and works of the Troubadours, their customs, morals and history. What interests us here is the extraordinarily rapid rise in the quality of the Provencal language. The first Troubadour poet was William, Count of Poitou, who flourished at the end of the 11th century and the beginning of the 12th - he died in 1122 AD. The first poem in this genre was composed, it seems, about 1080 AD. It was the first Romance language to come to perfection. French was still in the archaic stage and Italian had not been fashioned by the hand of Dante (1265-1321). Moreover, as the oldest examples of Provencal show a relative perfection, it may be concluded that poetry in this language had developed quickly.

Although the Provençal language began in Limousin and Poitiers to the northwest of what became Provence in The Kingdom of Burgundy, in 987, the mass of the people were in origin similar to the Ligurians, whose pre-Indo-European language had latterly become so celticised that some historians think of it as a Celtic language preserving in it only a few ancient words. However there is no doubt that the Ligurians had a predilection for certain sounds such as *asca, esca, isca, osca* or *usca; inca* or *inco; car* and *alb,* and *icna.* Sir Gavin de Beer quotes Pisani's suggestion that pre-Hellenic roots like *assa, asso* and *antho* and *intho* are related to Ligurian *assa* and *inco,* respectively.

Liguria and Ligurian-type Placenames

The distribution of Ligurian placenames is shown in Figure 12. Iscar, 26km SSE of Valladolid, in Spain, could be added, and the river of that name. According to Jannoray, indigenous culture of the coastal Langedoc to the Roussillon area had by no means been "véritablement hallstattisée", but the Ligurians were under pressure and some made their way, according to Festus Avienus, in his poem *Scyannus,* of the late 4th century AD, up the West coast and on to Britain. Others arrived in Britain as Roman mercenary soldiers (Diodorus XXXI, 3).

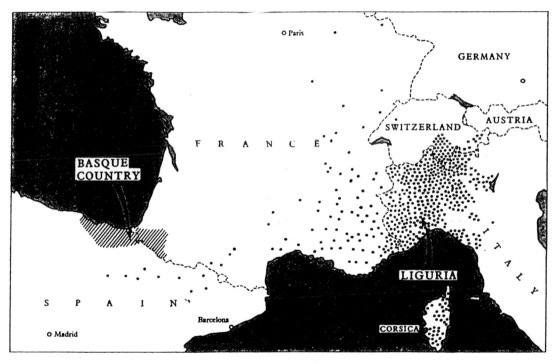

Fig. 13
Distribution of Ligurian place-names, represented by black dots.

One or other of these groups may have given some Ligurian placenames to Britain or else there was not much diversity among pre-Indo-European languages when they were used for naming rivers. I suspect that Isca Dumnoniorum means the river of the Dumnonii tribe; this became the Exe. The Axe is not far away. In the southeast of

Wales was Isca Silurum (Carleon), the watering place of the Silures tribe. Tacitus *(Agricola, 11)* "made no bones about calling these primitive inhabitants of Wales Iberians" and "Hibernia contains the form *iber* unaltered " (de Beer,p26). Only six miles west of the Usk at Caerleon is an urban district called Risca, near the confluence of the Sirhowy and Ebbw rivers. This could come from Ar-isca, rather than meaning Rhisga's bank. Risca, a small island on the south coast of Ardnamurchan, gives a hint of its meaning "surrounded by water". Could the urisk be pre-Celtic?

In Oxford the Upper Thames, a pre-Indo-European name, is called the Isis, formerly Isca. Oliver and Boyd's *Pronouncing Gazetteer of the World* (1883) derives the name from the British isca = water, but I suspect that both the British (Brythonic) and the Gaelic *uisge* are derived from an older pre-Celtic word *isca*, which required no latinising. The only place where a river cuts Hadrian's Wall is called Aesica. Isca survives today in *whisky*, but the Ligurians habit of drinking beer and milk mixed (Strabo, lv,6,2) has fortunately died out. Of course whisky is short for *uisge beatha, aqua vitae,* water of life. The word for wine too, has a splendid etymology. In early Greek it began with a digamma, so the stem of the word was originally *woin.* And this has remained unaltered in Cockney English!

The Gaels seem to share with the Ligurians a liking for the -sc- sound. A Gaelic dictionary has a very large number of words containing the letter sg, many of which belong to objects or actions known, shall we say, 3000 years ago. Sg names are common in Skye, but not in the Outer Hebrides; see Appendix 3b for a list of these, collected by Robbie the Pict. The names Gask, Lisk, Fasque and Throsk in Scotland may be of ancient origin. The last part of Monymusk could belong to this group. In the south Thirsk in Yorkshire, though said to be derived from Danish and to mean fen, may mean a water logged place. There are three villages and a river bearing the obviously ancient name of Wiske in this part of low-lying Yorkshire.

Two more Wessex names in -sc- may be mentioned. A king called Aescwine, 674-676 AD, was followed by Centwine, 676-685 AD. (Kent is also pre-Indo-European, though *wine* (pronounced ween-ah) is Old English for friend). And in 871 AD the Danes encamped at Reading, where they defeated Aethelred and his brother, but later in the year the English won a great victory at 'Aescandum' (the *Saxon Chronicle*, sub anno). *Aesc-* could well mean water.

Alba and Alps are cognate with the Latin for white according to Watson (1926), but I doubt this much copied derivation, because *Alp* and *Alb* names are numerous in Ligurian and are presumably pre-Roman. Places bearing this root are usually beside upland pastures and are remembered best by the Alps themselves; few of these places seem to be particularly white, though the houses could have been white-washed with lime. Alba longa in Latium was traditionally founded in ca 1200 BC by *Ascanius,* son of Aeneas; he had been saved from the flames of Troy by his father, whom he accompanied on his voyage to Italy. The Julian family claimed descent from him. Livy described the place thus: *'ab situ porrectae in dorso urbis Alba longa apellata'* (it was called Alba longa because it stretched along a narrow ridge). Similarly Albi (Albiga in Latin) occupies a commanding position on the left bank of the Tarn, between the high Plateau Central of France and the plain of Toulouse.

The two countries which bear this ancient name are Alba = Scotland and Albania. The earliest settlers in Scotland were on coastal sites, but as the growing population sought game inland they settled often on dry, glacial sands on the flanks of rivers, which at lower levels were thickly afforested, wolf-infested and subject to flooding. Albania, called by the natives Shkiperi (from *shki*pe, a rock; an *sc* word), today speak an Indo-European language, but many older names survive.

The country is divided into two parts; north of the river *Sh*kumi, the people are called Ghegs; south of it they are To*s*ks, who have a more advanced state of civilisation. Of the nine prefectures, four appear to have ancient names - Durazzo, Koritsa (Korça), S*c*utari (Shkodra) and *Elb*asan.

The Albigenses or Catharists in France were an anti-sacerdotal party in permanent opposition to the Roman Church and raised a continued protest against the corruption of the clergy of their time. They were originally based on Toulouse, but first appeared in Limousin between 1012 and 1020, where they were protected by William IX, duke of Aquitaine, otherwise known as Guilhem VII of Poitiers. The people were attached to the *bons hommes*, whose asceticism and anti-sacerdotal preaching impressed the masses. In 1209 Pope Innocent III ordered the Cistercians to preach a crusade against the Albigenses. The whole of the nobility of the north of France were thrown against the south till the Treaty of Paris (1229) destroyed the brilliant Provençal culture, though the massacres of heretics continued until 1246, when 200 Cathari were burned in one day.

Although their religious beliefs are not now well-understood they were in a sense early protestants, though not so early as Saint Martin of Tours, who in the 4th century had founded a monasterium, or *muinntir* in Celtic, where Christian preachers, teachers and research workers lived and travelled afar, leading an austere and simple life.

Saint Ninian was trained there and brought to Casa Candida in Wigtownshire in 397 AD a style of Christian teaching and living to Alba or Pictland. His most famous journey from 420 to 423 AD was to take him and his party as far as Orkney. *Muinntirean*, such as that of Deer in Aberdeenshire, were founded on the way.

Swiss place-names

The distribution of place-names, which de Jubainville regarded as Ligurian, is highly concentrated south of the Alps from near Nice to the Engadine. The area of highest concentration includes the Piedmont and Lombardy (Po valley - the river was once called Bodincus in Ligurian). Three prongs can be seen entering the Etruscan land, and a very dense area runs into south-east Switzerland, the canton of Ticino or Tessin.

In Vaud and German-speaking cantons of today only Petinisca, near Bienne, has been plotted on Fig. 12, but we can add the Latinised Ligurian place-names of Viviscus (Vevey), Aventicum (Avenche) and Geneva. We can safely infer that Ligurian place-names are recognisable only in Ticino because the Italian language preserves them with little or no alteration. These names are given in Appendix 3.

In German-speaking Switzerland old names can rarely be recognised. De Jubainville noted that the place and small river Urnasca in Appenzell has become

Urnäsch today but did not comment on the rarity of Ligurian-type names in Suisse romande. Hughes (1975) admits that the names of some great rivers, the Rhône (Rotten), Reuss, Limmat, and Ticino, "are probably from some remote tongue innaccessible to us and unidentifiable, formerly happily called Ligurian or Etruscan. Ticinese village names in -asco are romantically ascribed to the same origin." Why the immense scholarship of de Jubainville was totally neglected by Hughes and by Bossard and Chavan (1990), I cannot imagine.

On both sides of Lake Léman and over the whole of French-speaking Switzerland, names ending in *x, y* or *z*, preceded by a vowel, are astonishingly common. They are so common also among surnames that one can find as many as three of them in a single book-reference, such as "Raoul Domenjoz, par Georges Peillex, Editions Marandaz, Le Mont-sur-Lausanne". Names in -iz are rare; and -uz surnames are brought to mind by Charles-Ferdinand Ramuz.

Another group of place-names has -y (or -ie), after one or two consonants. I shall call these the -az groups and the -y group.

The -az group of names

Bossard and Chavan (1990) give a table of common suffixes of the place-names of Suisse romande. The names are arranged in three columns (1) Latin suffix, (2) Development into present place-names and (3) Examples. We can therefore have no feeling for true antiquity of most of the names, even though some of the Ecclesiastic Latin quoted from date from the 3rd century AD. -az, for example, is shown to have come from -ariu(m), -éaz from -eta, -u(z) from -utu(m), and -y from -ariu(m) or -aticium. In these names, and in names ending in -ens, the *x, z* or *s* is no longer pronounced except in canton Fribourg.

I do not suggest that all -az to -oz names are ancient. Estraz, for example, is derived from Via Strata; but I am sure that many of the names are pre-Roman. I maintain that homogenous peoples often show a taste for certain vowels or clusters of consonants. One may think of the -ac names of western France, from Carnac, through Cognac, Polignac, Veyrac to Armagnac, which appear to be ancient. In Mexico the tl cluster survives at the beginning of words (Tlapa, Tlaxcala), the middle, and the end of words (axolotl; Popócatepetl; Quetzalcóatl, the snake god; and the names of the months in the Aztec calendar.

In the country around Lake Léman I counted 293 placenames ending in -az, 51 in -oz, 18 in -ez, and 5 in -uz. Surnames seem to follow the same distribution. A few of the placenames are given in Appendix 4.

No -asca names have survived, even if they were once present more commonly, in Suisse romande, because French is a strong solvent for sibilants. In standard French these often survive only as a circumflex, such as château from castellum. The most extreme example of this tendency is même, which started life as *meum ipsissimum*, Latin for my very own self, and went through a number of changes to the present s-less word.

The -y group of place-names

With the held of Bossard and Chavan, a book about vineyards, several large-scale maps and many signposts, I counted 82 disyllabic and 41 trisyllabic names ending in -y,

8 disyllabic and 13 trisyllabic names ending in -gny, 9 names in -i, and 17 in -ie. These are given in Appendixes 5 and 6. They are followed by a selection of Scottish disyllabic surnames in -ie, which also fascinate me, Appendix 7. These names are most commonly found in the northeast of Scotland, in what was Pictland; I had arranged them in five categories; diminutives (Addie for Adam, Davie for David, Robbie for Robert); pejoratives (rare), place-names (Fyvie, Tweedie - not very common), Gaelic (Revie), French (Rougvie), unknown (Poustrie and many others). Craft names are uncommon. Urie, Hurrie have the old word for water, ur, as in Basque.

Hamish Henderson, poet and a founder of the School for Scottish Studies, has a hunch that the intonation and phrasing in the whole area north of the Grampians and of Inverness may be all that is left of how the Picts spoke their pre-Celtic language. Their taste for disyllabic names ending in -y and the use of diminutives ('yon sheepie on the briggie') may also continue a Pictish taste in speech.

The Swiss -y names have been traced to their Latin forms; a few are Gaulish and many are of unknown etymology. There is no doubt that the inhabitants of the Lemannic coasts have a strong liking for the -y sound. Bossard and Chavan put their latinised endings into 8 categories; diminutives, pejoratives, collectives, localisation (-atorium, -atoria), words which underwent the changes - adjective -> noun, agents and others.

The meaning of ancient words

All is not lost when comparative philology and the written history of a placename do not reveal its meaning. The gestural theory of the origin of speech (Paget 1930) may come to our rescue. Paget made a model of the human larynx and learned how to make it speak syllables. He also saw how words were formed by looking through holes in people's injured faces. Words, he observed, were pantomimic mouth gestures. Hand gestures are far more expressive than words, and it was obvious that not everyone would instinctively describe by mouth gestures a thing or action by the same consonants. When you refer to something distant you have w, b or p to choose from; something close would be c (k) or g, or ch as in loch.

L, m and n often denote a curved or woolly object. T, in which the tongue touches the palate, describes the top or tip of things. Others had noticed that certain clusters of letters such as str represent a smart movement away, as in strip, strike, strand. The first two come to an abrupt stop, the last ends in a rounded way; nd is the end of the beach.

When Paget was put to the test in Chinese, of which he had no knowledge, he 'translated' about a half of the words spoken to him correctly. The other meanings he suggested were to be found in Mandarin Chinese, and they were. Paget gave many examples of similar words occurring in totally unrelated languages and showed that people's surnames were acceptable as words to describe things only if they were gestural; thus boycott is gesturally related to picket. Shrapnell, Wellington and Hoover are gestural; they would not have become accepted if the eponymous gentleman had been called Smith. I have shown that this principle can be used when coining new words in science (Robertson 1962). Polythene is more meaningful gesturally than polyethylene.

Asca (feminine) or - asco (masculine) is the commonest ending of the group plotted on de Beer's map (Fig.12) prepared from H. D'Arbois de Jubainville (1894). The word survives in the Gaelic as *f(h)asgadh*, a shelter. Esca survives in the Norwegian word for a river at the edge of or coming from a glacier, in English esker or eskar. The meaning of isca, water or river, has already been given.

The ancient place name endings of the -asca group were given a new lease of life when the Romans adopted them in such names as Aemiloscus, Arriasca, Buriasca or Severascus, meaning the place belonging to Aemilius, Arrius, Burrius and Severus, respectively. Other names in northern Italy are named in a similar way after Granius, Romanius, Sallius, Villius, Charisius, Fabius, Cassius and so on.

Let us look at isca again but this time as if we were prehistoric explorers. When we look up a river, having landed recently, we see its narrow (i) course running from the distance (s) towards us (c); but when the pioneering days are over and the interior of the country has been settled, we turn about and look down the river. That is why La Rive Gauche in Paris is on the west side of the Seine.

And in Scotland, when you welcome a stranger to your home, you say "come awa' in", you ask them in. The opposite sense of direction is preserved in the Greek and Latin ex or ecs, away from, both pure gestural.

In Ireland the English word box is written bucsa in Gaelic but is pronounced busca. This is an example of the persistence of the pre-Celtic taste for the -sc- sound. Scottish Gaels, likewise, give a Pictish rather than a Gaelic rendering of the surnames Robertson, Morison, Finlayson and Ferguson; they say, and now write Robasdan, Moireasdan, Fionnlasdan, and Fearghasdan. Sometimes a t is used instead of a d.

The vowel may describe the shape of the river or home. Some asca homes may have been on flat ground, escas on a narrow terrace, oscas may be blocky (isodimensional) and uscas circular. Originally an osca might be a wider, bigger cave than a tunnel-like usca. Asca rivers may be shallow, and the others progressively deeper, as in the sequence Ask, Esk and Usk today. Even in Russia Omsk is on the Om, Tomsk is on the Tom, though Smolensk is on the Dneper.

Not all -sc names have the same origin, but most appear to be pre-Indo-European and many of them truly Ligurian. Even with the uncertainty of the history of all -sc names which have caught my eye, I should say that their distribution may give a hint as to the limits of late prehistoric Europe - even the Eastern limits.

Damascus in Syria, for example, is not far from Tyre and Sidon of the Phoenicians, and Askelon/Askalon/Ashquelon, north of Gaza, is in the southwest of what was once the land of the Philistines.

Alexandria on the Gulf of Issus became Alexandretta, and eventually in Turkish, Iskenderun. This change appears to reflect the phonetic taste of the pre-Indo-European inhabitants, and to indicate its eastern limit, which could have extended to Aleppo, for which it is the port. Was Issus ever *Iscus* one may ask.

Gaelic speakers also prefer sg (pronounces sk) to cs (x) and therefore change Alexander to Alasdair, bringing the g forward to something like a t. Lowlanders solve the problem by using Sandy in familiar speech.

Sk names are also common in the Americas, some of these are given in Appendix

3c, following Sc names in Switzerland (Appendix 3a) and Sc, Sg, Sk placenames in Scotland (Appendix 3b). A mixed bag of Sc names in history is given in Appendix 3d.

The -ac, -ec, -ic, -oc, -uc names of Old Europe.

Between the megalithic monuments of Carnac in Brittany and the Egyptian tombs of Thebes, near the village of Karnak, the -ac group of place names are commoner in the west of France than anywhere else in Europe. Loudiac and Perros-Guirec are in the Côtes du Nord, but the most memorable names of this group, are associated with the wine trade, Appendix 3e.

The Pict Calgac-us had one of these names, as did Caradoc (Caractacus) and Toulouse-Lautrec of *Albi* and many others.

For Larzac see p.167, and Kormak, see p.46.

Switzerland and Scotland compared

Where in the pattern of history does Switzerland lie? Is it a country where most traces of prehistoric culture have been erased by Celtic, Roman, Burgundian, Frankish and Germanic tribes? Or is it similar to Scotland where the original population has been diluted by immigration only to a small extent?

Switzerland was not so heavily glaciated as Scandinavia and Scotland in the Quaternary Ice Age. Whereas in the northern countries huge thicknesses of ice swept the record clean, evidence of Mousterian (Middle Palaeolithic) man has been found in twelve sites in the Jura and six in the Alps. As the climate deteriorated the people would have moved away from the permanently frozen land and remained away until, many generations later others returned in search of wild life for food and places to live. The last glacial period ended about 10000 BC and people began to return to the areas affected between 7000 and 6000 BC, in the Mesolithic period.

The early Neolithic began about 4375 BC, which coincides with the top of the diagram Fig 9. It lasted till the end of Period I. Cup markings without concentric rings, seen on a now recumbant stone at La Praz in Vaud (H. Meylan 1973, p.9), may be of an early type. They are similar to many in Scotland, Brittany and Galicia (Spain). Very small cups surrounded by one to seven rings, not unlike those of Newgrange in Ireland, were found in 1965 at Carshenna (Sils in Domleschg, Grisons) near Thusis (cf Tuesa, the ancient name of the Tweed). The inhabitants of Switzerland had a conservative taste in design. Sauter's Fig.40 shows a bracelet, ornamented with two concentric circles, of Hallstatt B age from Auvernier, Neuchâtel. I have a Victorian brass plaid brooch with a similar design!

Those who settled in these once uninhabitable lands would have 140 to 170 generations of relative peace in which to increase their numbers - within the carrying capacity of the land. In Switzerland the question hardly arises as to whether the 'Beaker Folk' came in numbers because the ceramic ware was probably of local manufacture all the time. I see no sign of startling innovations in shape or design until Hallstatt times, from say 750 BC, in the late Bronze Age. The whole of Switzerland as well as the whole of Scotland may remain substantially of Stone Age stock. The proportion in the present genetic inheritance of the Swiss is less than in Scotland because of later migrations into Switzerland.

The cultural history is more varied. Sauter (1977) was reluctant to enter into the debatable question of the ethnic and linguistic origins of the Swiss of the late Bronze Age and contented himself with summarising the commonly accepted view that the population of the plateau de Jura was linked with the vast entity which was later to be called the Celts. They have been called Proto-Celts (cf. our Picts). In the Alpine regions the picture is less clear. In the east the so-called Melaun culture of the Bronze Age, which covered the Rhine valley and Grisons, as well as the Austrian Tyrol, the north Italian Trentino, and extended as far as Lake Constance and the Inn Valley, came to be assimilated in the ethnic group which was to become the Rhaetians. According to Vogt (1948) the rest of the alpine population could have been of non-Indo-European origin.

The passage from the Middle to the Recent Bronze Age about 1250 BC was in a very troubled period, especially in the East (Sauter, p117); north to south migrations by the Dorians entering Greece and the movements of the 'sea-peoples', The Protocelts may have moved towards Switzerland or they may have driven earlier people to seek refuge there. The Ligurians seem to have moved in about 750 BC from the south of France and the neighbourhood of Nice and the Piedmont and southern Savoy along the north of Italy, the Po Valley, through Lombardy and round by Lake Como to Tessin. This was at the beginning of the First Iron Age, known after Hallstatt in Lower Austria. Their culture affected a huge area of southern Europe including the fringes of Switzerland. The succeeding culture of La Tène penetrated further inland and sites of this Second Iron Age are far more common north of Lake Léman. This began about 450 BC and radiated from northeast of Lake Neuchâtel. Hallstatt culture began on the Painting Line and La Tène at the Mechanics line of the (Picto-Scottish etc) Period VI´.

These cultural events were contemporary with the Etruscans. Both the Etruscans' and La Tène art required the highest skill in metalwork, which may have been their expression of mechanics. In both people the peak of wealth was about 300 BC.

The Swiss Dark Age

The now Celtic-speaking tribes led by Helvetians defeated the Romans at Agen on the River Garonne in France in 107 BC. The Roman threat was so unbearable that in 58 BC 263,000 Helvetians, 36,000 Tulinges, 14,000 Latobriges, 23,000 Rauraci and 32,000 Boii burnt their homes and set off to settle in France. Julius Caesar caught up with them by forced marches and routed them at Bibracte (Autun in Burgundy); only a quarter survived the slaughter and they were compelled to return and rebuild their homes. In this undoubted Dark Age, the eastern part of their country was subjugated by incoming German tribes. Although celticised for a few centuries they became heavily romanised as the Province of Transalpine Gaul, administered from Vindonissa near Schaffhouse and other centres.

The Latin language in the west of Switzerland gradually changed into a sort of Franco-Provençal, though never to the standard of Provençal at its best in 960 AD and thereafter. Instead it has become a much-loved or sometimes ridiculed "patois". René Merle (1991), a French specialist in Occitan literature, thinks the language , which he prefers to call "the idiom" deserves to have official support. Merle records that Python, an advocate in Fribourg, once translated Virgil's *Bucolics* into "l'idiome" and cites other literary works in this tongue. I must thank Luc Weibel for his interesting review of *Une Naissance Suspendue,* Merle's book.

Last year (1991) the Swiss celebrated their 700th anniversary, though the events of 1291 and the Federal Charter are obscure; but there is no doubt that the men of Uri, Schwyz and Unterwalden defeated Leopold of Bavaria at Morgarten in 1315 and so began a series of battles in defence of their freedom and of accessions to the Confederation, beginning with Zurich in 1351 and ending with Geneva, Valais and Neuchâtel in 1815. Myths such as William Tell have entered the story but the fact is that a complicated history of freedom is the proud heritage of the Swiss. The feeling of Swissness is based on the development of political structures to suit their needs, former military aid for other countries, social aid for the world (the Red Cross) and other services.

The Swiss wars of independence happened at exactly the same time as William Wallace and Robert Bruce. Bannockburn and Morgarten were fought a year apart. Both episodes fall on the line of period VII′ where a "mindless war" would be expected. The contemporaneous experience of Switzerland and Scotland is further proof of their being in the same, non-European (or rather Old European) phase of history.

The peak of wealth in Switzerland about 1500 can be judged by the date of many fine buildings and churches which are still the glory of villages and ancient town centres. An important source of wealth was the Foreign Service. J-R Bory (1965) tells how representatives of the Eight Cantons and of the City of Basle, stung by the disastrous battle of St Jakob on the Birs, near Basle, signed a treaty with the Dauphin of France at Ensisheim on 28 October 1444 stipulating that there should henceforth be "a good and lasting friendship" between France and the Swiss Confederation. This marked the beginning of a long and glorious saga. For four centuries, from Charles VII to Charles X, sixteen kings of France, five queens, one Prince of the Blood and an Emperor were to rest the authority of the Throne and the prestige of the State on Swiss arms, closely linking the destinies of the two nations. Bory continues "The Peace of Geneva was signed on 7 November 1515. The King (Francis I) undertook to pay the Swiss the 400,000 crowns promised by Louis XII for raising the siege of Dijon, and, in addition, 300,000 gold *écus* to cover campaigning expenses in Italy, and 300,000 more for the repurchase of Locarno, Domo d'Ossola and various other lands. He reaffirmed all the trading privileges granted to Swiss merchants. In return, the Cantons promised the King fresh troops for his wars..." "The service was costly to the Crown but so useful it lasted for 300 years."

Scotland's peak of wealth, by contrast, was shattered at Flodden. Until then the two countries, Switzerland and Scotland, were firmly on the line of Period VII′. The slide down to the Dark Age had less malevolent consequences in Switzerland than in Scotland because the changes which occurred between 1653 and 1715 were internal in Switzerland and in Scotland between 1690 and 1747 were the result of rivalry between Scotland and its neighbour. "In 1653 occurred the greatest of the peasant rebellions in Switzerland... Then, between 1712 and 1715 there was a final disturbance, a shake-up, which established a balance between the underlying facts of power and the institutions"

" .. but after 1715 the dynamic element, the element of innovation, was overwhelmingly confederative, ... though there was no perceptible change in federal law in this period." (Hughes, pp 88-90)

In both Switzerland and in Scotland, the Union, confederative and incorporative respectively, removed internal strife and allowed people to develop their talents without constant threat to peace. To illustrate similarity between the countries, we may compare two remarkable families. These rather compressed biographies not only show hereditary genius but also show that the phenomenon of the Enlightenment had roots going back for a century and a half before the peak about 1815.

The Clerks of Penicuik

Portraits of Taste and Talent is the title of a booklet by Iain Gordon Brown (1987) on a remarkable family. "Through five generations between 1630 and 1830 members of the family were leaders of artistic and literary taste and patronage, or prominent in all the sciences from medicine to geology." A sixth member of the family James Clerk Maxwell was one of the greatest figures in the history of science. See under Maxwell in the bibliography.

The Gregories

1. Rev. John Gregorie (1598-1653) of Drumoak on Deeside and his wife Janet Anderson were the progenitors of a remarkable family, which could possibly find a place in the *Guinness Book of Records*. Agnes Grainger Stewart (1901) first published a book about them and Paul D Lawrence (1971, 1980) followed their history over nearly 400 years in a much more scholarly way. He most generously amended my script:

2. James Gregorie (1638-1675), son of John was a mathematician of great genius, a contemporary and correspondent of Newton. He laid down the principles of the reflecting telescope. His son

3. James Gregorie (1674-1733) was appointed (mediciner =) professor of medicine at King's College, Aberdeen in 1725 and was followed by his son,

4. James Gregorie (1707-1755) who succeeded his father as mediciner in 1732 until his death in 1755. His son

5. John Gregory (1724-1775) studied at Leyden and was appointed Professor of Philosophy, Aberdeen 1746-49; changed the spelling of his name when he went to London to practice medicine, and returned to Aberdeen as mediciner 1755-66. His wife died in 1763 and thereafter he was never so happy in Aberdeen. When the Chair of Practice of Physic became vacant in Edinburgh in 1766 he was appointed having already been living and practising in Edinburgh for two years while still being mediciner in Aberdeen. His grandfather was Chalmers, Principal of King's College, from whom the family was reputed to have inherited gout which plagued them for several generations.

6. James Gregory (1753-1821) took over from his father as Professor of the Institutions of Medicine at Edinburgh although still only a student at the time of his father's death. He wrote the *Institutes of Medicine* 1776-89 and the *Practice of Medicine* 1790-1821. The dreaded Gregory powder was invented by him. His son

7. William Gregory (1803-58) was Professor of Chemistry at Edinburgh 1844-58. He was an excellent teacher of the "new" organic chemistry and translator of much of Liebig's work from the German. His brother

8. Duncan Farquharson Gregory was a brilliant mathematician, but as he died young, did not realise his full potential. And his cousin, son of his aunt Dorothea,

9. William Pulteney Alison, was Professor in three medical subjects between 1820 and 1855.

The older brother of the first James of this line was

10. David Gregorie of Kinnairdie (1625-1720) who had 32 children. His son

11. David (1661-1708) was Professor of Mathematics 1682-91 and of Astronomy at Oxford 1692-1708, where he wrote his name with a -y, like his cousin John (No 5). His brother

12. James (1666-1742) was Professor of Philosophy at St Andrews, 1685-89 and of Mathematics 1691-1725. His brother

13. Charles (1681-1754) occupied the Chair of Mathematics at St Andrews 1707-1739 and his sister Isobel married Patrick Innes, whose son

14. Alexander Innes became Professor of Philosophy at Marischal College, Aberdeen, 1739-42. No. 11 David's sister Margaret married Lewis Reid, whose son

15. Thomas Reid, was Professor of Philosophy first at King's College, Aberdeen 1751-64 and then at Glasgow 1764-1798.

Gregory and Gregorie descendants of this family are still around to this day.

Bernoulli family

Bernoulli or Bernouilli is the name of a Swiss family of scientists and mathematicians, who made their home in Basle.

1. Jacques Bernoulli (1654-1705), mathematician, University of Basle. Travelled in England, France and Holland. Returned to Basle in 1682, opened a public seminary for experimental physics. 1687 became professor of maths there; later rector. First to solve Leibnitz's problem of the isochronous curve. He proposed the problem of the catenary and elaborated on Leibnitz's construction of the curve. Studied other curves, and discovered Bernoulli numbers.

2. Jean Bernoulli (1667-1748), his brother, under whom he studied before working under the marquis de l'Hôpital in Paris. Then 10 years as professor of maths at Gröningen; in 1705 succeeded Jacques in his chair at Basle. Like his brother he was a great mathematician. He discovered the exponential calculus, and the line of swiftest descent. His writings were published in Lausanne and Geneva. (Jacques' in Basle and Geneva).

3. Nicolas Bernoulli (1695-1726), eldest son of Jean, was for three years professor of jurisprudence at Berne. He and his brother Daniel were appointed professors of maths in the Academy of St Petersburg, but he died 8 months later.

4. Daniel Bernoulli (1700-1782), Nicolas' youngest brother. Seven or eight years as professor of maths at St Petersburg before returning to Basle, where he became professor of anatomy and botany and afterwards of experimental and speculative philosophy. His most important work is his *Hydrodynamica* (1738). He dealt with liquid jet

propulsion; and wrote a memoir on making a clypsydra for use in ships and though only 24 years of age he got a prize for this at the Academy of Paris. He shared prizes with his father, Euler, Colin Maclaurin and another competitor. He introduced a parallelogram of forces and a doctrine of probabilities in reference to practical purposes in later years.

Because of his close association with the Bernoullis and of his amazing output of works in mathematics, I feel I must make a few notes about Euler.

Euler

Leonhard Euler (1707-1783), Swiss mathematician, was born at Basle the son of a Lutheran pastor, who was also a good mathematician. In 1723 he graduated at Basle university, where he studied geometry under Jean Bernoulli, at that time one of the first mathematicians in Europe and became a close friend of his sons, Daniel and Nicolas. He then took up theology and oriental languages, and medicine. In 1727, at the invitation of Catherine I, he joined his friends in St Petersburg, where he became professor of physics in 1730; in 1733 he succeeded Daniel Bernoulli as professor of physics.

The severe climate and overwork caused loss of sight in one eye in 1735. Nevertheless in 1741 he was commanded by Frederick the Great to go to Berlin where for twenty-five years he contributed many memoirs to the Prussian Academy. Even so, he sent many papers to the academy of St Petersburg. In 1766 he was allowed to return thither. He was now nearly blinded by cataract, but with the help of his sons and Krafft and Lexel he continued his labours. In the next seven years he sent in 70 memoirs to the Academy and left in his papers some 200 more. He died of apoplexy 18 September 1783.

Although he is remembered mainly for his work in pure mathematics and especially for the discovery of Euler numbers, he was a man of wide culture, and made important contributions to astronomy, hydrodynamics and optics. "His *Theoria motuum lunae* (1772) ... was completed under terrible difficulties. His house had been burnt down and some of his papers detroyed; he was nearly blind, and had to carry all the elaborate computations involved in his head." (J Ginsberg, *Encyclopedia Britannica*, 14th ed., (1929), vol. 8 under Euler).

de Saussure

Horace Benedikt de Saussure (1740-1799), physicist and Alpine traveller, was born at Conches near Geneva. He was a professor at Geneva University 1762-1786 and was elected FRS 1768. In 1772 he founded the *Société pour l'Avancement des Arts* at Geneva. Early devotion to botany led him to study the geology and physics of the Alps and also chemistry, mineralogy, palaeontology. (Thus we may say that the anorthosite of Rodel, Harris, has been in parts of the mass saussuritised, that is converted to a rock containing zoisite, albite and attractive green minerals). He ascended Mont Blanc (1787) - the second time known - Col du Géant (1788), Crammont (1784, 1788), the St Théodule pass to Zermatt (1789) and the Klein Matterhorn (1792). These journeys were described in *Voyages dans les Alpes* in four quarto volumes 1779-1796 and eight octavo volumes 1780-1796; and popular editions were issued from 1832. He invented the hair hygrometer (*Essai sur l'hygrométrie*, 1783) and was one of the pioneers of meteorology. His great grandson

Ferdinand de Saussure (1857-1913) was famous as the author of a *Cours de linguistique générale*, which is one of the foundations of the modern science of linguistics.

Summary

We can now see close similarities between Scotland and Switzerland. Both countries were repopulated after the Ice Age; their histories are in phase; the Wars of Independence were simultaneous; their peak of wealth around 1500 AD was short-lived. They both reacted with great vigour to the late 18th century Enlightenment and produced famous family pedigrees. Both have prehistoric roots and have a special relationship with the much more numerous late comers to Europe.

Beowulf

The epic of Beowulf is the only Old English poem of great length to have survived. The single manuscript of 3200 lines in which it is preserved was written about 1000 AD but the poem was composed a good deal earlier, possibly before 700 AD. It is thus the earliest complete surviving work on such a scale in any Germanic language, perhaps in any European vernacular... The poem was written in the alliterative metre of all Old English verse. Each line, divided into two portions by a caesura, contained a number of alliterative, stressed syllables. There was no rhyme and it went something like this:

> Many learned, linguistic   scholars of Scandinavian
> have sought to specify   the beginnings of Beowulf's
> superhuman story   with its mix of mythical
> giants like Grendel   and historial characters -
> Swedes, (but no Saxons),   Danes, Angles, Ostrogoths and Frisians,

yet there is no agreement about who was the compiler of this "cyclopaedia of German tradition."

Beowulf's style illustrates the late archaic approach to a peak of literature, which in Period VII´ would be 960 AD. The subject matter could not be more Indo-European but the writer appears to have been one of the Old People, even though he lived in England.

Iceland

Iceland was always famous for song; but it produced no major poets. Yet, within Icelandic literature is a group of poems displaying "high imagination, deep pathos, fresh love of nature, passionate dramatic power, and noble simplicity of language, which Icelandic poetry lacks. The solution is that these poems do not belong to Iceland at all. They are the poetry of the Western Islands; the coastal areas of Ireland, the West and North of Scotland and north-east England." (Sigfus Blöndal and Richard P Cowl; *Encyclo. Brit.* 14th ed., Icelandic Literature).

The Western Isles School, in the beginning of the 9th to the end of the 10th century, produced the *Helgi* trilogy, Dramatic poems, Didactic poetry, Genealogical and Mythological poems, as well as Dirges and Battle songs. They result from the contact of Scandinavian colonists, "living lives of the wildest adventure, with an imaginative and civilised race, that exercised upon them a very strong and lasting impression." Some of the songs of praise are written in a form of the old Teutonic metre, which was used by Beowulf (Blöndal and Cowl).

The peak of this literature is hard to pin-point, but is close to the date of the first Troubadour songs, 1080 AD. The earlier poems known as the Elder Edda show a transition from the highly stylised poems. Hallfred, Olaf Trygvason's poet, who was buried in Iona by the side of Macbeth, and Kormák, (930-960), the mystic and 'hot-headed' champion, may have been firmly in the archaic stage, but rhyming verse was introduced for singing at weddings, feasts and the like at the end of the 11th century - the *rimur* or ballads. About the same time love and humour were part of the repertoire of poets, - the skalds.

The subject matter of the sagas was also widened about that time. *Eyrbyggja* (890-1031) is the saga of politics; *Laxdaela* (910-1026) is the saga of romance. Its heroine Gudrun is the most famous of all Icelandic women. The *Banda-mannia* saga (1050-60) is the only comedy among the sagas.

Ari Fröði Thorgilsson (1067-1148), who was descended from Queen Aud, (who founded the famous historical school of Iceland), produced its greatest monument in a work which can be compared with the English Domesday Book - the Book of Settlements *Landnámabók*, which listed all the inhabitants of Iceland, giving all their genealogies. In contrast the Domesday Book (1086) is incomplete. The Norman administration presumably secured the services of church scribes; thus the most complete areas are around Ely and Winchester. There were far fewer entries in the north of England, where the people no doubt objected to having an inventory made of their assets for taxation purposes, - a pre-run of the Poll Tax imposition!

Erling Monsen in his introduction to Snorre Sturlason's *Heimskringla* (1931) held that the Nordic people had little in common with the Celts and Slavs of Germany; rightly so, since they were essentially of pre-Celtic, indeed Stone Age, origin.

Phoenicians

In about 4500 BC, at the beginning of the pattern of history, as shown in Fig. 9, something like a large village was built above the present port of Gebeil, formerly Byblos on the Phoenician coast, now Lebanon. Primitive huts were made of branches, their walls and roofs daubed with mud and the floors covered with limestone grit. By 2900 BC, not long after the peak of wealth in Period III, stone houses and a canal had been built, but in 2200± 100 the town was burnt, at a time corresponding with the Dark Age between Periods IV′ and V′. In the next Dark Age, centred on 1400 BC, Phoenicia was subservient to Egypt. This was the beginning of Period VI′.

The alphabet may have been invented in Sinai about 1500 BC, according to Herm (1975) just after the wealth peak of Period V′ and used to a small extent in

Canaan in 1000 BC (when one would expect calendrical reform to have occurred in that period). In coastal Phoenicia it was used mainly for mercantile purposes from about 750 BC, a little before the literature line of Period VI'. The Greeks began to use a similar alphabet also about 750 BC. The Phoenicians never had a great literature, the import-export business being their forte. For this, meticulous book-keeping was essential. Latterly, the Phoenicians' most famous literary and religious works were written in Greek or Latin and thus had a very wide readership.

The famous circumnavigation of Africa was authorised by the Egyptian King Necho II under whose benign rule Phoenicia had temporarily fallen. The journey, begun in 609 BC, occurred not at the frustrated peak of literature of the Phoenicians but at the peak of calendrical reform of the Egyptians in Period VII. Necho "was passionately interested in all nautical and overseas trade matters and therefore well disposed to the people of Lebanon" (Herm, p. 140). He was so impressed with the circumnavigation that he got the Phoenicians to begin work on the first Suez canal in 600 BC. This was used on and off until the 8th century AD.

Herodotus records that Xerxes, in 480 BC, allotted to various nations the digging of a canal through the Mount Athos peninsula. Only the Phoenicians battened back the sides, the span at the top being twice the width required at the base - sufficient for two triremes to pass side by side. In this work the Phoenicians showed the same skill as in everything they undertook (Dickson, 1989). The Phoenicians of Tyre and Sidon were clearly near their peak of mechanics in Period VI' of the Middle East.

By 264 BC their colony Carthage was rich and powerful enough to threaten Rome and cause the First Punic War. Scipio's victory at Zama in 202 BC in the Second Punic War, however, did not prevent Carthage becoming strong again. Yet, when Cato gave his opinion on any subejct he always added his famous words *"Ceterum censeo, Carthaginem esse delendam"* (moreover I am of the opinion that Carthage must be destroyed). This was during the Third Punic War, 149-146 BC. I am not surprised that this Dark Age event occurred a generation before the calculated date of 120 BC; the might of Rome was sufficient to hasten the end of the Carthaginians.

On the other hand, Rome rebuilt the city, providing it with academic institutions and a theatre, and, after Rome had been Christianised for some time, two men of notable spiritual character appeared on the scene, Tertullian (ca 155 - ca 222 AD) and Augustine (354-430 AD), both Carthaginians. Herm (p. 266) traces some of their religious thinking to the works of Zeno of Citium (ca 336 - ca 264 BC), who was almost certainly pure Phoenician. "Ridiculed in Athens for his Phoenician appearance - anti-Phoenicianism seems to have been a forerunner of anti-Semitism - he developed a doctrine whose basic concepts still serve as ethical and moral landmarks: stoicism."

Tertullian wrote vehemently (in very difficult Latin) on previous religious ideas and in the end gave up trying to comprehend inexplicable phenomena intellectually and owned to complete irrationality.

A more moderate and altogether more important figure than Tertullian was his fellow countryman Aurelius Augustinus, author of *De Civitate Dei*, "the City of God" and many other books. In his work was one of the most thought-provoking concepts imaginable, the doctrine of predestination, or predetermination, about which religious leaders have agonised and written many volumes. Although this idea was based on St Paul's *Romans* 9:16, it cannot be said that the many distinguished contributors were writing about the same thing. The kindly Roman Catholic priest in Pitlochry, Fr Rupert Loughlin, has come to my rescue.

"Predestination can be defined as God's eternal decision to assume certain rational creatures into heavenly glory. Before we ever asked about God and His Grace, before we sought to prove ourselves worthy of Him through a good life, God has already chosen us out of pure love and predestined us to communion with Him"."The problem has been whether God's eternal decision has been taken with or without consideration of human freedom. Catholic teaching holds that predestination by God does not deny the human free will.

"The choosing and calling of every pers on implies that God accepts man's free response and consent. In His love God makes the realisation of His salvific will depend on our freedom. That means that through our own fault we can also miss salvation. While respecting our free will God provides the spiritual help or Grace to accept or reject the commands and requirements he expects of us".

According to Herm (p268), Luther almost despaired of the doctrine and Melanchthon adroitly overcame the problem, but Calvin made it his central truth, calling it his "terrible decree", yet Calvin's theories were the exact opposite of St Augustine's teaching and were naturally condemned by Catholics; he was not reviving, many centuries later, the teaching on predestination as taught by Augustine. Fr. Loughlin continues.....”Calvin's system was that as a result of Adam's fall man has no longer any internal freedom of the will; he is a slave of God. Everyone according to him, is eternally predestined either for heaven or hell absolutely independent of his personal efforts. The (Catholic) Church has always agreed, with St Paul, that predestination is an unfathomable mystery. We believe that a mystery is a divinely revealed truth completely beyond the grasp of a created intellect but it is not opposed to reason. People generally will not accept the existence of mysteries in the field of religion, yet, in the natural world, we are surrounded on every side by mysteries."

Herm may also have misunderstood these opposing concepts, but was probably right in assuming that the powerful teaching of Calvin in Geneva would have traceable consequences in Scotland. "Calvin's theory that everyone could determine from his own material conditions the measure of love God had apportioned to him gave propulsion to the rocket which carried medieval Europe into the modern era. The 'protestant ethic of capitalism' was established, wealth and the striving for riches theologically justified, and the day not far off when 'the invisible hand' would be glorified. This idea was promoted by Adam Smith, the Scottish father of political economy, and also by modern neo-liberals, to regulate the equilibrium of markets. Its highest altars are in Manhattan. Was it by chance, however, that this doctrine was founded by a descendant of precisely that merchant race, which had always been convinced that economic prosperity was the surest sign of godly grace? Our capitalistic ideas are not so very different from those of the Carthaginians" (Id., p.269) And, finally, perhaps the Scots took to the idea of predestination because they were in phase with the Carthaginians and took more readily than continental Europeans, except the western Swiss, to the apparently predestined nature of cultural history, as shown in Figure 9. Not all Scots of course fell for this line of thought. James Hogg parodied and pilloried it in his "Confessions of a Justified Sinner".

The Jewish People

Of even greater antiquity and importance than the Phoenicians were the Israelites. The town of Jericho had been built before 6000 BC. Although it was some 250m below sea level and 8km west of the River Jordan where it enters the Dead Sea, settlement was possible around its freshwater springs. Around 2000 BC, the time of Abraham, Isaac and Jacob, life there was already quite civilised. In tombs from about 1600 BC fine pottery, wooden furniture, basket work, and boxes with inlaid decoration have been found, (Alexander 1980).

For Israelites their sojourn in Egypt was a Dark Age, between Periods VI´ and VII´. Moses led his people from slavery in Egypt to nationhood in the Promised Land, the Exodus of the Bible. This great journey was early in the 13th century BC in the reign of pharaoh Rameses II. About the same time the 'Sea Peoples', Mycenean Greeks, reached Egypt by ship and their families with their household goods trekked down the coast of Syria and Canaan. The two groups met each other again and founded the Philistine towns of Ashdod, Ashkelon, Ekron, Gath and Gaza. The Judges of the Old Testament tell of the lawless times between 1220 and 1050BC, from the conquest of Canaan to the crowning of King Saul.

The hymns, prayers and poems known collectively as the Psalms were composed over centuries. A few, before King David, may represent the religious consolidation of the people of Israel, whose Ten Commandments had already been given to Moses on Mount Sinai during the Exodus. King David who wrote many of these poems was not allowed to build a Temple in Jerusalem because he had sent Uriah the Hittite to his death in war and had married his wife Bathsheba when she became pregnant by him. Nevertheless their son Solomon was allowed by God to build the Temple ca 986 BC. The building and workman for the Temple were supplied by his fellow Semite, the Phoenician King Hiram. It was destroyed by Nebuchadnezzar, King of Babylon, in 586 BC, just after the peak of literature. Indeed the last Psalms were composed by Jews in exile in Babylon.

You may have noted that in Period VI´ there was no peak of sculpture about 800 BC. This was because the Jewish religion forbade the making of graven images, yet in spite of a very turbulent history during which their people had begun to disperse during Egyptian, Assyrian (722 BC) and Babylonian (586 BC) conquests, their culture had risen undeterred. In the Exile of 587-538 BC the Israelites were free to practice their religion and they made such good use of their leisure that they set down many of the books of the Old Testament in their present form, - one of the greatest feats of historical and religious research and compilation the world has ever known and one with the greatest consequences. See Bacon and Gilbert 1990.

The editing of the Old Testament to that time and the writings of Shakespeare fall close to the line of Literature; the former in the Middle Eastern phase and the latter in the modern European - that is, in Periods VI´ and VIII.

The diaspora continued when Judea was conquered by the Greeks (301 BC) and by the Romans (63 BC). Resistance ceased on the Heights of Masada in 73 AD and by 138 AD even the Philistines had left Palestine. But Rome fell and the Jews have continued to provide the world with philosophers, State advisers, lawyers, bankers, artists, musicians and poets out of proportion to their numbers; they are the most gifted people on earth, (Weyl, 1966); and the Scots are in phase with them.

Etruscans

The Etruscans, who lived between the Arno and the Tiber, recognised what may have been a period of civilisation. They called it the Great Year and it came to an end in the turbulent times of Sulla in 87 BC. This period appears to be VI′, which began about 1400 BC. Their cultural history belongs to the pre-Indo-European one. Indeed their alphabet, derived from the Greek, was introduced about 700 BC, a century before a peak of literature would be expected in this period. The defeat of the Etruscans by the Greeks in a naval battle off Cumae in 474 BC corresponds to a setback of the 'mindless war' type; certainly they were no match for the Roman army when it began to annexe the territories of Etruria in the 4th century BC, (A. Piazza et al, 1988).

The greatest artistic development of these people occurred about 600 BC, when they also enjoyed their greatest wealth and influence. By about 450 to 425 BC the line drawings on hand mirrors were already stylised and must have been made long after a peak of art in the Petrie sense. All the same, the style and execution of these mirrors suffered little further decline in the years 425 to 200 BC, in spite of mass production. The subjects portrayed on them were often Greek but the artists were clearly not. The Etruscan language and grammar have been ingeniously unravelled by Larissa Bonfante (1990) and many previous scholars. The first six numerals were inscribed on a gaming die in the usual way, opposites adding up to 7; the pairs have been differently interpreted but we shall follow Bonfante. We are so used to seing some sort of similarity in the first ten numerals of Indo-European languages that we are astonished at the strange appearance of numbers in ancient languages. To make the point let us compare only Ancient Egyptian, Etruscan and Basque with Greek, Latin and English.

Table 4

Ancient Egyptian	Etruscan	Basque	Greek	Latin	English
uā	thu	bat	eis mia hen	unus una unum	one
sen	zal, es(a)	bi	duo	duo	two
✗emet	ci	iru	treis, tria	tres	three
fṭu	ṡa	lau	te^{ss}ares tt	quattuor	four
ṭua	mach	bost	pente	quinque	five
suu	huth	sei	hexa	sex	six
se✗ef	semph?	zazpi	hepta	septem	seven
✗mennu	cezp?	zortzi	octo	octo	eight
patu, pseṭ	nurph?	bederatzi	ennea	novem	nine
meti	ṡar	amar	deca	decem	ten
t'aut	zathrun	ogei	eicosi	viginti	twenty

The Etruscans called themselves and their country Rasna or Rasenna. The *-sc* spelling may have crept in later, as with Faliscan and Oscan. Placenames in *-isca* etc. are rare in ancient Tuscany; the only one I have noticed is in the south - Gravi*sca*, the port city of Tarquinia.

Words in *-sc-* are rare in Etruscan; a garden was eka*sk*. *Aska*, a vase or container, is clearly from the Greek *askós*, but both may be ancient words continuing. Tes*inth*, a caretaker, has a Ligurian ending.

Other words of interest are *mi* = I, *am* = to be, *clan* = son. Clann in Gaelic = children. Mi is a gestural word pointing to myself. *Am* is one of the several forms of the verb to be in English; I suspect that as it is not found in other Indo-European languages it may be an ancient relic.

Oscan was a P- language like Greek and Welsh. Latin and Gaelic are Q or KW languages. The *kw* sound in certain words changed to a P a long time ago. Noone has explained why this happened. We can be sure that Varro (first century BC) must have been amused to hear *quidquid*, the Latin for 'whatever', pronounced *pitpit* in Oscan!

The generally accepted view of archaeologists today is that the Etruscans developed their culture *in* Italy in the Bronze and Iron Ages. They borrowed much from the Greeks and Romans and gave much to the Romans. They were an ancient, autochtonous people.

Chapter 16
Music, 1120 AD

No twelfth century Scottish music has survived; there could have been a peak about 1120 AD, since Giraldus Cambrensis records in the 1170s that "in the opinion of many, Scotland today has not only equalled Ireland, her instructress, but even far surpasses and excels her in musical skill. And therefore they now seek there as it were a fountain-head of the art "(of harp playing). John Purser (1992, page 50) quotes the preceding paragraph which suggests to me that the music had become free from stilted formalism, as in the phrase "By their faultless art, the melody is sustained through the most complicated arrangements of notes - with a velocity that charms, and a varied rhythmic pattern, and a judicious use of elements of concord and discord."

At least about this time there would have been a great demand for music by the great abbeys which were built then; and a musical people would have risen to the occasion, provided the choirs and perhaps composed some of the music. Thus:-

Selkirk (later Kelso) Abbey was founded by monks
    from Tirón (Burgos) Spain in 1113.
Dunfermline Priory, founded by Malcolm III and Margaret,
    was raised to an Abbey in 1128.
Holyrood Abbey was founded in 1128.
Melrose Abbey was founded by monks from Rievaulx Abbey in Yorkshire 1136.
(GWS Barrow,1981)

The archaic phase of 'Gregorian' plainsong or monody may have been between ca. 800 AD and ca. 1120 AD. Some of the loveliest melodic lines in the vast repertoire of plainsong were preserved in the 13th century *Inchcolm Antiphoner*. The monastery of Inchcolm, an island in the river Forth, was founded in 1123 and dedicated to St Columba. The manuscript contains the only certainly identified music of the Celtic church. The wide vocal range and tunefulness of some of this music do suggest that it was written not long after the foundation.

The famous manuscript *Carmina Burana*, though written at Seckau, west of Graz in Austria, was found in Benediktbeuren only 30km from once Ligurian Switzerland.

Plainsong eventually gave way to harmony which began in the 11th century. This was in the European tradition and developed to a peak about 1790. The Abbey of Cluny established abbeys all over Europe - a Scottish example, being at Paisley. Both Beuren and Cluny maintained their love of music, their feeling for which could have come from the older people of Europe. Cluny, meaning a pasture in Gaulish as in Gaelic, is only a few kilometres from Mâcon, which comes from the Ligurian name Matiesco (Caesar, *Bellum Gallicum*, VII,90,7).

The distribution of pentatonic music

More information about our early ancestry is oddly enough provided by a study of folk music. The very oldest surviving music not only has but five notes in the octave but also a small compass.

Pentatonic music has 5 notes in the octave, heptatonic 7, the 8th completing the octave. The mathematical ratios of vibrations in pentatonic music can vary among several possible modes. Pentatonic music is therefore not in tune with heptatonic music, especially with the compromise which the piano dictated. The Highland bagpipe is an ingenious solution to the problem of playing three keys of pentatonic music on one instrument. In the flageolet only one key is played on a given instrument, or, better put, one needs a set of flageolets to play different keys.

I continued in my article *Music a clue to bright ancestors* (1984):

Cecil Curwen (1940) showed that the proportion of melodies of this type was highest in the Outer Hebrides, lower in the Inner Hebrides, and lower still in Ireland and the Highlands of Scotland. Curwen concludes: "Down to the late Bronze Age therefore, we have reason to suppose that Scotland, Ireland and part of Wales were occupied by a more or less homogenous culture-group that was in the main descended from the old megalithic stock... It is difficult to resist the conclusion that the pentatonic tradition is a legacy from the pre-Celtic Picts, and that the latter, whatever their language may have been in historic times, represented the old megalithic stock blended, no doubt, with Beaker and other Bronze Age elements". He also concludes that ..."the spread of the heptatonic (7 note) scale at the expense of the pentatonic is a measure of the spread of musical instruments such as the harp, lyre or flute and that the heptatonic distribution corresponds roughly with the spread of the Indo-European and Arabic languages". See Table 5.

Country	Number of Melodies	Pentatonics of small compass	Pentatonics (total)	Hexatonics	Heptatonics	Others
Lapland	848	0	67	30	2	1
Scotland						
Outer Hebrides	241	18	46	33	21	
Inner Hebrides		14	38	50	12	
Highlands		4	41	37	22	
Lowlands	336	0	31	33	36	
Ireland	1500	4.5	13.5	34	52.2	4.5
Finland, secular	100	0	9	25	66	
Faeroes	100	0	8	54	38	
France	60	0	5	40	33	
Norway	100	0	4	50	46	
Iceland	20	0	5	20	75	
Basque country	48	0	4	25	67	4
England	169	0	4	20	76	
Brittany	60	0	3	28	67	2
Russia	100	0	2	50	48	
Germany	100	0	2	15	80	2
Wales	312	0	1	32	67	
Sweden	50	0	0	46	54	
Finland, church	112	0	0	34	66	

From E. Cecil Curwen (1940)

Table 5
Pentatonic and other scales in different countries.

Curwen's Table places England firmly in the European musical tradition and in fact nearest to Germany. The rather similar position of Iceland may not be true - only twenty tunes were analysed. The secular music of Finland appears to be old, but the church music seems to show Swedish influence. France has a curiously low proportion of heptatonics, much lower than Brittany, Wales or the Basque country, but Curwen's figures are not wholly reliable. More detailed analysis by this method is called for - perhaps England could be divided into a few large regions; but we cannot escape the fact that the Celtic peoples of Wales and Brittany no longer preserve many pre-Celtic tunes.

Performance Coefficients

Another method of comparing one area or country with another is to count the numbers of people bearing surnames which are known to have started in a particular area. Nathaniel Weyl (1961) obtained from the Bureau of Old Age and Survivors Insurance computer a list of the 1514 most common names in the USA in 1956. He then compared their frequency in BOASI with their frequency in 75 books of reference, such as *American Men of Science, Who's Who in America, Poor's Register of Directors and Executives* and so on. The ratio x 100 he called the Performance Coefficient. Before we start using Performance Coefficients in our study of racial origins, we should say something about its reliability. A good test is provided by the names Clark, Clarke or Palmer; they were first assumed about the time of the Crusades by the brightest young men who had been to the early universities or had been taught to be literate by the Church. Thus John le Clerc might have been a clerk in Holy Orders or Richard le Palmer an educated pilgrim. Now if this kind of brightness were genetically inheritable and if men bearing these names had the instinctive knack of marrying the right kind of woman, then we should expect, even after 700 years, this clerical surname group would still show high performance coefficients. And so they do: 153 in Who's Who, 186 among physicists, 194 among biologists, 186 among social and behavioural scientists. As one might expect, the name is less common among army officers and state bureaucrats, where security is preferred to competition, conformity to creativeness.

The validity of the method of using Performance Coefficients as a test of human ability is provided by such pairs of names as Green, Greene; Clerk, Clerke; Brown, Browne; Smith, Smythe; Low, Lowe and so on. An e was added to their surnames by people who had "a fine conceit of themselves". What is interesting is that people with names ending in e have, without exception, highers PCs than their unadorned fellow citizens. One must stress that in this study all people called Green or Greene are examined and the numbers involved (n) are large.

Not only do we have a strong indication that intelligence is inherited, in spite of what the egalitarians and environmentalists have to say, but we can now compare one country with another. After the Jews, who are exceptionally able, the Scots, Dutch, Welsh and English have higher performance coefficients than other Europeans. In the graph I have combined Curwen's data with Weyl's (in the latter I have taken the PC figures of the earlier immigrants to the USA).

I think one can safely conclude that survival of an ancient musical taste and high performance go together. Put another way the oldest inhabitants of Britain had to be very clever or they would not have survived.

We notice, however, that Ireland seriously underperforms, and France does so to some extent. The French deficiency may be due to the drain of clever sons into the priesthood, a celibate profession, or to the persecution of intelligent minorities. In Ireland the church robbed society of an even higher proportion of bright sons and the potato famine of the mid-1840s caused the physically strongest to secure escape to the UK and America - though only some of the more intelligent and hardy were able to make the taxing journey. In any case about a half of the Irish genetic inheritance is English.

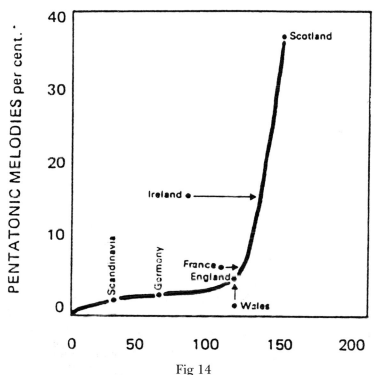

Fig 14
Performance Coefficients relative to tonic scale.
Average performance of people coming from different countries to the USA,
plotted against proportion of pentatonic melodies (Weyl/Curwen).

It is fair to state that Francis Collinson, the famous musicologist at the School for Scottish Studies at Edinburgh University, believed that pentatonic music was earlier than heptatonic music when he was writing *The Bagpipe* (1975) but shortly before his death he recanted. In *Bagpipe, Fiddle and Harp* (1983), he implied that the oldest surviving musical instruments from a number of difference countries suggested that the two scales could have been 'invented' at about the same time, - a view still held by his successors at the School for Scottish Studies. I can only say that music is likely to have progressed from the simpler to the more complicated, as in the series pentatonics of small compass, pentatonics, hexatonics, heptatonics, octatonics, a 12 tone scale and finally atonal music, - the last two would have been designated by Petrie as decadent; that present-day Scots are musically more conservative than Continental Europeans and that many of them have 'Stone Age souls'.

Curwen also reviewed the proportion of pentatonic and more elaborate scales outside of Europe. The Arabs, for example, "have a highly developed heptatonic system in which pentatonic scales have little or no place. The same may be said of the Hindustani system, except that in this case an earlier pentatonic system persists. In India pentatonic scales are specially common in the Himalayas and in Bengal, as well as among the hill villages, and they seem to be particularly associated with the pre-Aryan population. Persian music is said to resemble the Hindoo (heptatonic), and we thus begin to suspect a possible correlation between heptatonic scales and Indo-European languages.

Elsewhere in Asia pentatonic scales are common, if not predominant, almost everywhere - in Mongolia, China, Japan, Siam, Annam, Java, Sumatra, the South Sea Islands, and New Guinea. In China they exist side by side with a very ancient heptatonic system.

Later, Curwen points out that "the Sumerian flute, called *ti-gi* or *imin-e* (seven voices) was carried as far as China, and the Chinese records tell us that in the third millenium BC the Imperial Master of Music was sent westwards to study its proper ordering. In due course he found a people in western Asia whose musical scale he adopted, and he cut his bamboo tubes to accord with the notes he had heard. On his return the scientists proceeded to develop the mathematic theory of this western scale, which was definitely heptatonic".

In Africa five note scales have been reported from the Sudan and from Zululand, as well as from Nubia, Abyssinia, Basutoland, and South Africa generally.

In North America pentatonics are common among the Indians, Eskimos and Negroes. Curwen obtained the following figures from collections of songs:-

People	Melodies Examined	SCALES			
		Pent.	Hex.	Hept.	Etc.
N. American Indian[38] ..	9	7	0	1	1
Eskimo—ancient[39] ..	32	18	12	1	1
Eskimo—1750–1900[39] ..	19	1	7	10	1
Eskimo—modern[39] ..	14	1	2	7	4
Negro (Jubilee Singers)[40]	61	(49%)	(38%)	(13%)	—
Negro Slave Songs[41] ..	148	(36%)	(24%)	(36%)	(4%)
U.S.A. (all classes of population)[42]	32	15	12	4	1

From E. Cecil Curwen (1940), p. 354

[34] Hj. Thuren, *op. cit.*, 193-203.

[35] Cecil Sharp, *English Folk-Song : Some Conclusions*, 45.

[36] Carl Engel, *The Music of the Most Ancient Nations*, 157-162.

[37] *Oxford Companion to Music* (1938), s.v. ' Harmony ', §4, and ' Scales ', §10.

[38] Thurlow Lieurance, *Indian Songs* (Chappell & Co., 1913)

[39] W. Thalbitzer, *Inuit Sange og Danse* (Copenhagen, 1939). I am indebted to the author for a copy of this work.

[40] Rev. G. D. Pike, *Jubilee Singers* (London, 1873). A characteristic example is ' Swing low, sweet chariot '.

[41] W. F. Allen, etc., *Slave Songs of the United States* (New York, 1867).

[42] *Botsford Collection of Folk-songs*, I. This mixed group includes Negro, Indian, Creole, Kentucky, Texas, Middle-West, Cowboy, and a chantey. See also *Oxford Companion to Music*, s.v. ' United States ', §§6, 7.

Table 6
Pentatonic music among American Indians, Eskimos and Negroes.

"As a contrast, Spanish influence in Mexico and Latin America tends to eliminate earlier, transilient scales altogether, but pentatonics appear among the South American Indians". Jacques Martin wrote (16 January 1991) concerning Inca music of the aboriginal Amerindians of Peru and Bolivia, their past music was pentatonic and their present one largely remains so, "the chromatic scale having been introduced by the Spanish conquerors. The simplest and best proof to my mind is that their basic instrument, *la quena*, a sort of flute, which they have used for centuries could play only the pentatonic scale. They now have types that can play the chromatic scale". The history of the instrument was told by Ernesto Cavour in his undated book *La Quena*.

Even Curwen thought "that the seven note scale is an instrumental scale, and that it is introduced with the instrument wherever the latter is adopted by pentatonic people", but this is not always true as we learn from the Incas' experience. As I have said above the ancient Chinese were playing pentatonic music on bamboo woodwind instruments long before heptatonic music was introduced to them, and the older music has not yet lost its charm. Moreover the Scottish Highlanders adapted the nine notes of the bagpipes so that three pentatonic scales can be played. in the keys of G, A and D (Seumas Mac Neill, 1968). "The Gael shares with the African Negro and the American Indian a love for music in the pentatonic scale doh, ray, me, so, lah, do. Many Gaelic tunes are pentatonic, and an examination of piobaireachd shows that it is overwhelmingly pentatonic also. Francis George Scott (1954) found as long ago as 1931 that 22 out of 26 tunes in GF Ross's collection of piobaireachd are pentatonic. Further investigation indicates that about this proportion is correct for all piobaireachd".

A characteristic of modern pipe music is the note interval 27/25 or 133 cents known as the *limma*. It also occurs in the Phrygian scale of ancient Greek music, but Lenihan and MacNeill (1960) think that it is only a by-product, and probably never appeared in older tunes.

Francis Collinson (1965) came to the conclusion that some of the ancient airs of Scotland may have as long a history as christianity in this country. This could have been true only of recorded tunes, but the types of music they exemplify must be very much older. In *Piobaireachd and its Interpretation* MacNeill and Frank Richardson (1987) have done much to reveal the unique nature of the art of Highland composers who were oblivious to the European tradition; and MacNeill even claimed that the great Highland bagpipe was "in its death throes in the 16th century". True: the music belongs to the Picto-Scottish period VII´, which is not in phase with the Continent, and as the music peak of that period was about 1120AD, decline would have become apparent by the 16th century.

Scottish drumming is outstanding in its rhythmic vitality, ingenious syncopation and worldwide renown of its drumcorps. Their style is said to have been derived from the playing of drummers brought to Scotland from North Africa and amply supplied with good instruments. A similar tradition is found in and around Basle in Switzerland, but not, it seems, elsewhere in Western Europe.

Pitch profiles

Faced with the daunting task of bringing some sort of order into the cataloguing of thousands of melodies Denys Parsons, librarian of music at the British Library, had the neat idea of dividing the tunes according to their first three notes. The first note was represented by an asterisk, and the next two notes by whether they went up, were repeated or went down. Obviously there were nine categories. In his book *The Directory of Tunes and Musical Themes* he showed that the frequency of tunes was in the following decreasing order:

*UU, *UD, *DU, *DD, *RR, *RU, *UR, *RD, *DR, where U means up, D down and R repeat. European tunes, whether classical or folk, most commonly begin with two rising notes (UU) Fig 14a. On the other hand Dr Graham Pont and his colleagues Nigel Nettheim and Jenny Nevile in the Centre for Liberal and General Studies at the University of New South Wales showed in an article on "Geography and Human Song" (*New Scientist*, 20 January 1990) that nearly 58 per cent of the songs of the Pintupi in central Australia began with RR (Fig 15b), 56 per cent of the Menominee (Northwest American Indian) tribes' music also began in this way, but other tribes had fewer tunes beginning thus; Peyote 49, Teton-Sioux 47, Yuma/Yaqui 34.4 and Flathead 21.7 per cent (Fig 15c)

These research workers were surprised that Gaelic songs "of the rebellious Scots", as they put it, tend to deviate from the classical European "norm", as plotted by Parsons. Thus waulking songs, for an unknown reason, had 26.3 per cent RR tunes, South Uist music 18.3 per cent and Scottish Gaelic music 13.3 per cent (Fig 14b). Parsons' three very large European collections had only 11.1, 10.8 and 9.9 per cent of RR tunes. These extraordinary differences deserve to be looked into more deeply.

Denys Parson's Research

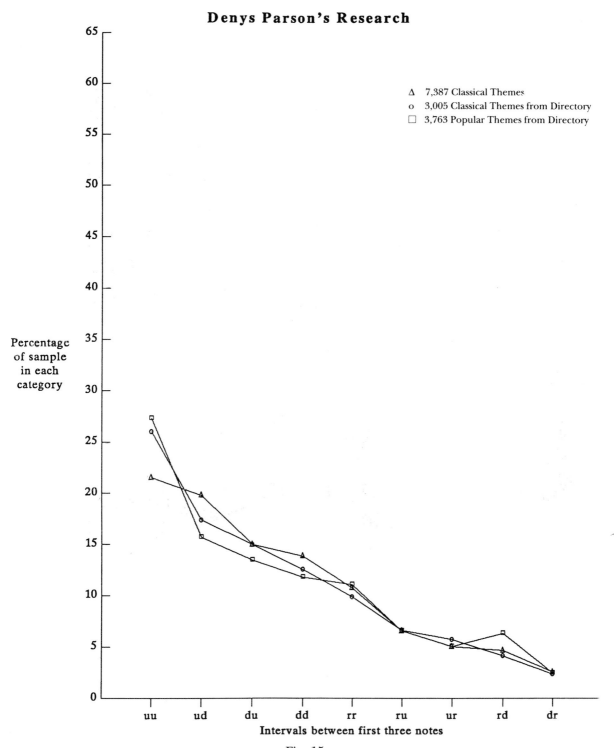

Fig. 15a
The classical European norm mapped by Parsons.

Scottish Gaelic Songs

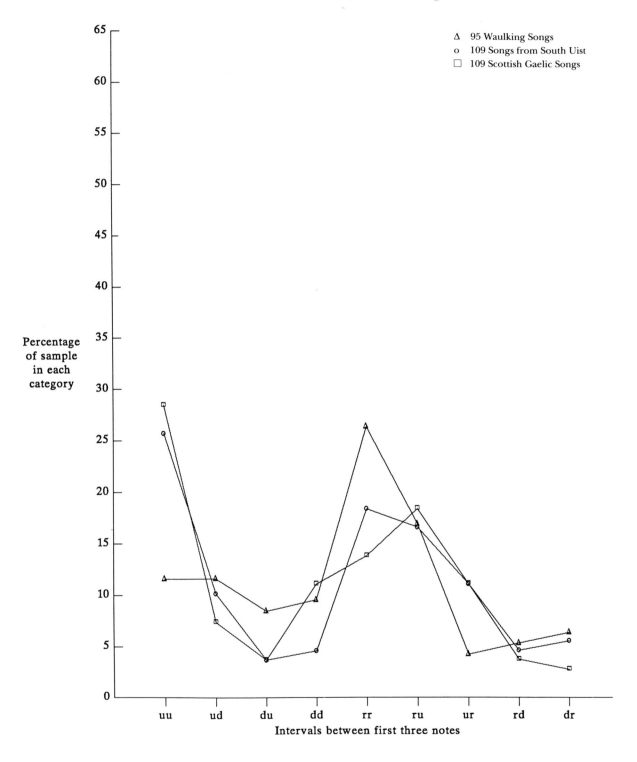

Δ 95 Waulking Songs
o 109 Songs from South Uist
□ 109 Scottish Gaelic Songs

Percentage of sample in each category

Intervals between first three notes

59b

North American Indian Songs

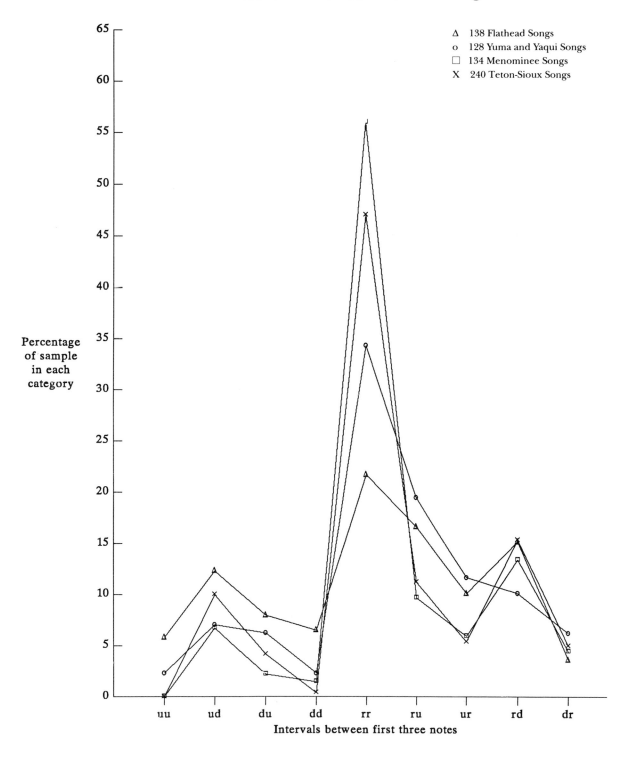

Australian Aboriginal Songs

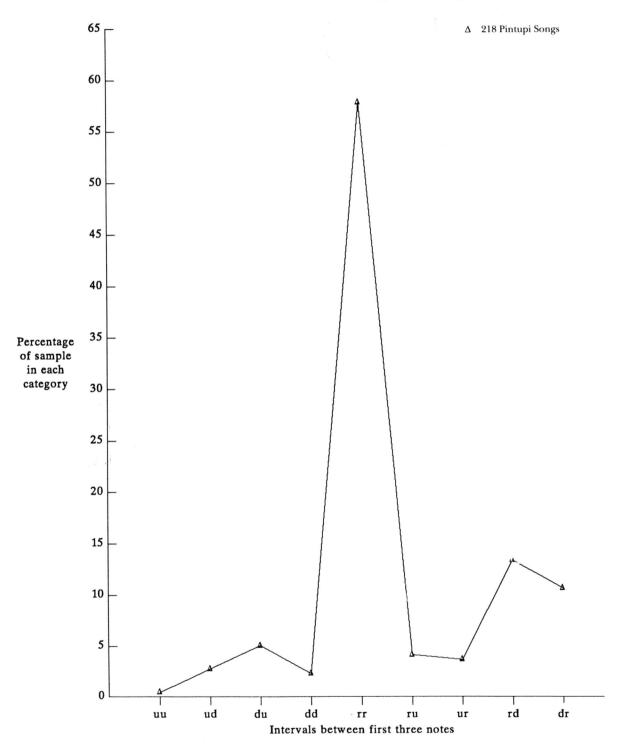

△ 218 Pintupi Songs

Percentage
of sample
in each
category

Intervals between first three notes

uu   ud   du   dd   rr   ru   ur   rd   dr

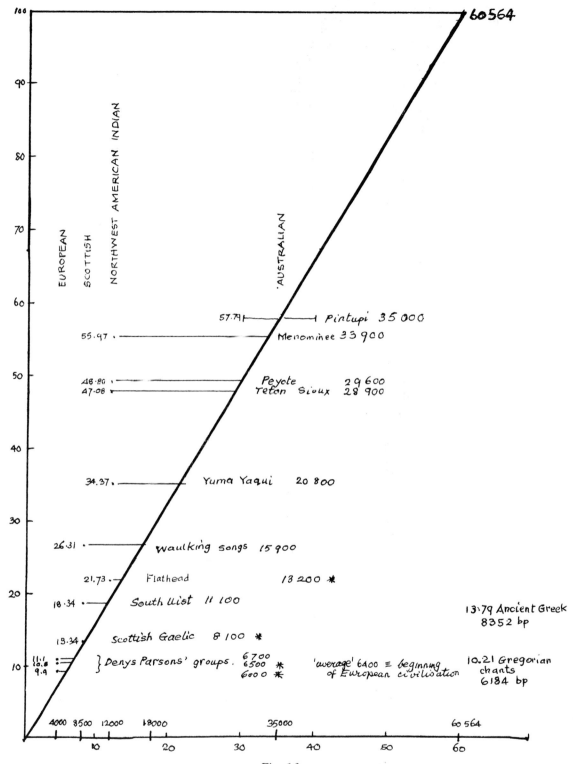

Fig. 16
Proportion of RR tunes related to time of settlement.

I'm not so sure that the Scots are rebellious or that Europeans are normal! Perhaps the Scots have been singing their sorts of music much longer than the comparatively modern Europeans. Perhaps the oldest music was of the RR type and the other eight categories came into use at later dates. We know that people arrived in different countries at different times; they may have brought much older music with them or, more rarely, they may have begun a new musical 'tradition' immediately on arrival at the end of their long journey. In Fig 16 the proportion of RR tunes is plotted against the number of years since each people or tribe have been said to have arrived at their destination.

A line drawn on this graph between the origin and the 57.79 per cent of RR tunes of the Pintupi tribe, who may be supposed to have been in Australia for 35,000 years, passes through one of the three Scottish collections but lies below all the remaining points. If Scotland were first settled about 8500 years ago, the music brought into the country may have dated from 11000 to 16500 years before the present (bp), - the Magdalenian period.

The Bering Straights became a land bridge about 35000 years bp according to some authors and about 18000 to 12000 years bp according to others. André Langaney (1990) director of genetics and biometry at the Museum of Man in Paris and professor at the University of Geneva says that this polemic has remained unresolved. It is possible that migrations from Asia (and Europe) may have occurred at more that one period up to 12000 years ago - or even later in the case of the Inuit. At least the graph supposedly relating time of settlement of tribes and musical development may be regarded as as aide-mémoire to do some more research.

In the United States the 'Flatheads' may refer to tribes of Salish stock in Western Montana, who may have had music dating from 13200 years bp. The music of the Sioux of the south and west of Minnesota appears to date from 28900 years bp and far to the southeast of there the Yenominee's music in South Carolina seems to be 33900 years old. Far to the south of Montana the Yaqui of Sonora, Mexico, had music dated by our graph at 20800 years bp. The last three are all much older that 'Clovis man' whose culture was dated as 12000 years old. However, for what it is worth, the statistically too few Inca tunes available to Martin are 18.75 per cent RR, equivalent to an age of 11400 years ago, soon after the Bering Straights were dry and equivalent almost to South Uist music which is apparently 11100 years old.

Also inexplicable to the 'Clovis school' of archaeologists at Stanford University, California, were the findings of Niède Guidon and Bernadette Arnaud, who examined the rock paintings of Petra Furada in North East Brazil (Harrois-Monin, 1990) and their associated living sites. Their first hearths were found in 1978 to have a corrected C14 date of 25000 years bp. Deeper, at 5.5m, the age was 39000 (1987) and in 1990 they believed the site had been occupied 48000 years ago.

If the sloping line in fig 16 has meaning and is straight, one would infer that RR tunes are the oldest of the nine possible sorts of tunes measured in this way and that they would have begun just over 60000 years ago. In fact, the discovery of a well-preserved hyoid bone about 60000 years old at Kebara in Israel suggested that Neanderthal man, who lived in Europe and the Middle East between 100000 and 35000 bp, must have been able to communicate by speech when the owner of this bone was alive, (Arensburg and Tillier, 1991). Its owner would have had the capacity to sing too.

Only with the development of speech would leaders have been able to plan and direct the long journeys which are known to have occurred at least 50000 years ago.. Thermoluminescent dates suggest the arrival of people between 50 and 60 thousand years ago in northern Australia (Roberts, Jones and Smith 1990); indeed these authors finish their piece with the words "the absence of artefacts in deposits older than 60 kyr at this site (Malakunanja 11, at the base of the Arnhem Land escarpment) suggests an upper limit on the time of arrival of modern humans in Australia". An interesting but controversial book on the development of speech has been written by Philip Lieberman (*Uniquely Human*, 1991).

North American research into the earliest arrivals into the American continent is in disarray (Morell, 1990). Dennis Stanford had for long persuasively argued that no one had come from Asia before about 12000 bp since the Clovis culture of New Mexico was established about 11500 bp, but by 1990 he said in public that "It's time to acknowledge that we do have a pre-Clovis culture in the New World", even though Joseph H Greenberg's grouping of the hundreds of languages in the Americas suggested that there were three waves of migration from Asia, the last occurring 12000 years ago and giving rise to the Clovis culture. Christy L Turner II gave dental evidence for three similar sub-groups, the Aleuts and Eskimos, the northwest coast Indians and all the other Amerindians, coming in the reverse order but all after 14000 bp. However, excavations at Meadowcroft Rockshelter, Pennsylvania, have given a site-date of 16000 years bp and Monte Verde in Chile of 13000 years bp, which are consistent with pre-Clovis settlements. Those who have claimed much earlier dates, up to perhaps 40000 years, are thought of as 'mavericks' or at the worst misguided.

Dating of very ancient tribes by linguistic means is in any case unreliable because very few of the most ancient words can have survived. Gavin de Beer (1965) noted that the Basque word for knife, *aitz*, is the same as the word for flint - an obvious neolithic connection! My guess is that the English word *adze* is our oldest word and has the same pedigree.

Dance

Religion and dancing literally grew hand in hand. They cannot be plotted on a line in our diagram, Fig 9, because they are eternal, the former being transcendental. They sustain people at any time in history. Dancing could be older than human speech itself, but as it is usually associated with music and song, I have found room for it here - after the discussion of the great antiquity of Scottish music. The ancient Greeks did not recognise the primacy of the dance because they originally worshipped only three Muses, as on Helicon in Boeotia; and their names were Melete, Mneme and Aoide (Practice, Memory, Song). How very modern that sounds! Three Muses were also worshipped at an early date at Sicyon, near Corinth in the Peloponnese, of whom one was called Polymatheia (Much Learning). From the beginning these groups of Muses were associated with Thrace.

In Homer, the Muses, whose name was derived from Montiai or Monsai, the 'mindful ones', are represented as singing to the gods, to the accompaniment of Apollo, as well as inspiring or instructing poets generally.

Hesiod, the didactic poet, who lived near Ascra in Boeotia in the 8th Century BC, (whether at the beginning or at the end of the century is uncertain), said there were nine Muses, all daughters of Zeus and Mnemosyne (Memory); their names were Euterpe, Thalia, Melpomene, Terpsichore, Erato, Polyhymnia or Polymnia, Urania, and Calliope. According to the *Encyclopedia Britannica* the assigning of different functions to individual Muses is late and erratic. This is hard to believe because the names must have been either well-known or self-evident even in Hesiod's time. There is no mystery why Thalia (good cheer in festivities) came to mean the goddess of comedy; but Euterpe (well-enjoyed) oddly came to mean the Muse of flute-playing. However there was never any doubt that the Muse Terpsichóre presided over dancing, since the name means 'she that delights in the dance'.

Jane Harrison (1961) quotes the scholiast on Lycophron's *Alexandra* who "says that the women who worshipped Dionysus Laphystios wore horns themselves, in imitation of the god, for he was imagined to be bull-headed and is so represented in art" (M Gimbutas, 1974-1990). Gimbutas continues (p. 227): "The key to a more complex understanding of the male god and the Bull God of Old Europe lies in the Dionysiac festivals - Anthesteria, Lenaia and the Greater Dionysia. In these festivals which have elements of deep antiquity, Dionysius appears as a year god. The idea of renewal is predominant throughout the festivals of winter and spring. Each re-enacts an orgiastic agricultural scenario with phalli, phallus-shaped cups, ladles, cult dishes and the bull-man (Dionysus) marrying the queen (goddess)."

Maenads, the devotees and ecstatic dancers in the Dionysiac festivals, were dressed in festive attire, with exposed breasts, snake collars and belts. As part of the celebrations offerings were made before Dionysus' image, including porridge poured with a ladle, a custom reminiscent of the serving after dancing of Atholl brose in a quaich.

An essay on *The Circle and the Cross* by Graham Pont (1990) caused me to attempt the hermeneutics of the Eightsome Reel, but before this I must say something about its composition. According to Piper Bill Clement recent research has shown that the *Blair Atholl Eightsome Reels* were dedicated to the Atholl Highlanders, arranged by Helen Lady Forbes and published by J Marr, Wood & Co, Piano Makers to H M The Queen and H R H The Prince of Wales, 183 Union Street, Aberdeen (Price 2/- nett). In the programme of the Blair Atholl Eightsome Reel Ball, 30 September 1989, Margaret G Brander points out that Helen was the second daughter of Sir Thomas Moncreiffe of that Ilk (7th Baronet) and married to Sir Charles Forbes of Newe. Lord Frederic Hamilton's memoirs state that "she was the most perfect example of classical beauty I have ever seen". Indeed all eight of Sir Thomas' daughters were celebrated Victorian beauties. Another of them, Louisa, became the wife of the 7th Duke of Atholl.

According to the (now Royal) Country Dance Society (1930) the dance was worked up by the Earl of Dunmore and several friends from their recollection of 'Round Reels', which were in danger of being forgotten. They spent a week in the early eighteen seventies evolving this dance in time for the Atholl Gathering Ball. The young gathering at Blair Castle at that time were mostly in their twenties and thirties and must have enjoyed trying out the components of the eightsome reel as we know it today. Later that season, or possibly the following year, it was introduced at the Portree Ball, and at Perth. It caught on throughout the country and became a feature at the Royal Caledonian Ball in London from 1890. There are examples of round dances to be found in old books, but none with the same figures.

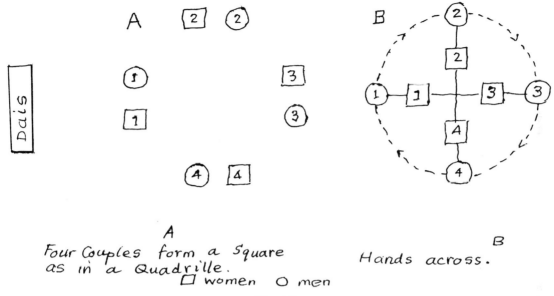

Fig. 17a
The Blair Atholl Eightsome Reel.

The Blair Atholl Eightsome Reel

The starting position, A. The square represents the earth; its four sides the seasons. The first movement (8 slip steps to the left, 8 slip steps to the right) represents the circle of the sky and the universe (heaven), for this is a cosmic dance. The second movement (bars 9-12) is hands across, B, the women first in the centre; then men's hands across to return to base (bars 13-16). The cross within a circle was the emblem of the prehistoric Great Goddess. It symbolised life itself and fertility and the Four Seasons, Fig 17b.

Bars 17-20 Set to partners twice. Bars 21-24 Turn partners. Bars 25-40 The grand chain (the women moving in the direction of the sun) may represent the epiphany of the Great Goddess in the form of interweaving serpents. (The undulating serpent symbolises among Australian aborigines the life force. The turning point half way round the grand chain represents the cosmic egg, as shown in Fig 17c.) The men in the grand chain have the less important role in that they move anti-sun in direction.

One may note here, with George Bain (1951, p. 59) that the Scottish Highlander's sword-dance, being a war dance, is anti-sunwise, but finishes sunwise symbolically of victory.

The second part of the dance is quite different. Seven of the eight dancers are in their original square formation, representing the earth or land. The first woman goes into the centre of the dance and dances alone, usually the Pas de Basque. The other seven take hands and dance around her, eight slip steps sunwise and eight steps back. The first woman sets to her partner, or season, and turns him; then to the opposite man (no 3) and turns him; then all three do a reel of three, probably a bee dance. (The epiphany of the Great Goddess as a bee is discussed by Gimbutas (1990, p. 181). A bee dance survives among the Hopi Indians. Then she dances to the man on her right (no 4), and turns him; and finally with the man opposite to him (no 2); and has thus visited all the 'quarters' of the year.

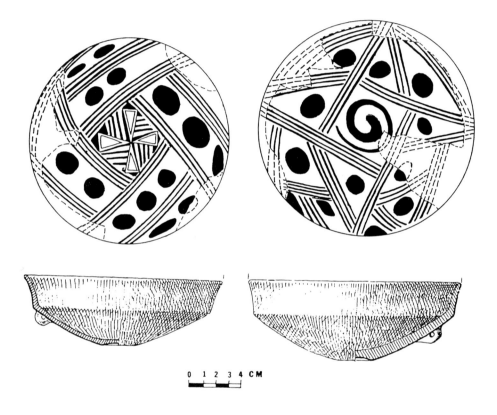

Fig. 17b
Graphite-painted dishes with cross and snake motifs in the centre of the cosmos.
Tangîru mound, Romania. East Balkan civilisation. Mid-fifth millennium BC.

When all four women have danced from the centre, all four men do the same. Then the first half of the dance is repeated as in bars 1-40.

This cross and circle dance is apparently of great antiquity; its continuing popularity today confirms the heritage of their Neolithic ancestry by Scots all over the world. Indeed as soon as the eightsome reel is announced and *The Deil among the Tailors* is played, those who are triggered by the music feel that they will soon be in a state of ecstasy. Even those who cannot dance will throw themselves into action in a manner they would never be seen doing in ordinary circumstances; but the better dancers are visibly carried away and often have a faraway look in their eyes.

Fig. 17c.
Cosmic snake and cosmic egg compositions painted on Lake Cucuteni vases from Sipinstsi, western Ukraine. c. mid-fourth millennium BC.

From *The Goddesses and Gods of Old Europe* by Marija Gimbutas, published by Thames and Hudson, London.

Marghanita Laski (1961) in *Ecstasy: a study of some secular and religious experiences* quotes the definition of ecstacy as "extraordinary to the point of often seeming as if derived from a preternatural source". Transcendant ecstasy "takes one right out of this world." In a pleasant and happy evening of Scottish Country Dances only the Eightsome Reel seems to induce this unusual state of mind.

In country places a rather clod-hopping jig step may replace the ballroomish slip step and some parts of the sequence tend to be left out. Even the Royal Scottish Country Dance Society allows that in stead of the slip step the Pas de Basque may be used. However the Dunmore-Blair Atholl reconstruction seems to have preserved a great deal of what had deep religious significance thousands of years ago, long before the Indo-European Celts brought their languages to the British Isles. On the other hand the country or contra dances were nearly all composed during the last 350 years.

In the Eightsome Reel the men raise their arms when setting in a pose usually thought to resemble a red deer's antlers; but the pose more likely represents a bull's horns and forms a link with ancient Greece. Two heads of the aurochs found in the clay of the Cuilc, a reedy lochan in Pitlochry, have been preserved in Blair Castle. However, it is said that the Celtic god Cernunnos (from 'cornu', horn) carried deer's antlers (M Eliade (1989), p. 96).

In 1937 the Scottish Country Dance Society was invited abroad for the first time. Miss Jean Milligan came to the London branch to give the team led by Mrs Anne Law a final training session. She and the bagpiper, Angus Macaulay of Benbecula, were both created bards at the Gorsedd held at the Crec'h à la Clarté not far from Peros-Guirec on 26 July, under the Taldir or Chief of the Druids, François Jaffrenou, who had founded with Camille Le Mercier d'Erm, the Parti nationaliste breton (Strollad Broadel Breiz) in October 1911 in the same month that the Monument de la Honte nationale, symbolising Brittany kneeling at the feet of France, was erected. (The Union with France was in 1532).

In the open-air Concert held the day before, Gweltas Jaffrenou played the Great Highland bagpipes. Angus helped him and his colleagues to tune the pipes which are now played in commendable style in Brittany as a national instrument in addition to their own biniou and bombarde. Today the Vale of Atholl Pipe Band plays a number of Breton melodies in its repertoire.

On Saturday 5th March 1938 the London Highland Club provided 32 dancers for the Polytechnic Tours Jubilee Reunion in the Albert Hall. Although I was appointed *chorodidáskelos* or trainer of the dancing team, I could never bring so many dancers together for a rehearsal. We had to do without. Instead, four leaders were appointed to drill their own teams of eight and every dancer was given a set of instructions. Pipe-Major Ian Macdonald-Murray led the party so that all the men faced all the women for the country dance Petronella. Then the dancers moved neatly so as to form a great star of eight Foursome Reels. The pattern then dissolved into a waltz, during which three fresh dancers were exchanged for tired ones at an exit, and the waltz suddenly recrystallised as four Eightsomes, at the end of which another country dance was performed, - 23 minutes non-stop!

Before the concert began the four leaders met in the empty hall, illuminated only by a single vertical spotlight focussed on the centre of the floor. After we had paced out the floor and memorised exactly where we had to go between dances, and the piper knew how many bars to play, we laid down swords and danced the Argyll Broadswords alone under the vast dome of this magnificent building. Recollecting this fifty years afterwards, Dr David N Lowe said that it was the highlight of his life, even though he had had many interesting experiences as Secretary of the British Association for the Advancement of Science and then of the Carnegie UK Trust. David was the son of a teacher of dancing in Dundee and his two brothers were judges of Highland Dancing at Annual Games. Another long line of dance teachers began with John Lowe of Brechin (fl. 1790s). His sons Joseph (d. 1866) taught in Edinburgh and Inverness and Robert (d. ca 1852) taught in Glasgow, Montose, Brechin and Forfar. This teaching family continued until 1971 (A MacFadyen 1992). My own great great great grandfather, Robert Robertson, born in Moulin in 1721, was musician to John Jenkins, Master of Manners or teacher of deportment and dancing in Dundee from 1749 onwards. (The reason why the dancing Lowes have an e in their surname was given under Performance Coefficients in Chapter 16: of course, dancers have a 'fine conceit' of themselves').

We were unfortunately too busy on that memorable day to see the 'Bella Nissa' Folklore Group from Nice in the French Riviera dance La Nissarda, La Nicoise and Les Rondes Niçoises, a Quadrille, but when David Lowe visited Nice after the War he noticed that a solo Provençal dance was strikingly similar to Highland dancing; the accompaniment was by a man playing pipe and tabor.

Dr Jacques Martin consulted *Les danses de Provence* by Marcelle Mourgies (1983) and found that the pattern of, alas, only 15 dance tunes would have been like the Scottish pattern if there had been many more RR tunes and some more RU tunes. The absence of RR tunes is surprising since some dances describe ancient rites: thus UU tunes accompanied a fertility dance, which survives also in England; UU and UR tunes accompany two different fights between summer and winter; a myth of the cosmic tree (like a maypole) has a DD tune; and nature's awakening is RU. Perhaps the music is Celtic and therefore later than the music of the Highlands. All the other dances seem to belong to the present millenium, judging by subject and style, - *la fricasséio militari; lou brandi gavot; la danso dei fielouso; la dansa dei jardinièro* (a hope dance); the *volto renaissenço* (quoted by Shakespeare in Henry V); *u guiardo* and two others including *la farandoulo classico*, the national dance. Further work is needed on dating these dances and their tunes since the sample was too small.

In this century Scotland had the reputation of being 'dancing-mad'. George Morrow (1992) wrote that Scotland had in the 1950s more dance halls and ballrooms per head of population than any other country on earth.

Roy Castle, in preparing for a BBC 3 programme (30 June 1991), 1840h), was told by a local historian that the Maltese place an Easter egg on an edible base in the shape of the Mother Goddess, similar in outline to the most famous of the Neolithic temples of the island. In the same programme a courtly dance was performed: the 12 dancers began in a linear arrangement reminding one of the 18th century. Their costume was of the same period, but the dance itself depicted a square becoming a circle and then the grand chain or serpent's dance. The dance also included a 'hands across' element, the whole representing the Mother Goddess, with emphasis on the sky and the sea of an island.

The dances of Scotland in their subtle and intricate footwork and in their remarkable 'elevation' reveal the desire to show personal excellence of performance. In team dancing grace, elegance and accuracy in the 'drill' give expression to the other side of the social duality, seen also in the crofting culture, in which crofters owned cattle personally but sheep communally in 'township committees'. (This system was discouraged by the Crofters Commission and finally eliminated by the Highlands and Islands Development Board (1969-1990). Yet we had here a model for a social structure which was more moral than unbridled competition and the 'devil take the hindmost' system of the world we live in today).

At the beginning of World War II, during the 'Cold War', a problem was to maintain fitness and morale in the army building up in Britain. I was asked to run a class of

Scottish Country Dances so that the officers of the Canadian Seaforth Highlanders could learn them with the women of Blechingley in Surrey. Many dances were learned and the 'discipline' was exemplary. The officers thereafter introduced the dances to the men, making fitness and co-operation a pleasant aim.. The officers led from within and got to know their men better.

I have said nothing about *accelerando* in dance music. Scottish dances are characteristically in strict tempo, whereas some Hungarian dances increase in speed throughout the dance. Certainly in Scotland the slow Strathspey is followed by the fast Reel-time in a Foursome Reel. *Accelerando* seems to have survived in Northwest American dancing if H.W. Longfellow's *Hiawatha's Wedding Feast* is anything to go by. When I went to a boarding school in my fourteenth year new boys in my group were obliged to sing a song. I asked if I could fetch my music; and then I sang 'The Beggar's Dance' to the music by S Coleridge - Taylor (op 30, no.1) (1898). I was laughed at for being a horrid little prig! Never mind. I love it still and here are the words:

" You shall hear how Pau-Puk-Keewis,
—
Danced at Hiawatha's wedding;
———
First he danced a solemn measure,
Very slow in step and gesture,
In and out among the pine trees,
Through the shadows and the sunshine.
Treading softly like a panther,
Then more swiftly and still swifter,
Whirling, spinning round in circles,
Leaping o'er the guests assembled,
Eddying round and round the wigwam.
Till the leaves went whirling with him,
Till the dust and wind together
Swept in eddies round about him".

What a dance!

Religion

Stuart Piggott in his book *The Druids* is of the opinion that religious practices may also have such an ancient history. There were, it seems, three main antecedent phases in Celtic religion; the first, predominantly Indo-European, goes back to about 4000 bp and perhaps to its beginnings. Behind this again would be the wholly obscure religions of the Neolithic agriculturalists - from the end of the fourth millenium BC (say 5200 bp) and "finally, underlying all, there would be beliefs and rites of pre-agricultural Europe which might well have contained elements surviving in shamanism. It is a pedigree which could be a good 20,000 years in length". Perhaps a study of the music in the Altai Mountains, Scythia and Lappland, which preserve elements of early shamanistic religion, would throw light on their prehistoric development. The Scottish musical evidence needs to be reworked to see if the pre-Pictish, Gaelic and Anglic contributions to music can be disentangled; such a study could be extended to Norway and, especially, to Iceland as well as to Orkney and Shetland.

Marija Gimbutas in *The Goddesses and Gods of Old Europe* (1974) provoked a tremendous reaction. She was branded as a feminist, whose explanation of the Balkan figurines as evidence for a Mother Goddess was quickly adapted by parascientific cultists. Close inspection of this evidence does not allow one to make any firm conclusions about the gender of the deities worshipped in pre-Christian times, maintains Hutton (1991). To this author "it now seems that the Picts were probably another set of the Celts, indistinguishable in their culture from other tribes in Britain". He goes too far in the opposite direction since he fails to consider Anthony Jackson's detailed analysis of the importance of women in the succession of tribal chiefs (1987).

Part of the history of religion in aboriginal countries will be treated in the next essay - on the Land.

The Land

In Stone Age Australia, "every major topographical feature was endowed with mythological significance. It was not part of Aboriginal culture to build monuments such as megalithic tombs or pyramids. Natural landmarks are the centres of religion and ceremony. The places where Aboriginal people gather for the great ceremonies are not marked by formal structures - the land is their cathedral" (Flood 1983).

American Indians were and are also deeply religious, and felt their relationship with rocks, trees, animals and the landscape. They believed in one creator and that the land was a gift not a possession. In two moving BBC programmes *Savagery and the American Indians* in the *Timewatch* series (23 and 30 January 1991) the impact of Europeans on native culture was described. To the English the natives were 'lazy, shiftless' and the land was visited by them only occasionally. The land appeared to be empty, boundless and there to be taken, built on and 'developed'. When forced to cede land by treaties the natives argued that "our land is more important to us than your money. We cannot sell what was put there by the Great Spirit. It is not ours to sell". See also the *Book of the Hopi* (F Waters 1963).

Among the few remaining Indians, who have not been forced into the American melting pot, some are trying to reassert their old culture and to take over their own destiny. To them the main idea is a sustainable entity or universe; an exploitable entity is or rather was the European idea, for now we too have the seeds of a green philosophy and ecology is better understood. Lovelock's *Gaia* palely reflects the Indian's view "that the earth is my mother". The Indian thinks of quarries as 'wounds'.

The Scottish Highlanders and Islanders still retain a very strong sense of affinity with the land. James Hunter in *The Making of the Crofting Community* (1976) discusses the traditional belief that they owned the land they occupied from time immemorial; that deer, fish and game birds were theirs; "he considers them the unconfined bounty of heaven". More important still was "the concept that the tribe, clan or community which lived and worked upon the land had a right to permanent occupation of it".

Hunter decided that this notion which has its origins in the remote antiquity of the Celtic peoples could not be traced back to its origins in his book because it deals especially with its expression in nineteenth century crofting life. I should add that 'pre-Celtic' would be more apposite.

When Lord Leverhulme outlined his commercial fishing schemes for Lewis to a group of his dissident tenantry about 1918, he painted a vivid picture of what life would be like when he would provide "steady work, steady pay, beautiful houses for all", one of the ringleaders made in impassioned tones a short speech in Gaelic, which in English went "Come, come men! This will not do! This honey-mouthed man would have us to believe that black is white and white is black. We are not concerned with his fancy dreams that may or may not come true! What we want is the land - and the question I put to him now is: *will you give us the land?*"

As the Board of Agriculture's representative reported, "Lord Leverhulme's picture, so skilfully painted, was shattered in the artist's hand!" (Hunter, id, p.198)

Louis Macneice's poem *Leverhulme* in *I crossed the Minch* records the great man's arrival in his (European) heaven.

> Lever started the heavenly climb,
> He went up the stairs two at a time.
> St Peter said, Make room, make room.
> Here come Viscount Leverhulme.
>
> St Peter said, 'Don't be cross with me
> But this is a mere formality;
> Have you any failure to confess?'
> And Lever truthfully answered 'Yes'.
>
> 'All through my life I've made my bit
> From my day of birth to my obit
> And all my life I've done my best
> In the cause of enlightened self-interest.
>
> I've asked for nothing but a little rope
> And I paved Piccadilly with Sunlight Soap.
> Organisation was my flair—
> Organisation and savoir faire.
>
> In any deed that I had to do
> The thought of failure was taboo,
> Only once in time till now
> Did I take my hand from the racing plough.
>
> I left my programme incomplete,
> The Western Islands had me beat'.

St Peter said 'I'm not surprised;
To tackle Lewis was ill-advised.

The Scottish Islands are a rotten deal
Those Celts are terribly difficile;
We find them unwilling to pull their weight
When we let them in at the Golden Gate.

They've no team spirit, they won't take part
In our study circles and community art
And at garden parties they won't concur
In speaking English - which is de rigueur.

No one here will consider it
The least reflection on your native wit
That the ignorant crofters, penny-wise,
Should have sabotaged your enterprise'.

The instinctive feeling for the land which has led to land raids even in the twentieth century, as in Knoydart, will survive as long as Highlanders remain in their own country. One can still hear them condemn the sale of huge estates, often to foreigners as 'ridiculous', 'wicked' or 'obscene'. The view is expressed with the greatest vehemence when the sale is of holy ground such as Iona.

Chapter 17
MECHANICS 1220 AD

No strong signs of a peak of native mechanical prowess have been noticed in medieval Scotland. It may have expressed itself in the building of cathedrals, a Continental import rather than a Picto-Scottish art-form. Certainly St Andrews Cathedral Church, the largest single medieval building in Scotland was in use by the 1230s, and as Barrow (1981) says "most of the Scottish cathedrals as we have them today, whether beautiful even in ruin, like Elgin, or splendidly restored, like Dunblane, belong structurally to the period 1220-1280 AD, a wonderfully busy time for the Scottish stonemason."

'Mindless Wars'

Peace and tranquility were not to last long, because after the peak of mechanics, appalling devastation followed. Perhaps such wars should be expected when advances in mechanics can be used for warlike purposes. Fig 9 shows the interpolation of a 'wedge' from the time of Nero, through the Scottish Wars of Independence to World Wars I and II. In the Treaty of York between Alexander I and Henry III, the Scots' claim to northern English counties was finally abandoned (1237 AD). This is the equivalent of 1945 or thereby in England's Period VIII; Bannockburn (1314), equivalent to about 2000 AD, represents a recovery of spirit and the recovery of freedom and some measure of prosperity.

Events in Switzerland, traditionally dated to 1291 and 1315, beginning in Schwyz, Uri and Unterwald, led to a common resolve to assert their freedom from external overlordship and eventually to the Helvetic Confederation of today. A fuller account was given in chapter 15.

The last two decades of the Scottish struggles were also bimodal, led in the one case by Sir William Wallace, fl. 1297-1305, and in the other by King Robert I the Bruce, fl. 1306-1314, a total span of 17 years.

World Wars I and II, 1914-19 and 1939-45, bimodal again, had a span of 31 years, 5 years longer than one would calculate from a straight-sided wedge beginning in 60 AD. The wedge seemed to be widening even further during the Vietnam war and the invasion of Afghanistan by the USSR. Was this split unstoppable?

The succession of mindless wars may be looked at more closely. The first of them, as we have said, was in the reign of Nero (54-68 AD) who, after a few years of quite good rule under the guidance of Seneca, "had espoused complete absolutism in Rome. This, and his profligacy with imperial resources, encouraged him to look around the Empire for more funds to replenish the depleted treasury. His gaze soon lit upon Britain, whose wealth had not so far produced the expected flow of revenues. This was due in large part to the Silures and Ordovices, who denied access to the lead and copper deposits in the Welsh mountains... Suetonius Paulinus, the Roman Governor, was appointed specifically to defeat these tribes" in 60 AD.

Anna Ross and Don Robbins (1989) not only wrote these words but revealed the importance of the gold road from Ireland, via Anglesea, to East Anglia as a most desirable source of wealth for transmission to Rome. The history of the year 60 AD is brilliantly reconstructed from events surrounding *The Life and Death of a Druid Prince*, based on a study of the bog-body known as the Lindow Man - a fascinating, true detective story.

The late spring and early summer of this fateful year was a darker hour for Britain than 1066 or 1939. The Celts suffered three appalling disasters: a huge army of them supported by Druids were slaughtered on a beach on Mona (Anglesea) at the Menai Straights; their sacred groves were destroyed, and the defeated Queen-Priestess Boudicca fled from a disastrous battle probably at Mancetter near High Cross in Warwickshire and committed suicide. Finally unrest caused by the rebellion led the farmers to abandon the planting of the spring crops.

We may note that the 'line' of mindless wars traced backwards in time meets the line of Period VI´ at about 450 BC. Such a date may represent the rapid spread of the Brythonic language into southern Britain.

We may see in this dreadful progression from Nero, through Edward I to Kaiser Wilhelm and Hitler of 'the intrusive wedge' - a technical intensification of mindless death-dealing which could end not only European culture but civilised life itself. Starting again with a new set of values becomes imperative. We shall return to this theme when we have completed this review of Scotland's Period VII´, for we cannot rule out the possibility that European civilisation itself may have already come to an end.

Chapter 18
Wealth, 1500 AD

When we come to the wealth line we have no difficulty in pin-pointing the peak date in the reign of King James IV, 1488-1513 (mean 1500) AD. Jenny Wormald (1981) writes of the "sheer exuberance of Scottish cultural and intellectual life in the late 15th century and early 16th century" and says that there was sufficient surplus of wealth to encourage patronage of the arts. It is no coincidence that the oldest surviving company in Britain, the Shore Porters Society of Aberdeen, was established in 1498 at the peak of Scotland's prosperity (*Guinness Book of Records*).

There was still a ready market for wool in Flanders, and the Scots made enough cloth for sale to the urban poor in Flanders, while importing much finer Flemish cloth. The staple had been established in Bruges by the end of the 14th century and had access to the first bourse. The Scottish warehouse, still to be seen there, was about the same size as the English one next door on the waterfront. The staple, now miles from the sea, moved to Middleburg in 1467, and finally settled at Veere in 1541.

Prosperity in Scotland, however, was not long-lived. The King and most of the Scottish nobles fell at the battle of Flodden in 1513. A weakened Scotland, deprived of leadership, was dealt a further blow by the Regnal Union in 1603, when James VI became James 1 of Great Britain, a fictional nation, ridiculed in Shakespeare's time by the parody "Fee, fi, fo, fum, I smell the blood of a British man!" Scotland was left to decline under a series of *gauleiters*.

Chapter 19
The Dark Age, 1693-1747 (pessimum 1707) AD

Scotland had become demoralised by bad harvests in the early 1690s. The country was financially ruined by the Darien Scheme and Scotland's ruin was plotted in London in the late 90s. Certainly no country in full vigour would have sold its freedom as the Scottish Estates did in 1707.

The incorporative union with England was in effect an Anschluss leading to the formation of Grossengland. The Highlanders held out until their culture was annihilated in 1746-7 by various punitive acts of parliament following the Jacobite rising of the '45, which was probably a more anti-Union phenomenon than the older history books conceded. The lowest point of the Dark Age is taken as 1707.

Thus a period of history in Scotland died with the dream of a great world emporium or free town on the Isthmus of Darien to be set up by The Company of Scotland, founded in 1695. Alas, noble ideals were smothered by greed; about a half of all the specie or cash in the land had been invested and lost. It may not come as a surprise to note that the Banks of England (1694), Scotland (1695) and France (1716) were founded in Scotland's Dark Age by Scots, whose contribution to these countries was to transfer the issue of money to individuals for their own profit at a high rate of interest (usury) - a truly Dark Age phenomenon.

Another country on the edge of Europe suffered a Dark Age at the same time. In 1640, when Philip IV attempted to deprive Catalonia of its rights and privileges, it gave itself up to Louis XIII of France. It was restored to Spain in 1659, and was once more occupied by the French from 1694 to 1697. Under Philip V, in 1714, Catalonia was deprived of its cortes and liberties. In 1715 the Catalan language was banned.

Genocide

The Acts of 1746 and '47 were in effect a cultural genocide - a crime recognised by the United Nations as a variety of genocide, which is usually associated with mass-murder. It is a crime none-the-less, and there are no amends. The Highlanders' dress, language and music have barely survived, but the destruction of a tribal society and the creation of a neofeudal landowning class has left apparently insoluble problems of land use.

Historically, of course, the crime of genocide was not recognised until the Nuremberg Trials in 1945 and 1946 to describe the Nazis' attempts to eliminate not only Jewish people, but also all signs of their way of life, institutions and culture. In the declaration of the United Nations in 1946 against genocide cultural destruction, as well as mass-murder, was recognised as a criminal act. In 1948 a Convention of the United Nations declared both forms of genocide a crime punishable by international law and stated that those who were guilty of this crime, soldiers and private citizens alike, should be considered personally and individually responsible for the crime itself. 'Obeying orders' was no defence.

Apparently there is no legal redress for the victims of genocide, *sensu stricto* or *sensu lato*, if the crime was committed centuries ago. In Scotland the perpetrators were at first Lowlanders. By the end of the 16th century the practice of genocide was being practised fairly systematically "so that the fate of the MacGregors was by no means unique" (Thomson and Grimble, 1968): "In 1605 the head of the Gordons offered to take in hand the service of settling the North Isles ... and to put an end to that service by extirpation of the barbarous people of the Isles within a year". Thus one of the most literate peoples in Europe was reduced to almost total illiteracy". Is there no redress in international law for genocide and memocide? Can reparations be assessed and paid? Or does time alone make all such crimes acceptable?

The scene then shifted to Westminster. "This identification between the cause of the Stewarts and Gaeldom proved to be fatal. It brought together the three principal sources of human cruelty, greed, religious intolerance and racial hostility in a policy of genocide in both Ireland and Scotland, that gathered momentum throughout the 18th century and continued into the present one". One must always be on the alert.

There has never been a perfect state or nation. When schoolchildren studied Ancient Greek they learned about great works of literature, architecture and art, and the beginnings of democracy, but their minds seldom dwelt on the slavery which sustained the privileged classes. Nor was the Fall of Melos, 416 BC, given much emphasis. Only thirteen years after Pericles died, the Athenians attacked the isle of Melos "with no other justification except that an autonomous island was an anomaly, threw a strong force ashore and summoned the Melians to submission. When the islanders refused to surrender ... the Athenians slew off the whole male population, and sold the women as slaves. This action was perhaps the most atrocious political crime committed in the whole" of the Peloponnesian war (Oman, 1913, p. 349). I am reminded of the Scots women who were deported to Birmingham and the like at the beginning of WWII.

Memocide

Dr Richard Dawkins, lecturer in animal behaviour at the University of Oxford, pointed out in *Memes and the Evolution of Culture* (1976) that while the gene, the DNA molecule, is the replicating entity among biological organisms on earth, cultural items, such as language, replicate non-genetically and at a far faster rate. He calls the unit of cultural replication the 'meme', a monosyllable similar to 'gene', inspired from Greek words which also give us 'mime'. We can therefore talk of genocide (*sensu stricto*), which means killing populations, and memocide, which means destroying cultures. Genocide (*sensu lato*) covers both.

The techniques used in memocide have been studied by Craig Beveridge and Ronald Turnbull in *The Eclipse of Scottish Culture* (1989). They developed the theme of Frantz Fanon (1967), who in *The Wretched of the Earth* "uses the idea to describe those processes in a relationship of national dependence which lead the native to doubt the worth and significance of inherited ways of life and embrace the styles and values of the coloniser ... it is through the undermining of the natives' self-belief and the disintegration of local identity that political control is secured," the process being known as 'inferiorisation'.

Memes can be erased by various techniques. Political prohibition is the most effective, such as the one-time laws against the sale of alcohol in the USA (though the laws were disobeyed), the elimination of a religion and its adherents in Germany (1930-1945), and the attempted extirpation of a language as in Brittany and in Scotland. The bureaucracy's usual method is by intimidation. In schools ridiculing can be wickedly effective. In a wider sphere personality destruction can be effected by the use of barbed words like 'crank', though Fritz Schumacher, author of *Small is Beautiful* (1973), was not hurt by being called a crank because, as an engineer, he knew what a useful tool a crank can be! Social ostracism keeps memes at bay: the rebellious mind may be black-balled in a club or society; a brilliantly creative member of staff may not be invited to join the board of a company even if he has the ability to serve well in the wider capacity. The Chairman of a meeting may prevent a radical solution being accepted. (On one occasion a meeting was called to discuss a new use for powdered peat: I had brought with me the research worker who had carried out the laboratory work and a letter from a company expressing a wish to finance the new product. The Chairman carefully avoided my eyes and never spoke to me. Consequently the industry was established in another country! In this case the 'power' through intimidation failed, though Scotland lost a new industry.)

Dawkins writes of the meme for blind faith in religion. The meme for blind faith also exists in politics, though, fortunately, it is no longer so common and many countries are achieving freedom. He also points out that, whereas genes can be advantageous to progeny, memes evolve only because they are advantageous to themselves; one can see examples in churches, the banking system, monetarism, government ('administrative convenience' rather than benefit to individuals) and other 'sets' or milieux.

Memocide can become a subconscious habit of mind. An example of this in the permanent civil service in London is given in Chapter 26. Far more common are the arrogant attitudes of members of the obducting classes towards the cultural heritage (memes) of the people under their control (Chapter 27). Rational discussion may not be possible between these two layers.

However, in the normal course of events, memes are much more long-lived than genes. The meme-complexes of Socrates, Leonardo, Copernicus, and Marconi are still going strong. Petrie dealt with the rapid spread of memes in his first law and of their slow decay through poor imitation. One could add to Law No 8 that most political ideas are bad mutations, though some of these can be eliminated by computer studies.

Memetics do not readily explain Petrie's Laws 2 and 3; but his Law 4 could be rephrased as "the rise and fall of a civilisation is genetically and memetically caused". Law 5 likewise needs now to be changed to "all periods begin with the infusion of new blood and/or new ideas"; of the two modes of transmission the latter can be the more effective and longer-lasting.

Memes in education are particularly powerful. The arrival of a single English-speaking (or 'Anglo-saxophone' as the late Oliver Brown used to say) child in a Gaelic-speaking class can oblige the schoolteacher to switch from Gaelic to English. University lecturers cannot use a single Scots word in lectures because some of the students might not know its meaning. One of the small-scale effects of meme-travel may be illustrated by the splendid surname H. D'Arbois de Jubainville, the first volume of whose great work on *Les Premiers Habitants de l'Europe* was published in 1889. His name may have fired the imagination of his contemporaries: Thomas Hardy's novel *Tess of the d'Urbervilles* came out in 1891 and Sir Arthur Conan Doyle's *The Hound of the Baskervilles* was published in 1902. The large-scale memetic effects of the 'media', if treated here, would unbalance this book and its writer.

Since culture is transmitted memetically we may be sure that Scottish culture cannot long survive too high a proportion of English students in Scottish universities, especially when students' societies are taken over by the wealthy, private-school-educated students, whose accents, clothes and attitudes can be seen or heard by all to be foreign. They have taken over the Kate Kennedy celebrations in St Andrews and ski-clubs in several universities. At Edinburgh Rob Brown (Scotsman, 28 December 1987) wrote that a group of Scots have set up an 'alternative ski society' called ScotSki as a refuge from the main club, which has long been dominated by the 'Yahs'. St Andrews University, where the proportion of Scottish domiciled students fell from 44 to 34 per cent between 1980 and 1986, tries to take into account a 'significant Scottish connection' of some sort when selecting British students, through their parents, for instance, or through their having been to a Scottish school, but no positive steps are taken to provide first year students with courses which would increase their cultural Scottishness. After all, the Yahs are a social group which is "notable for its indifference to - or disdain for - alternative views or habits. They usually fail to appreciate that in Scotland a unique set of values and historical traditions exist which do not defer to Anglocentric metropolitanism." The very existence of introductory courses to Scottish culture would also stimulate interest among the natives. Universities in other countries are more enterprising in this sphere.

At the University of Frankfurt-am-Main, for example, I was happy to attend a *Deutschkurs für Ausländer*, at Cambridge, scientists, at least at Caius College, had to write weekly essays for the Dean to criticise; and one of the best-written MSc or PhD theses I ever had to examine was by an Algerian, for, at Leeds University, post-graduates coming from certain countries spend a year perfecting their English before beginning their research. Language memes must be handled in a positive way, but they can be extirpated.

A national library one would imagine would be safe from destruction; but no! Look at the deplorable history of the great libraries of Pergamon and Alexandria. The latter was founded as the capital of Egypt by Alexander the Great in 322 BC and became the centre of Hellenistic culture until Julius Caesar destroyed the library in 30 BC, an appalling example of memocide. Mark Antony ingratiated himself with Cleopatra by transferring the immense library of Pergamon to Alexandria later that year. Thus the country around and north of Izmir (Smyrna) was deprived of its greatest riches because Antony was so besotted with the Egyptian queen. All the same the books and manuscripts (parchment was invented in Pergamon) were poorly curated and many were dispersed in 380 AD as Rome approached its Dark Age. The city was taken by Chosnes, King of Persia, in 616 AD, and in 640 AD by the Arabians under 'Amr, after a siege of 14 months, during which Heraclius, the emperor of Constantinople failed to send a single ship to its assistance. The library came to an end in 642 AD when the Muslims captured the city and burnt it. Mayan libraries were destroyed by the Spanish in 1528.

Hardly comparable but worth mentioning is the sale to the one-time Soviet Union of the only library of patents existing in Scotland. Admittedly the files were virtually inaccessible and gathering dust in Glasgow, but one regrets the loss of this valuable tool for industrial development. The recent removal of the reference collection of fossils from the British Geological Survey's offices in Edinburgh to a place called Keyworth in England is also an unwarrantable removal of one of Scotland's intellectual resources (1992).

Chapter 20
Scotland's New Period (VIII'), after 1707

The Treaty of the Act of Union did not bring immediate prosperity to Scotland. The 'final solution' of the 'Highland Problem' after the '45 ("whose problem?" one may ask) and the guarantee of peace after centuries of bellicose behaviour between the Scots and the English released the long pent-up energies of the Scots - in poetry, prose, science, technology and philosophy - the so-called Scottish Enlightenment, a phenomenon unmatched on such a scale in England. The Enlightenment was a European phenomenon within the century 1750-1850. Robert Burns was one of the few who remained true to Scottish traditions; Sir Walter Scott was ambivalent. Scott preserved many ancient customs and linguistic treasures, but had in mind an English or touristic audience. Other authors took pains to remove all Scotticisms from their written work. Thomas Sheridan the second saw an opportunity and taught English pronunciation in Edinburgh. (If only one could hear a tape-recording of him at work!) The Scottish Enlightenment relates more to the ferment of ideas in Napoleonic France than to the early stages of recovery from a Dark Age, which was the true position in which Scots lived.

In *Scotland's Scientific Heritage* A.G. Clement and I selected as objectively as we could over 200 Scots who had made major contributions to science, engineering and medicine in the time-span 1600-1950. Their births were first plotted in each decade, Fig. 18. It is obvious that they were most numerous between 1760 and 1850; and that the peak was at about 1805. This corresponds with the time generally known as the Industrial Revolution.

Fig. 19 provides a closer analysis of the dates of each person's most famous contribution since the numbers have been divided by the population. In this way we arrived at the output of inventions or discoveries per million per decade. The blocks, at 1600, 1700, 1750, 1800, 1850, 1870, 1900 and 1950 were chosen for statistical reasons ('smoothing'). The peak of achievement at 1830 corresponds with the birth peak at 1805.

The rising part of the curve is exponential and may be explained by bright and creative people 'meme-infecting' several others in their life-time. An excellent educational tradition inspired even more.

One would have expected the curve to even off to an S or sigmoidal shape. If nothing disastrous had occurred a high proportion of bright Scots would have been born for a very long time; but from about 1830 the output of inventions and discoveries by Scots plummeted from about 7 per million per decade to only one in 1930; in other words this valuable group in Scottish society has been decimated more than eighteen times (7 x 0.9 x 0.9 x 0.9...) Clearly this disaster requires some explanation.

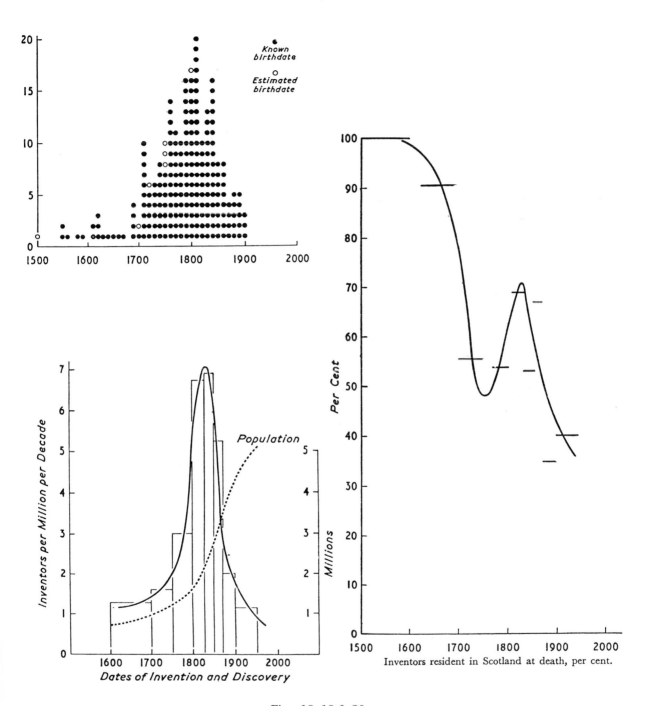

Figs. 18, 19 & 20
From A. G. Clement and R.H.S.R. Robertson, *Scotlandd's Scientific Heritage*, Oliver & Boyd.
Edinburgh and London, 1961,

The most incriminating cause of this decline has been emigration of the most illustrious. Bright people do not remain in a cultural backwater; they go where the scientific 'bright lights' are to be found. Medical men from Scotland flooded even the English countryside. 'Lads o' pairts' proverbially became 'heids o' depairtments'. The London theatre, press, and scientific institutions attracted the brightest, hardiest Scots for generation after generation. The promise of a fine recovery after Scotland's darkest times in the early 18th century was shattered.

The damage done has been measured by Lynn, who showed (1979) that the average IQ of children in Scotland has declined by $3^1/_2$ percent in this century. The damage done is irreversible unless many bright Scots return home in their prime of life. The most effective political act which could be made to restore Scotland would be to vote huge sums to the universities and to newly established institutions where discoveries and inventions could be developed commercially under good management. On the other hand further colonisation by the English would hasten the demise of Scottish culture at a time when it could and should be healthily progressing. See Fig. 20.

Very rarely in history do different arts flourish together. I discussed the resurgence of the arts in Egypt when the heavy burden of administration by the Hyksos Kings was removed (Chapter 29). We have noticed a similar phenomenon in the Scottish Enlightenment (Chapter 20) and we can now see signs of renewed artistic creation. These phenomena can be related to the relief of tension, such as would be felt by the removal of an unwanted government or a long-drawn-out threat of war. Scotland is moving away from its Dark Age around 1720- fitfully it would seem, Fig. 22. Paul H Scott said (1989) in his Rectorial Address to the University of Dundee "It is another aspect of the same upsurge that Scottish literature, music, the visual arts, historical research, journalism and publishing are all now more vigorous and assertive than at any time since the collapse of intellectual nerve at about the end of the 1830s. The recovery in both political and cultural terms began about a hundred years ago and has been gathering pace ever since", (Scotsman 24 April 1989). The present upsurge runs parallel with the growing feeling that independence is desirable and within grasp. Why! even Sir Peter Swynnerton Dyer, who chaired the University Grants Committee and the Universities' Funding Committee for many years, said on his retirement (often a moment of truth!) that he felt that Scottish university education should be funded within Scotland, and not in the future from Bristol of all places (Scotsman 28 March 1991).

Chapter 21

Who are the Scots today?

In 1954 A.E. Mourant published his great work on *The Distribution of the Human Blood Groups.* He and J Morgan Watkin had already related blood groups to anthropology and language in Wales and the western counties of England. The biologist W.T.W. Potts (1992) has reviewed the ABO blood group evidence in the British Isles in the light of the fact that it is the proportion of genes (p,q,r) which gives the proportion of constituents in a hybrid population, whereas the proportion of blood groups does not. The distribution of genes in Europe shows that the populations of the north and west of Britain and Ireland have a very distinctive genetic make-up, whereas the people of the east and south of England closely resemble their continental neighbours. Even today the inhabitants of Lincolnshire and East Anglia are strikingly similar genetically to the inhabitants of northwest Germany and Schleswig Holstein, but the Welsh, the Scottish Highlanders and Islanders, and the western Irish must be descended mainly from much earlier settlers.

The present Scottish population, Highland and Lowland together, is in origin about 75 percent Mesolithic and Neolithic and only about 25 percent from later incomers, which include 'Beaker Folk', Brythonic, Gaelic, Anglic, Lithuanian, Ukranian, Polish, Chinese and others. Scotland is not a Celtic country; the inhabitants are essentially pre-Celtic aboriginals.

The English component in Scotland may be under-estimated by this method because there is a cline or gradual decrease in the proportion of 'Old People' from the northwest of Scotland to virtually none in East Anglia, where the people are almost wholly of Germanic origin. The line where half the population is of ancient origin must be somewhere in the north of England, so, when a 'Geordie' or a Yorkshireman looks for a job in Scotland he (or she) may be attracted by the thought or instinct of going to live among a similar and not a foreign people.

For the same reason, I believe, so many Italians settled in Scotland during the last century. Many of them came from Barga, and the country around there, in the middle of the Tuscan group of Ligurian place-names (Fig 12); these include Forno Vel*asco* and F*osci*ano. Another group came from around Picinisco, northeast of Naples. The National Library put on an exhibition *The Italian Scots*, 1 July to 31 October 1991. "Maybe the most significant thing about their role in our lives was their cheerfulness, a natural gaiety, which brightened even the most trivial transaction, and a dignity which sensed the precise line between service and servility". (W Gordon Smith, *Scotland on Sunday*, 1 Sept 1991) Among their families one can count literary, artistic and scientific people of distinction. Dr Terri Colpi has recorded their contribution to Scottish life and culture in *The Italian Factor* and *Italians Forward* (1991).

By way of contrast, I noticed when writing *Scotland's Scientific Pioneers* that only two of those who had made their name in Scotland's Golden Age were English - Roebuck and Lister. But there is still an attraction to Scotland from countries where there are live descendants of the 'Old People, and Scots are interested in their countries.

James Boswell, a Scot, was the champion of General Pascal Paoli, the leader of the Corsican nation, whom he visited in 1765. The French consul in Edinburgh towards the end of World War II and afterwards, Joe Chiari, a Corsican, was warmly received by literary folk and contributed verses to some of their publications.

A Ph.D thesis on Scottish nationalism was awarded in France to a Nicois; the Sorbonne also sponsored theses (1990) on medieval clan leadership in Rossshire and on Scottish ethnozoology by a half-Corsican. All of these are examples of the Auld Alliance among pre-Celtic peoples. So is the connection between the Royal Bank of Scotland and the Bank of Santander.

A representative of the 'Old People' of Iceland is Magnus Magnusson, who is fully identified with the cultural life of Scotland; and his family keep up the tradition.

Scottish culture was held in such low esteem by University professors in Scotland about 1964 that a very low proportion of all student theses had any Scottish content and the Social and Economic Inquiry Society of Scotland, who found this to be true, itself withered away and died in 1973.

But the message may have been accepted because a great deal of outstanding work on Scottish subjects has been published since then, - a veritable upswing at last.

Let us take another look at the Icelanders. Although they speak a Norse language, they are closely akin to the Irish and Scots. A detailed analysis of their genetic characters by Thompson (1975) showed that, at the most, only 7 per cent of the ancestors of the modern Icelanders came from Scandinavia. At least 93 percent were Scottish or Irish. They were probably taken along as serfs by the Viking leaders, although some Gaels reached Iceland before the Norse.

 At first one may be astonished that a stable society could be managed by such a small élite class - only a twentieth of the whole population; but this was small compared with the government of the sub-continent of India where 50,000 soldiers and administrators of the British Raj ruled 6,000 times as many people for a long time and with considerable success, a subject discussed by John Lawrence (1990).

As we have said, Potts' work proved that the Scottish population to this day are mainly Mesolithic. They are aborigines * with only a quartile of later admixture. Even the English, apart from East Anglians, are Mesolithic to some extent, especially in the north. The editor of *Nature*, (29 March 1964, 308, 387) once asked rhetorically "Is Britain a part of Europe?" The answer to this must be 'yes' for one cannot exclude our prehistoric heritage. The question was born of insularity. Europe is a huge and variegated *pizza*. The filling represents the familiar nation states speaking Indo-European languages; the sides and bottom holding the thing together represent the Stone Age basis of European civilisation. Perhaps one should call it the *Flan* of Europe, rather than a pizza, the edges of which would be too narrow for it to be a good metaphor. Gesturally, a plan has sharp edge, but a flan's edges are wider and less distinct.

---

* Early use of this word to describe British subjects was by the Rev. Donald Sage, son of the Gaelic minister of Kildonan. He was an eye-witness of the Sutherland Clearances in 1819. He describes in his *Memorabilia Domestica* how he was summarily bereft of his 'flock of aborigines' (Milne, 1942 p.61-62).

Recent research has shown that a modern city's genetic structure reflects its tribal past. Jones(1989) in a review article began with Hiroshima and Nagasaki, whose populations are, for tragic reasons, genetically the best known in the world. Japan was first settled about 30,000 years ago. For much of its history it was divided into a series of warring clans not unlike those found in South America today, where each Indian tribe is genetically isolated from its neighbours by geographical and social barriers which are impermeable enough to allow individual tribes to accumulate unique genetic variants called ' private polymorphisms' which do not spread to adjacent groups. Many of these are characteristic of a particular tribe as are surnames in Europe. Thus the genes of the inhabitants of the modern Sicilian town of Messina still show strong affinities with those of modern Greece, - Messina was one of the centres of Magna Graecia founded about 800 BC.

Piazza and others (1988) constructed a genetic history of Italy on the basis of 34 gene frequencies and illustrated the cline which exists from north to south, a fairly stable feature which persists also in the elongated British mainland. "The genetic history of Italy is not a classification of different kinds of environment, but more likely the result of the ancient history of peoples with their settlements and movements. Genetic drift was the probable cause of differentiation among the different ethnic groups who settled in the country". So it happens that in Italy languages and genes have a similar distribution and therefore a probable common ancestry.

The dispersion of the Indo-european languages began about 3000 BC, before or in the Early Iron Age. "It seems plausible that they were not brought to Italy through massive migrations, but rather by a moderate number of carriers originating roughly in the Danubian area, who reached Italy with metallurgical skills by a transalpine and/or an Adriatic route (Pulgram 1958; Devoto 1962).

Harding and Sokal (1988) widened the scope of study to the whole of Europe and concluded that the results indicated that European gene pools still reflect the remote origins of some ethnic units subsumed by the major linguistic groups and that affinities between modern European gene-pools have been formed primarily by relatively short-range gene flow between geographically adjacent populations. Their work confirms that the transmission of languages is from brain to brain rather than from body to body and is a cultural, memetic phenomenon.

In his latest work, summarised in *Science*, 4.9.1992, p. 1346 by Leslie Roberts, Robert Socal has tried again to show by genetic analyses whether the Indo-Europeans swept into Europe from north of the Black Sea in horse-borne warrior bands or migrated in from the Middle East as an agricultural people; but his new data showed that both hypotheses were wrong. However, he seriously doubts whether the former "Kurgan" people were Indo-Europeans. On the other hand Cavalli-Sforza, Gimbutas and Renfrew think that these invaders spoke a primitive form of Indo-European. The debate continues, but Petrie's revised diagram, discussed in the present book, suggests there is only one western civilisation but two time phases, the earlier of which still shows Stone Age 'symptoms'; the later is more solidly 'Indo-European' in culture. Perhaps Petrie can reconcile these doughty research workers. Perhaps a few gene groups will be found to coincide with the two major groups of people identified in this book.

To answer the question how the Scots inherited their undoubted ability we must try to disentangle that which has been genetically inherited and that which has been memetically acquired. This subject has been deplorably, though understandably, muddied by political views overriding scientific findings, by Hitler's crimes and by Sir Cyril Burt's fraud. The proportion of intelligence measurements which has been attributed to inheritance has ranged from 0 to about 80 percent according to the method of study, but Cavalli-Sforza (1983) hazards the view that "most modern and reliable investigations suggest an approximately equal importance for genetically and culturally transmissible factors". Nevertheless he and his colleagues at Stanford University Medical School in California have found that " racial differences that have been conclusively shown to be innate represent - perhaps without exception - adaptations to different climatic and other local conditions, or the effects of random events", and that "the transformation and differentiation of local populations, of which the formation of races is an outcome, is the elementary process of biological evolution. The forces behind it include *mutation, selection, drift* and *migration.*

In Scotland we are especially concerned with the *founder effect,* " a special case of random genetic drift, which comes about when a new population is established in a previously uninhabited land by a group of immigrants, 'the founders'. Except for later additions by immigration or changes by migration, the genes found in the population in future generations will be limited to those present among the founders. Genetic drift tends to generate homogeneity within populations but heterogeneity *between* populations".It is reasonable to suppose that the first colonisers of Scotland after the last Ice Age were hardy, enterprising and intelligent.

They may also have been musical and artistic; and some of their tastes may have persisted to the present time because later immigrations have always been of far fewer people that the ever-growing population of the aborigines. The bulk of the Scottish inheritance could be derived from people arriving 6 to 10 at a time in skin-boats, about 8500 years ago. Such boats were more seaworthy than dugout canoes, as was pointed out by H Shetelig and A Brøgger in *The Viking Ships.* Several times that number, perhaps, could have brought farming to the country in the 'Neolithic Revolution' about 5550 bp and maybe not many more in the Bronze Age influx of new genes about 4000 bp when the Beaker culture was introduced. I can visualise a few hundred Gaels sailing into Dalriada between 350 and 500 AD in rather bigger boats, yet in the end, in spite of small numbers, they won supremacy over the more numerous Picts, the original inhabitants.

Menozzi, Piazza and Cavalli-Sforza (1978) had calculated that the expansion of farming in Europe progressed at the rate of about 1 kilometer/year. The spread of farming could have been either demic or cultural - or it could have been both. However the genetic consequences would have been different. If both, they argue, *clines* would have developed, which they did. They are particularly clear in the maps of the Rh- (Rhesus negative) and HLA-B allele frequencies. Rh- may have been close to 100 percent in northwestern hunter-gatherers in Europe; Rh+ came later both from the east and from the southwest, apparently in different migrations. E-W and NW-SE clines or gradual transitions are shown in maps of different groups of alleles, usually several dozens of them taken at a time, the results of a colossal research effort. The NW-SE genetic cline parallels the diffusion of farming.

By the use of colours these authors showed how farming progressed from 8500 bp in the Middle East and then in bands of 500 years each towards the West. The dates are uncorrected radiocarbon dates and are therefore somewhat lower than true dates. Nevertheless, the bands representing 8500-8000, 8000-7500, 7500-7000, 7000-6500, 6500-5500 and ≤5500 bp (say 4000 BC) show a considerable amount of detail. As an example, one can see that Switzerland was occupied somewhat later than the country around.

Fig. 1 of these authors gives the "first principle component of gene frequencies from 38 independent alleles at the human loci of ABO, Rh, MNS, Le, Fy, PGM, HLA-A and HLA-B". Here in a band lie Scotland, the northern part of Ireland, Yorkshire and Lincolnshire, a prolongation south of Manchester, the north of Denmark, Scandinavia, all the Baltic States and a strip along the west of Finland. Their third figure links north-west Ireland with Iberia and Gascony. Another set of allele frequencies separates Liguria and Provence from Occitania; and also shows the old area of the English north-midlands. The HLA gene frequencies show the NW-SE cline very well (their Fig. 5).

How are all these maps, some of which reflect past movements of people, 'bearing gifts' one may say, to be construed when our pattern of history (our Fig 9) suggests that there has been but a single civilisation from the Aegean and Egypt to the Atlantic and to northern seas? The answer I think becomes apparent if you accept that the allele maps and the cultural peak diagram are both in the main genetically determined. Farming and languages and designs on pots and figurines are of course memes and are transmitted by people, who, compared with the learners, may have been few or numerous. Given a good meme, an artist or other gifted person, perhaps of a cultured caste among the older people, would bring the new art quite quickly to a high peak of perfection. Our methods of study have brought us to focus on our truly genetic inheritance. Cavalli-Sforza (1983) reminds us that "at least 50,000 years ago, not only had man achieved the biological structure found in all modern races, he has also perfected stone tools, had used fire for a long time, was developing artistic abilities comparable with modern ones, and had most probably brought communication by language close to present standards."

"Even some 10,000 years ago, however, the human population was still relatively small, almost 1000 times smaller than today - of the order of 5 - 15 million."

Genetic markers tabulated from over a thousand families all over France - originally to collect information on disease epidemics - showed instead a strong correlation between genetic make-up and language. There is a distinct north/south division between the language spoken in Paris and that of Provence (*Scotsman* WE, 21 Sept 1991, p.9, quoting a recent issue of the *New Scientist.*)

Marija Gimbutas (1990) in the latest edition of her classic The *Godesses and Gods of Old Europe* describes the myths and cult imagines of an area of autochthonous European civilisation, ca 7000 - 3500 BC (Fig 21)). In other words the figurine art and pictorial painting in this area illustrate the development of objects and designs which had meaning in the Upper Palaeolithic down through Neolithic times to much later.

The area would be more accurately called Southeast Europe, because the pre-Indo-European-speaking people of western and north western Europe were developing in a rather different way.

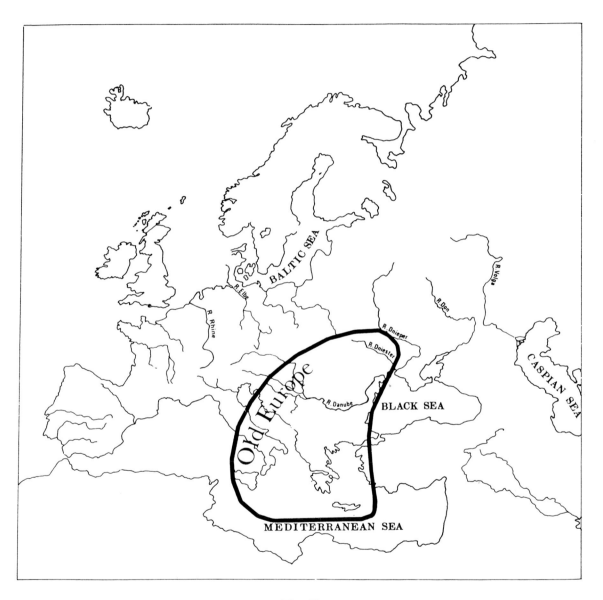

Fig. 21
Old Europe: the area of autochthonous European civilization,
c.7000-3500 BC in relation to the rest of Europe.

M. Gimbutas, p.16.

Chapter 22
A Summary of Scotland's Periods VII′ and VIII′

Scottish history during the last two millenia can be represented by a graph, Fig 22, the heights and widths of the cultural peaks being indicative only. The top line or envelope shows the general rise and fall of period VII′ and the fitful struggle to recover since then.

I have tried to plot here the serious setback during the Wars of Independence, a slow recovery to a modest peak of wealth, a check at the regnal union, and the final decline to the end of period VII′ in 1693 - 1747, mean 1720. The lowest point in this clearly defined Dark Age was 1707, the Parliamentary union.

Subsequent events are also shown graphically; the rise towards the Scottish Enlightenment and, 'dashed', the expected further recovery; there was, however, a disastrous decline which has been described. A slight recovery occurred in engineering and commerce between 1875 and 1914. In several years income per head was higher in Scotland than in England. Many excellently-designed mansions were built by the well-to-do. But again this brave recovery was nullified by World War I, and the hoped-for recovery is also indicated by dashed lines. No substantial recovery was seen between the wars, but from about 1970 there were signs of some recovery due to the electronics, oil and microcomputer industries. Continued recovery is doubtful because Scotland has been deprived of its oil revenues and any great improvement in the electronics industry relative to England may be 'scotched'. When the North Sea oil industry needed more steel pipes in early 1990, they were imported from abroad, at a time when the Scottish steel industry could have been improved so as to supply the tubes. Whatever the economics of the Scottish steel industry may be, the admission by the consultants appointed to report on the future of the Ravenscraig works without ever visiting it did not inspire confidence in the Scottish Development Agency, now defunct.

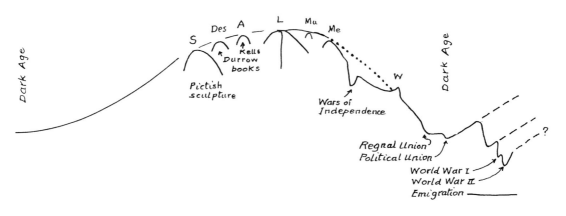

Fig 22
The Picto-Scottish Periods VII′ and VIII′

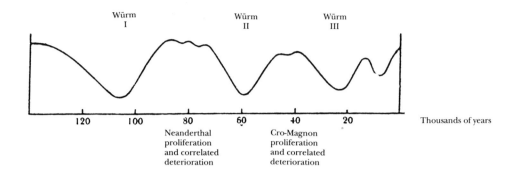

Würm I   Würm II   Würm III

120   100   80   60   40   20   Thousands of years

Neanderthal proliferation and correlated deterioration

Cro-Magnon proliferation and correlated deterioration

Fig. 23
Rise and fall of Neanderthal and Cromagnon man.
Humps: interglacial warm spells   Dips: glacial periods

Elmer Pendall (1977)

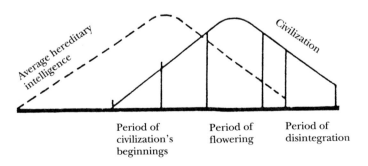

Average hereditary intelligence

Civilization

Period of civilization's beginnings

Period of flowering

Period of disintegration

Fig. 24
Lag of a civilization behind the rise and fall of the intelligence on which it depends.

Elmer Pendell (1977)

Chapter 23
PERIODICITY AND CATASTROPHE IN HISTORY
The mechanism underlying rises and falls in civilisation

The causes of the rises and falls of the periods of civilisation have seldom been carefully studied; and when they have been the authors seem to be trying to prove some preconceived theory. An example of this school is Paul Colinvaux's *"The Fates of Nations"* (1980) whose book was reviewed by William H McNeill (1981) under the title "Trap for the Unwary". McNeill's criticism is summed up in one devastating sentence: *With 1066 and All That* plus school-boy Latin as his guide, and Toynbee as guarantor of "facts", what does an intrepid ecologist discover in the human past? The answer is a rhythm of rise and fall, predictable in the light of ecological niche theory", - his particular specialty, of course.

Elmer Pendell in *Why Civilisations Self-Destruct* (1977) on the other hand related the rise and fall of Neanderthal and Cro-Magnon man to climatic changes (Fig 23) even though many prehistoric people of those types were not living in places where there were glacial periods. In spite of that he formulated a law of population dynamics, which accounted both for the rise and for the fall of these early periods of mankind's development.

1. Evolution tends to eliminate inefficient individuals in somewhat greater proportion than efficient individuals.

2. A considerable increase in an area's human population signals a more sparing application of evolution's winnowing process, due, for instance, to improved shelter or clothing, or better food storage methods.

3. When a group proliferates, the survivors include individuals further down the scale of efficiency.

4. When a group increases at a faster rate than usual, then it has fewer early deaths per thousand births than usual, and there is less weeding out than usual.

5. Since births are normally more numerous among the less efficient half of any specific group, there is a larger proportion of survivals among the less efficient half when the group increases in number.

His following diagram serves to illustrate these points (Fig 24). In his view civilisations are built by vigorous men and women of exceptional intelligence and character. In the period of construction the weak and inadequate tend to be eliminated; but when a civilisation reaches its peak, egoistic motives give way to altruistic ones and the less intelligent are preserved so carefully that their offspring eventually outnumber those of the more intelligent. The decline hastens towards its end. In other words (1) the cause of the rise in the civilisation curve is the antecedent rise in the intelligence curve, brought about by the survival of the most ingenious and tough in very difficult circumstances; and (2) the levelling out and downturn of the intelligence curve coincides with the rise in the civilisation curve.

I think it would be impossible to find enough evidence to prove the validity of this argument. To begin with, there is no single intelligence; there are many different intelligences - and Petrie considers some of these in his book more convincingly. Pendell went on to propose a set of marriage laws, which need not be summarised here because history has condemned them. Their chief fault lies in the proposal that there should be an imposed selection of what government officials would regard as superior people.

We know what disasters can follow from such policies but we should continue to think about stopping the "misery due to population pressure" as Professor J P Duguid calls it in the *Scotsman* (19 June 1991). He writes "This role of population pressure is discounted by philanthropists who urge the giving of food and medical aid to oppose nature's cruel control of population in distressed communities. It is, of course, true that droughts, floods, land erosion, wars and bad government are the immediate causes of famine, but these disasters are largely the consequence of overpopulation".``

C D Darlington (1958) concluded that "there is indeed much evidence of a genetic component in the survival of nations. The nation which takes most serious thought for its own genetical future is, therefore, most likely to have a future."

We have enough scientists to study this aspect of our future, but through governmental parsimony and mismanagement many have sought employment in financial services. These have now been saturated and good training in science is scattered and lost. Even in 1963 Colin Bertram recorded that "so great has been the population explosion that, it is calculated, of all the individuals of the species that there have ever been since *Homo sapiens* emerged, between 3 and 4 per cent are alive at this moment. Of scientists...90 per cent of all those who have ever existed are calculated to be alive today".

Pendell also comments on the wealth peak of any period of civilisation, when "the outward splendor manages for a time to hide the inner rot". We may be mesmerised by the dazzling brilliance of microcomputer devices but should think deeply, if you are living in Period VIII, on the downward social trend and ways of reversing it.

As I see it neither unbridled altruism nor unbridled self-interest are good for society. Egalitarianism opposes élitism. Every subject under debate, in parliament and press, is distorted by adversarial attitudes. Learning to compromise or agree should be everyone's aim;- that is consensus. Interestingly this word comes from the Latin *consentire* to think, an essential step towards agreeing; but to think straight you need to have facts and, of course, fact-finders.

The causes of cultural history's lengthening period

To a first approximation the slowing down of cultural history is inversely proportional to the growth of population. This relationship was touched upon in chapter 6. In so far as it is related to the number of interacting people,it is both a genetic and a memetic phenomenon. By looking at the history of the last 6400 years we have become aware of the basic pattern which can be plotted on the outside of a cone or, two-dimensionally, by flattening on to a sheet of paper, as in Fig. 9. History is therefore capable of being treated mathematically.

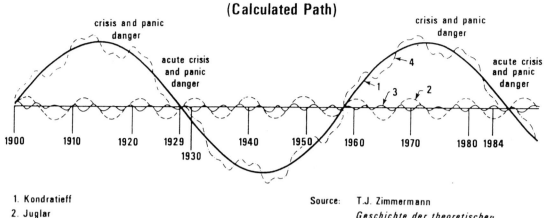

Fig. 25
The 20th Century Business Cycle and Crisis Points (Calculated Path).

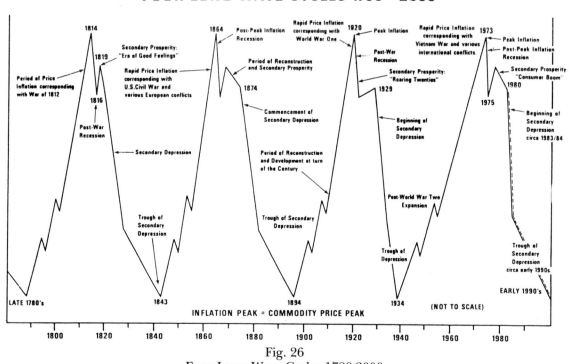

Fig. 26
Four Long Wave Cycles 1780-2000

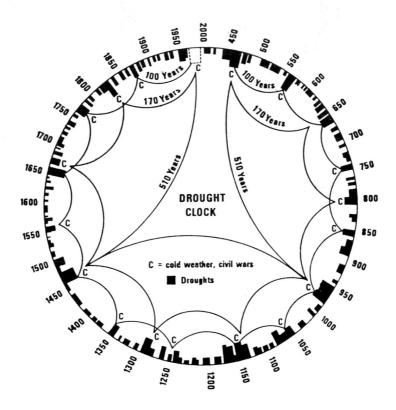

Fig. 27
Dr. Raymond Wheeler's Drought Clock.
R. Beckman 1983

It would be foolish to imagine that these ever-growing waves (or periods) are completely smooth. "Schumpeter combined the findings of three 'cyclical' economists, Kitchin, Juglar and Kondratieff (Fig 25). The Kitchin cycle involves a period of about 3 ¹/₃ years. The Juglar business cycle runs for 8 to 10 years, and the Kondratieff cycle about 54 years. Of greatest interest are those times when all three cycles have moved into tandem". So wrote Robert Beckman in Downwave (1983). Here he published a graph which illustrates the point, Fig. 26. This gives details of four Long Wave Cycles 1780-2000 AD. Raymond Wheeler's Drought Clock Fig. 27 was compiled from over two million data entries made over 20 years by a staff of over 200 at the University of Kansas, so it cannot be lightly dismissed. This work shows cycles of 100, 170 and 510 years. Juglar's cycle may be connected with sunspot activity; the other cycles may also be caused by variation in energy output by the sun.

Schove (1967) in his summary on sunspot cycles has shown that the mean length of the solar cycle in the 20th century has been 10 years, although since 500 BC the average length has been 11.1 years. However, since the magnetism of the leading spots is reversed in alternate cycles, the true solar cycle, known after Hale, is 22.2 years. Cycles of 55-100 years in the strength of solar emissions and of about 80 years in the length of the solar cycle have been demonstrated by Gleissberg (1965). Correlations with events on earth may be only faintly discernible. Other cycles which may have some effect on our planet's weather are the 205-year cycle of solar activity which has been traced in the growth of tree-rings; these also suggest an 80 year periodicity. A much longer cycle of 1265 years has been noticed in the postglacial period, but this has not yet been correlated with historical events.

Nevertheless, the self-perpetuating boom-bust economic cycle, most clearly expressed in the Kondratieff cycle, turns back at its crisis-points by a built-in 'hunting' mechanism, which may be modified by outside influences. (Fig 26).

Another example of a hunting periodicity is a 300 year cycle attributed by J D Unwin (1940) to the nature and degree of sexual control in society. A period of sexual liberality, such as in the 1660s and the 1960s, the 'swinging sixties', cures itself by satiety and boredom; a move begins to gather strength towards a stricter way of living, such as following the teachings of John (1703-1791) and Charles (1707-1788) Wesley, for example, the founders of Methodism. In some Churches threats of hell-fire for sinners turned people once more towards a more balanced life. The new move however could not be stopped until the cycle was complete, in spite of precepts and preaching. The imposition of this cycle is inevitable.

Petrie thought he had found a cycle of economy and waste covering about 130 years. The waste he asserted began at 1535,1660,1790,1920 and the more austere periods revived in 1560,1690,1820; and pointed to a revival in 1950 or thereabouts, (*Nature*, October 1, 1938) He also had one final shot at looking for regularities in the history of Egypt: "the long general cycle of civilisation in Egypt bore the best work in 3700,2600,1550,450 BC and AD 760, an average of 1115 years, resembling the 1100 years of the "Great Year" known to the Etruscans. (The first and last dates are very doubtful; the reworking of Petrie's peak dates after they were known through later scholarship provide far more information than this forced acceptance of only four "Great Years").

History we can now see can be affected by continuous and by discontinuous events. Of the latter there have been volcanic episodes such as Thera and Vesuvius and much rarer impacts of meteors, as in Russia. Of the former, Kondratieff's 54 year cycle has been found also in the Arizona tree ring widths going back to 1050 AD; both reflect rhythmic climatic changes, which ultimately depend upon the sun's radiation.

But there are two rhythmic variations which engineers would describe as hunting between unacceptable limits. The sexual cycle of Unwin, which has been mentioned, and the right-left swing in British politics this century. If the leadership is too much (or too long) to the right or to the left it becomes patently dogmatic, verging on the dictatorial or plain boring; and the voters swing away from the extreme at the edge of the band. Do you remember the bus which could run on railway lines? The hunting control mechanism was on such a small and delicate scale that the bus was steered within a few millimeters of the centre line. Political voting, especially in a two-party system, shows the same phenomenon of hunting. After a long time in office any ruling party will bore the voters even if they have not run out of good ideas. On the other hand hunting cannot occur in a dictatorship; there is no future but ultimate catastrophe.

The pattern of history consists of the cultural peak lines crossing the lines representing periods; they can be projected on to a cone or onto a flat surface; the lengthening of the periods appears to correlate best with increasing population since the time of the hunter-gatherers 'of no fixed abode'. The future of our civilisation may therefore depend upon controlling in a humane way the numbers of people living in each area in a sustainable and acceptable manner. Population density studies, of which there have been many, may throw light on the mechanism which causes linearity in the pattern of history.

Indeed, one of the most depressing features of the structured history of culture is the ever-increasing length of the periods. The European phase looks as if it would reach a peak of wealth in 2250 AD and a Dark Age at about 2450 AD. Beyond that if civilisation continues 'according to plan' there would be a long and dreary haul until the next peak of sculpture at about 3580 AD and a peak of literature at about 4100 AD. Even those who are in phase with the Scots would see no peak of sculpture until about 2700 AD nor of architecture till about 2800 AD. Obviously no one wants to wait as long as that to experience these cultural peaks, nor need they because there have been many humble to splendid architectural styles which, though not at a peak as defined by Petrie, still give great satisfaction. All the same the pattern of cultural history has occurred without human thought or understanding: it has gone on perhaps too long. But has civilisation already come to an end? I return to this question in the last chapter, but will say a little more about the world's prospects if the present trends continue.

Dr Eric Voice, an independent scientist now living in Thurso, has had a lifelong interest in the environment. He is pessimistic about immediate prospects. "We are going to have a catastrophe within 50 years" he said in an interview (*Scotsman*, 7 March 1990) The world population, already 5.5 billion, would rise to 11 billion by 2030 AD. Most of the world's good agricultural land was already in production; much land will be lost by swamping through global warming causing the sea level to rise. By then four times as much energy will be needed. Nuclear energy is the only major way to avoid fossil fuel's aggravating the greenhouse effect. Alternative energy would not be enough on a world scale, though it should be developed in addition to nuclear fusion and, possibly, the relatively clean and safe thorium route to nuclear energy.

As the West declines the threat to world peace will grow. Saddam Hussein's tactics since 1990 may be seen as a strong man phenomenon in a country, Iraq, which ought, like Scotland, to be beginning its rise from a Dark Age. The greatest conquests of the Ottoman Empire were made under Selim I (1512-1520) and Suleiman the Magnificent (1520 -1566)), when Mesopotamia as far as Basra was annexed. In the first half of the 18th century the Ottoman Empire began to lose ground. The misrule and state of neglect in which the Empire left its provinces gave rise to widespread nationalist movements in the 19th century. Since then the similarity between Mesopotamia and Scotland has been obliterated.

Saddam Hussein's use of chemical warfare against Kurdish civilians is characteristic of a 'mindless war'. He is not a strong man leading his country towards a higher state of civilisation. More likely he is out of his mind and should be added to 'Ailing Leaders', Appendix 8. Weyl (1967) believes that the murder by Genghis Khan's forces of poets, philosophers and other gifted people in the Middle East in the 13th century has done permanent damage, making full recovery impossible. Hülegü, a grandson of Genghis Khan, crushed the Moslems in the Middle East and destroyed Baghdad in 1258 (Morgan 1985).

As signs of decay begin to show in the West, Islamic countries thought they could break free from its influence. Religious fundamentalism and intolerance will not solve many problems. *Homónoia* or agreement could be reached by the generous sharing of technical resources, The West should recognise the good points of Islam, such as their better attitudes and practices regarding interest or usury. Islam should agree to respect the law of other countries; they could begin by cancelling the *fatwa* or sentence of death against Salman Rushdie, the British author of *Satanic Verses* , however unpleasant this work may seem to them.

Chapter 24
Catastrophe Theory

At this point we may turn to consider how a collapse comes about; how can one recognise a potentially catastrophic state? Fortunately, the French mathematician René Thom developed about 1963 an elegant treatment of recurrent identifiable elements which nevertheless have 'structural stability'. The former we can see is a good description of the rise and fall of the periods of civilisation and the latter is exemplified by the pattern of history, so clearly shown in the modified Petrie diagram (Fig 9).

Thom's procedure allows one to visualise the growth of instability in a system of multidimensional models. C H Waddington, professor of animal genetics at Edinburgh University, "had anticipated important parts of Thom's biological thought, and was the first scientist of great stature to acclaim catastrophe theory". The leading exponent in Britain today, Professor E Christopher Zeeman, shares with Thom not only a fascination with the variety and recurrence of form in nature, following D'Arcy Thompson (1917), but also a belief in the importance of special intuition. Alexander Woodcock and Monte Davis have written a highly readable account of *Catastrophe Theory - a Revolutionary New Way of Understanding how Things Change* (1978); and, by choosing, as a first approximation, one of the simplest three-dimensional models, they threw light on such diverse phenomena as the 'territorial behaviour of animals' and 'conflicting lobbies: ecology v. nuclear power'! Fig 28 shows a typical example 'Social order v. disorder in times of danger'.

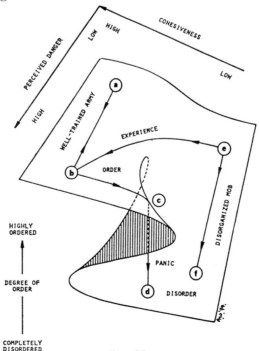

CATASTROPHE THEORY

Fig. 28
Social order v. disorder in times of danger. *A. Woodcock and M. Davis (1979)*

A similar diagram, made to suit this book, shows social order v. disorder in a time of increasing bureaucracy, Fig. 29. These diagrams are dimensionless but qualitative; they are independent of the time-scale and can depict events taking place from seconds to millions of years. In Fig. 29 the time-scale runs from 1600 to 2000 AD.

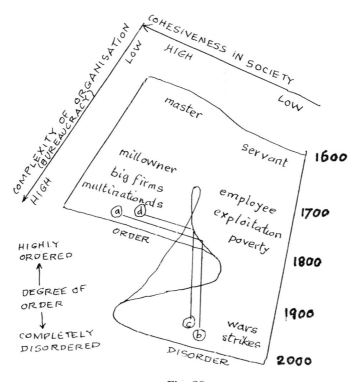

Fig. 29
Social order v. disorder in a period of increasing bureaucracy.
After A. Woodcock and M. Davis (1979)

In this simple model it will be seen that a relatively smooth state in a society unaffected by much bureaucracy gradually develops a steep plunge down from this happy condition to a division of society into employers and workers. The curve later bends right over like an S (here backwards), and in the end the system will totally collapse. (When you hear an employer saying "we are bending over backwards to find a solution" you may be sure that the speaker is poised on the arm of a catastrophe, just as when someone says "to tell you the truth" you may reply, as my father often did," Am I to understand that up till now you have been lying to me?")

Thom, defending himself from fierce but sometimes unfair critics, defended himself (1976,1983) by stressing that catastrophe theory (a term invented by Zeeman) is not a 'scientific' theory; it is a language, and as with ordinary language every author will use it to this own taste, with his own style...In the 'soft sciences' (biology and sociology) he knows of nothing better, and a good point in its favour is that it helps to dislodge the dogma of certainty and infallibility attached up till now to the 'scientific' tag.

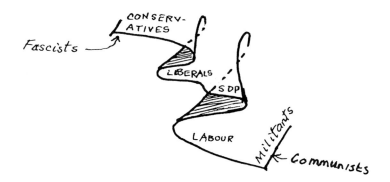

Fig. 30a

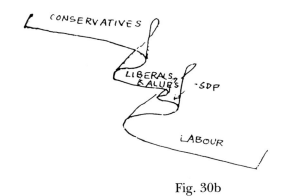

Fig. 30b

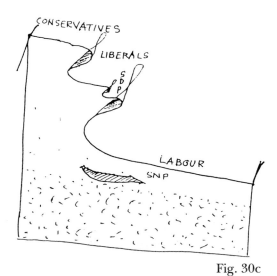

Fig. 30c

The sequence of happenings leading to the development of a cusp and eventual breakdown of the system has been found in engineering, zoology, botany, neurology, mineralisation, sociology (including the events leading to war) and politics.

The diagram suggests that some time before a final collapse no agreement can be reached between political parties occupying the wings of the model. Examples are the extreme difficulty of the National Coal Board coming to agreement with the National Union of Miners some years ago. There is no middle ground; this is a mathematical impossibility in a catastrophe curve. Arnold Toynbee, like others before and since, saw the great danger for modern civilisation lay in the estrangement of class from class. And Jowett wrote "I cannot help asking this question whether civilised Europe at the end of the 19th century has no means of preventing universal war".

Let us return to British politics. Fig 30a shows the alliance between Liberals and the Social Democratic breakaway from Labour. This came about because of the feeling that it would be nice to have a strong, stable middle ground in between the wings of right and left. Fig 29 shows how people can 'flip' from one part of the curve to the other; drop-outs fall to a lower level; creative people born in lowly surroundings do sometimes break through the rigid structure of class. But Fig 29 shows that the middle of the leading edge of the diagram already shows the sign of instability (before 1987). On 3 June 1990 the SDP was disbanded by Dr David Owen; this action introduced a secondary cusp as shown in Fig 30b.

In Scotland this curve represents only the politics of the blanket, except that the Conservative wing is much smaller than in England and the Labour wing is dominant. What the diagram does not show is the politics of the obducted masses, the Scots, the people of very ancient lineage. Here, in Fig 30c, we see the distorted diagram of Westminster politics overlying the poorly represented Scots.

A substantial minority of Scots have declined to join the parties of catastrophe. They are indicated in Fig 30c by a separate mass, shaded. They are there simmering away below the blanket, getting up steam.

Some members of the Scottish National Party make the mistake of calling themselves 'somewhat left of centre' a phrase which admits that they are bound to the decaying British system of government. They should stress that they care for social justice, a stable and secure society and that they are the only Scottish political party capable of leading the country to its rightful and proper place among the nations of Europe.

The SNP wrongly hope to have a majority of Scottish MPs in Westminster where they will remain firmly enchained and in a perpetual minority. In a Scottish parliament all political expressions will be represented.

The trouble is that they do not see the nature of the rigid blanket which obducts or covers them. It is made in the Workshops for the Blind but the designers have used not only wool to pull over people's eyes and a low permeability to deprive the people of oxygen for the brain but also steel wires pulled by them alone. The designers are not only Parliament and the permanent civil service but also the banking system, which will be examined in Chapter 34. It is enough to say now that Devolution of certain functions of government as practised by Westminster to a sub-Parliament in Edinburgh will be bound by financial wires pulled from outwith Scotland. But "freedom is a nobil thing" wrote Barbour, and it will be achieved when Scots realise what is constraining them and start to design their own bridge to a more stable world. This road will connect with a network of 'lands of manageable proportions' or small nations within the European Community. The Tories call such an idea idiotic; our study of history suggests that 'Scotland within Europe' is a meaningful slogan providing hope for the future.

NOTE: When a people are approaching a Dark Age or are suffering from such a catastrophe, they suffer from social ills collectively known as **addictions.** These are true illnesses of the mind and have much in common. They are discussed in Appendix 9.

Chapter 25
Evidence of Decline in Europe

Many observers have commented on the decline of civilisation in Europe. I shall quote only a few. Thomas Carlyle (1795-1881) in his hemi-autobiographical *Sartor resartus* saw his generation going to pot in a welter of materialism. Then "Britons, after proclaiming for so long that they would never be slaves, had succumbed in a coma of mental inertia" wrote Compton Mackenzie (1957) in *Rockets Galore*. Or "we live in a country where bit by bit, clause by clause, year by year, personal freedoms and democracy are being deliberately eroded" wrote Ruth Wishart in the *Scotsman* (12 Feb 1985), when discussing what she called the idiocy of Section Two of the Official Secrets Act which led to Clive Ponting's conviction in the Courts.

In the same newspaper there was a flock of memes on this subject attracted, I suspect, by the Editor's headline *Politics of decline* and phrase *Tories and Labour are caught in the politics of decline*, partly owing to self-inflicted wounds" (Id., 31 Dec.1981).

Football was once enjoyed without fear as a family entertainment. Hooligans penetrated the scene and caused violence and death. The English team were banned for several years from playing on the Continent.

Churches complain of falling membership and difficulty in recruiting enough people for the ministry or priesthood.

Decline is seen in other aspects of modern life. John Higgins, an ex-heroin addict made the profound observation (Id., 7 Dec 1983) that "heroin is a drug of idleness and despair; it kills time and pain; it is a crutch for people without work, realistic ambition and self-esteem". This lonely voice from prison hoped that the Government would replace the prevailing mood of apathy with hope for the future. A forlorn hope.

Another commentator, more comfortable placed, Stanley Eveling (Id. 31 March 1984) had been moved by a popular BBC programme to write "A society is in a state of irreversible decline when it gives itself up to the making of crude, violent musical sounds as its primary form of artistic, energetic expression. *Top of the Pops*, with its cretinous, burbling DJs, continues to send out distress calls, the death chants of a dying culture. Hordes of ambiguous, garishly-geared savages howl and whine and unintelligibly thump out their banal noise; and millionaire teenagers entertain the young unemployed. David A H Wate (Id, 10 Feb.1982) asked if rock music had now displaced religion as the 'opiate of the masses'.

The Central Statistical Office's annual report on *Social Trends* (Id., 8 Dec. 1983) confirms the view that Britain's moral standards are slipping, for during the previous year cases of sexually transmitted diseases increased, there were more illegitimate than legitimate births to the under-20s (for the first time) and spending on alcohol reached a record high. The move towards the Wealth Peak was shown by the fact that nearly every household in Britain had a television set, 59 percent had a car, and 76 per cent a telephone. There had been big increases in the ownership of dishwashers, washing-machines and tumble driers. On the other hand the decline which continues for centuries can be seen by the lower spending on books and newspapers - 15 percent down in ten years; and there were 65 per cent fewer admissions to cinemas than 12 years before.

Declaration of freedom from Soviet centralisation and misrule has fired the imagination and sympathy of the oppressed and the relatively-free worldwide. Estonia, Latvia, Lithuania, Poland, Czechoslovakia, Hungary, and Romania broke away in 1989. The unity of federal Yugoslavia ended with the secession of Slovenia and Croatia followed by other states seeking freedom from Serbian aggression. Freedom movements led to bloodshed in Georgia and Azerbaidjan. The Kurds are tragically caught between Iran, Turkey and Iraq. They have been sprayed with poison gas by the Iraquis, but in January 1991 the Turks wisely allowed them to speak their own language, Iraq had started a genocidic war of appalling cruelty against them in 1990. Signs of revolt have been reported right across the fringes of the USSR as far as Mongolia and the Ukraine; and the largest nation of all, Russia, has assumed a degree of freedom from Soviet rule.

All of these freedom-seeking peoples look to western capitalism as their model, but as we have seen in chapter 24 the East and the West are at the two extremes of a catastrophic curve. One must question the wisdom of the East copying Western ways unless the West makes adjustments, putting its own house in order.

America is in an era of decline, as are Europe and Australasia. As Albus (1988) puts it "We have just gone from being the world's largest creditor nation to the world's largest debtor...Consumer debt is also dangerously large, - in loans and home mortgages. The farm economy is in a state of depression. Bank failures are numerous and growing rapidly. The Los Angeles and other riots (1992) are further evidence of decline. Yet the whole of the West could create a golden age of mankind. If we have the wisdom and discipline to change our ways - to save our money and invest in the technology of the future - we could lead the next industrial revolution and enjoy the prosperity it will generate." This is a compressed version of what Albus says. The thing to stress is that everyone everywhere could benefit by adopting a conceivable strategy.

What divided the East from the West, primarily, was ideology. Speiser (1984a) pointed out that in the USA the ideology, capitalism, was based on the ownership of the means of production being in the hands of only 6 percent of the population, who were shareholders, but in the USSR the ideology, communism, was based on the ownership of the means of production being in the hands of the State, which was run by about 6 percent of the population, who had become members of the Communist Party. In both super-states the power lay in the hands of a small minority. It is not certain that Karl Marx's original ideas of socialised ownership were ever seriously considered by Lenin and his colleagues, for they all preferred state control. As Speiser (1984b) pointed out it was Karl Johann Kautsky (1854-1938), author and editor of the fourth volume of *Das Kapital*, who stated precisely in 1905 that in Russia it is the government, not the people, which already controlled the means of production.

The West as it is organised today has little to offer the East of Europe or the Middle East but a chance to join a declining system, admittedly via a peak of Wealth in about 2250 AD, but ultimately to a Dark Age about 2400 AD. The prospect would be gloomy indeed were it not for the ideas of Albus, Speiser and Bradbury. Capitalism on the other hand could be made truly attractive if all new investment in large-scale industry were financed so that all adults become in fact shareholders by the creation of "super stock".

In Britain the former Prime Minister, Mrs M Thatcher, helped only those with savings to become richer; and the proportion of people with a significant amount of capital has risen. The great majority, though, still have no or only a little share in the prosperity of the country. Too many tried to make a quick gain when the industries which they already owned, albeit on a non-profit-making basis (to them), were privatised. A great opportunity of spreading wealth more evenly was lost. Employee ownership, favoured by some, is essentially an unfair method of distribution. USOP, the Universal Share Ownership Plan, should appeal to the East and to the West, and could form the financial basis of measures to resolve the differences between the Middle East and the West.

Chapter 26
LESSONS FROM PETRIE

Evidence of Scottish distinctiveness

Very few Scots deny that they are Scots, however British or unionist they may be in politics. This strong feeling of a Scottish identity is in many Scots subconscious. When asked to explain how they reconcile their inner patriotism with their political adherence to a foreign party they sometimes lose their temper. (Lord Boyd Orr, medic and scientist, when wanting to obtain justice for Scotland, would approach a member of the permanent civil service in London, opening his remarks in a general way, such as "I think I'm right in supposing that rationed building materials are allocated to different areas according to their needs". "Oh yes of course". "Well, Glasgow's needs are more than twice those of the national average". "I won't discuss them, you have tricked me".

The notion that the Scots, like the Jews of old, were a 'peculiar people' (*Deuteronomy*. 14.2; 28.18) was used in many a sermon. Indeed at times Scots protestants felt themselves to be a 'chosen people'. Though such an extreme statement of their uniqueness is not fashionable today, annoyance is often expressed by such phrases as the 'Queen of England', 'Queen Elizabeth the Second', 'Anglo-American relations' and the like. Such prickliness is rare among English people, who quite commonly say with pride that they had a Scottish grandparent. The simplest explanation of this phenomenon is that the Scots really are a different people from the English; and that simple explanations are often right. If they are not strictly 'chosen people' they certainly are 'Pict Scots'!

Bill Forsyth, the world-famous film director, is reported by Kenny Mathieson in *Scotland on Sunday Magazine*, (18 April 1990) as saying "Scotland is a nice comfortable place to live, but to be honest, my commitment doesn't go much beyond that. I'm getting a bit sick of the current trend for self-analysis and self-consciousness about being Scottish. This endless reflection on our culture and our relationship with the English is tiring and slightly embarrassing. Other small nations seem to get by without it. We are more than a bunch of reactive emotions to England. Under the circumstances I'm not even sure we deserve to have a film industry". Forsyth, a left-winger, admits that he would willingly make a few party political broadcasts for Mr Kinnock and the Labour Party but would always remain non-political in his film making. If the Scots were better informed about their origins and nature there would be less need for such uncertainty and embarrassment. Have we forgotten what was inscribed on the Temple of Apollo at Delphi γνῶθι σεαυτόν — gnōthi seautòn – 'know thyself?

When Scotland is given a chance of playing a full role in Europe once more, it will surely be making a distinctive contribution. But can one measure any perceptible differences? D Elliston Allen found he could. In *British Tastes*, an enquiry into the likes and dislikes of the Regional Consumer (1968), he wrote " 'Except in Scotland'. So runs a favourite escape-phrase of marketing men. And so often as not it is abundantly justified. For Scotland differs from all the English regions in a myriad different ways, as is only to be expected of a land of five and a quarter millions - one Scotsman to every eight Englishmen - that remained a foreign, independent country until as recently as two and a half centuries ago. In many respects it is still half-foreign". Allen traces the many resemblances Scotland has with the Continent, especially with France, and notices that some of the difference appears to be of genetic and very ancient origin.

At one time when Scots met abroad they would exchange their tribal greeting "Here's tae us! Wha's like us? Gey few and that's for sure". There were variations of the last sentiment. I was taught never to use this drinking toast because it was often uttered in a rude and racist style of speaking. Originally the greeting was an expression of solidarity between strangers on discovering their common difference from sasunnachs surrounding them. It is not a declaration of superiority but simply of friendship; it was preferably given out of earshot of others.

No one reading descriptions of the Scots in *Early Travellers in Scotland* 1295-1695(ed P Hume Brown,1891) can fail to realise how very different the Scots were thought to be from the English or other foreigners. Some of the authors quoted there told much more about their own prejudices than about the Scots. A study of these is at least entertaining.

Aeneas Sylvius, later Pope Pius II, visited Scotland in the reign of James 1. He found the common people poor and destitute of all refinement. They eat flesh and fish to repletion, and bread only as a dainty. The men are small in stature, bold and forward in temper; the women fair in complexion, comely and pleasing, but not distinguished for their chastity, giving their kisses more readily than Italian women their hands". Hume Brown says in a note that "foreigners were struck by the same freedom of manners in English women and that Erasmus was amused by this custom of kissing among them."

Don Pedro de Ayala (1498) wrote "the women are courteous in the extreme. I mention this because they are really honest, though very bold. They are absolute mistresses of their houses, and even their husbands, in all things concerning the administration of their property, income as well as expenditure. They are very graceful and handsome women. They dress much better than here (England) and especially as regards the head-dress, which is, I think, the handsomest in the world".

Andrea Trevisano (1498), Venetian ambassador to England, reported that "the inhabitants of the country are called wild or savage Scots, not however from the rudeness of their manners, which are extremely courteous". He recalls that Don Peter "also says that all the Scotch nation are extremely partial to foreigners, and very hospitable, and that they all consider that there is no higher duty in the world than to love and defend their crown".

Estienne Perlin (1551-52) noted that "the Scotch who apply themselves to letters become good philosophers and authors". And "nothing is scarce here but money".

Henri, Duc de Rohan (1600) found Scotland "truly generous in the production of virtuous persons. For, besides the nobility whom I found full of civility and courtesy, the country possesses a multitude of learned men, and a people of such courage and fidelity, that our Kings of France chose from among them the soldiers who formed the special guard of their persons".

A pasquinade or wickedly satirical piece thought to have been written by Sir Anthony Weldon (1617) said of the ladies that "pride is a thing bred in their bones, and their flesh naturally abhors cleanliness, their body smells of sweat, and their splay feet never offend in socks". He concluded "the men of old did no more wonder that the great Messias should be born in so poor a town as Bethlem in Judea, than I wonder that so brave a prince as King James should be born in so stinking a town as Edinburgh in lousy Scotland".

Sir William Brereton (1636) was told that wives in Scotland never change, but always retain, their own names, though Thomas Morer (1689) implied that this was optional.

John Ray, the naturalist, noted (1662?) that "the people here frequent their churches much better than in England, and have their ministers in more esteem and veneration".

I may add to these early travellers' reports some later ones. S Birt in his *Letters from a Gentleman in the North of Scotland to his Friend in London* (1754, II,238) admitted that he had several times passed the mountain way from Inverness to Edinburgh with four or five hundred guineas in his portmanteau. Even though he was accompanied by a single servant he felt no apprehension of robbers on the way or in his lodgings at night; and added "I wish we could say as much of our own country, civilised as it is said to be, tho' one can't be safe in going from London to Highgate".

This short compilation may be ended by Dr Han Suyin (1952) who greatly admired the Scots James and Fiona, whom she found "heroes and classless". I wish we all deserved such praise.

Famous Scots

In his review of Forbes Macgregor's *Famous Scots: The Pride of a Small Nation* (1984 Gordon Wright), P H Scott (Sc.22 Dec 1984) wrote "When the Englishman, Henry Thomas Buckle, set out to write *A History of Civilisation [in England]* he was so distracted by the Scottish contribution that the only volume he completed was the one "on Scotland and the Scotch intellect". He was astonished by the ability of "so poor and thinly-peopled a country" to produce so many remarkable men. Paul Scott continued:"many others have reacted in a similar way. Macaulay thought that the people in Scotland were the most intelligent in Europe. Harold Orel said that Scotland had made a greater contribution to civilisation than any other small nation. Kenneth Galbraith proposed the Jews as our only serious rival and Harold Thompson the ancient Greeks. The least that one can say is that Scotland has a record of achievement out of all proportion to its size..." Robert Chambers produced 150 years ago the four volumes of his *Biographical Dictionary of Eminent Scotsmen*, which is still a valuable source. Scott deplored the fact that most people growing up in Scotland know little or nothing about this great record of achievement. "Even if this book does no more than stimulate a little healthy curiosity, it will serve a useful purpose". I would add that they might also turn to *Scotland's Scientific Heritage* by A G Clement and R H S Robertson (1961)!

Dr Desmond Morris, the noted behaviourist, now living in the house once owned by the Scottish lexicographer, James Murray, who died at the age of 90 having reached the word "Turndown" in the Oxford English Dictionary, wrote *The Book of Ages* in 1984. "This is a record of achievement by the famous at all ages of their lives. And, quite honestly, the Scottish entries are out of all proportion to the rest.... the Scots are the supreme inventors of all time" (Scotsman 14 Jan.1984)

Performance Coefficients

We have already used Weyl's performance coefficients (Ch. 16) in a study of national musical tastes but will now pause to consider the place of Scots among the American élite (Weyl 1966), 24-26) in the past, present and future. The average P.C.s, adjusted for Negroes who had taken surnames of the different nations or groups listed, were taken from 12 rosters of the type *Who's Who in America* (WWA) or *American Men of Science* (AMS) and the 58 rosters current in 1966. Figures for the future were derived from college enrolments and scholastic excellence in 5 rosters. Table 7.

Of the national groups people with Scottish names dropped, in perhaps a century, from the top position (151), through 125, the second position, to only 96, the fifth position. However, the English Puritan names, that is the names of the Pilgrim Fathers, declined to an even greater extent 948 - 253 - 89, showing the very marked loss of influence of this group in American life. The same pattern is seen in the Special English Occupational Names (Cooke, Draper, Miner & Potter) 346-197-119 and by the British Clerical Names (Clark, Clarke and Palmer) 198-118-117.

Table 7
Performance coefficients of populations; changes with time.

PAST 12 rosters		PRESENT 58 rosters		FUTURE 5 rosters	
Scots	151	Jewish	220	Jewish	362
Welsh	136	Scots	125	Chinese	215
English	132	Dutch	118	Dutch	117
French	114	Welsh	103	Scandinavian	100
Dutch	110	English	101	Scots	96
Irish	78	German	96	German	96
Jewish	66	Scandinavian	92	Welsh	92
German	60	Irish	91	English	87
Italian	38	French	71	Irish	83
Scandinavian	32	Chinese	65	Greek	66
Spanish	32			French	52
Slav	few	range		Slav	49
Chinese	or	from	41	Hungarian	38
Greek	zero			Italian	31
Hungarian		to	13	Spanish-speaking	17
Puritan	948		253		89
Special occupational names	346		197		119
Clerical	198		118		117

From: *The Creative Elite in America,* Nathaniel Weyl (1966)

The rise in performance coefficients of the Jews is remarkable , 66-220-362, and also of the Chinese 0-65-215. The Dutch are constant almost 110-118-117, as are the Germans 60-96-96. On the other hand the Scandinavians are rising fact, 38-92-100. The Welsh are consistently a little above the English, 136-103-92 against 132-101-87.

These figures are in agreement with the notion that the Scots emigrés were until say a century ago a very able lot of people, and that emigration has been disastrous for Scotland.

The Jewish scores 66-220-362 show the escape of many families who fled from Nazi tyranny and continued to flourish tremendously in the States. Greeks, Italians and Hungarians also show the release of creative energy among these groups in the land of opportunity.

The figures also confirm the policy of providing ample facilities for all kinds of creative work when Scotland and of course many other countries regain their freedom.

Using Weyl's data I made a map of the distribution of "genius" in Scotland ("Q", January 1976, p.15)

	AMS	WWA
Borders	116	179
Central	149	126
East Scotland (including Buchan)	165	159
Strathclyde	130	160
Western Isles & West Coast	129	129

The figures show the outstanding output of famous people in Buchan; the equivalence of the Western Highlands and Strathclyde in scientific potential; and the result of the Border preoccupation in anything but science, it seems! The highest scores in *American Men of Science*, all three editions combined, for those who may be pleased to find their names here, are Livingstone 269, Forbes 266, MacPherson 259, Guthrie 249, Cameron 244, Sutherland 235, Gordon 228, Carmichael 222, Sinclair 218, Kirkpatrick 214, and MacLean 209.

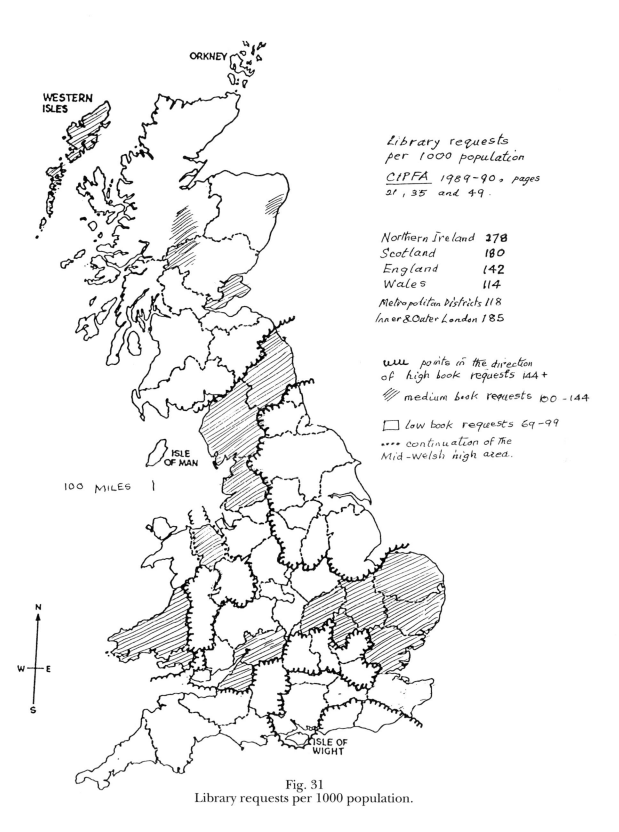

ORKNEY

WESTERN
ISLES

*Library requests
per 1000 population*

*CIPFA 1989-90, pages
21, 35 and 49.*

Northern Ireland	**278**
Scotland	**180**
England	**142**
Wales	**114**
Metropolitan Districts	118
Inner & Outer London	185

⟋⟋⟋⟋ *points in the direction
of high book requests 144 +*

/// *medium book requests 100 - 144*

☐ *low book requests 69 - 99*

···· *continuation of the
Mid-Welsh high area.*

ISLE
OF MAN

100 MILES |

N
W — E
S

ISLE OF
WIGHT

Fig. 31
Library requests per 1000 population.

Residual Brightness

Lynn (1979) showed that the average IQ of Scots had been declining in the 20th century and was in no doubt that selective emigration of the brightest was the main cause. Weyl (1966) pointed out that England, Wales and Ireland had also lost a substantial proportion of their potential leaders in many walks of life. But how do the four parts of the British Isles compare today?

Every year the Chartered Institute of Public Finance and Accountancy publish their Public Library Statistics. The most useful figures for our study are on pages 21, 35 and 49 of the 1990 report where a column 'Requests per 1000 population' shows:

Northern Ireland	278
Total London	185 (inner and outer)
Scotland	180
England	142
Metropolitan Districts	118
Wales	114

There are four large areas remarkable for their high proportion of book requesters. I Scotland; II Durham 463, Cleveland 277, North Yorkshire 190, Humberside 176, Derbyshire 150, Nottinghamshire 152, Lincolnshire 153; III London 185, Hertfordshire 199, Buckinghamshire 215, Oxfordshire 181, Wiltshire 189, Somerset 149, Devon 144, Cornwall 189, as well as West Sussex 168 and East Sussex 148 and IV the Welsh marches (see Fig 31).

The following local areas have more than 300 requests per 1000 population:

City of London 3559 (sic); the inner London Boroughs of Camden 369, Greenwich 309, Westminster 410; the Outer London Boroughs of Hillingdon 336; Doncaster 349 in South Yorkshire; Durham 463; Llanelli 551; Scotland: Stirling 345, East Lothian 428, Midlothian 312, Hamilton 361, Kyle and Carrick 330, Renfrew 389; Northern Ireland, Belfast 435, South Eastern District 336.

Requests for books not in stock are made for various reasons. One is that expenditure on books by an authority is low; another is that the bright and enterprising wish to borrow books of interest to minorities in the population; and there may be others. Until further research has been conducted in this subject one may conclude that the figures represent a fairly determined and intelligent readership to a first approximation but that there are some distortions due to limited stocks available in public libraries. After all, even high-spending authorities cannot supply more than a small fraction of all books published.

These library statistics show that Scotland has not suffered so much as the decline in IQ suggested for the population as a whole. Michael Yorke, marketing director of Reed Employment made a survey of female secretaries or personal assistants in Edinburgh and Glasgow (*Scotsman*, 4 July 1990). He found they were typically bilingual and cultured, with degrees, computer skills, shorthand and desktop publishing knowledge. They are willing to work hard, late and at home. The survey concluded that Scots secretaries have sparkling personalities, and are talented, superbly qualified and committed to their careers. In fact, "secretaries in Scotland are the *crème de la crème*".

The loss to Scotland of its most creative and able people remains a problem. Here is a comment made by an observer working in a large research organisation in England (December 1990): "all the Scots whom one meets down here are so talented and positive, so dynamic, organised and enterprising that one wonders how Scotland could ever experience social and economic problems of any kind, any more than Switzerland or Sweden, say". Precisely. These folk are no longer within Scotland nor able to contribute to the life of their own country. Politicians and journalists in England hardly give a clue as to the disastrous effects of emigration of the brightest.

Chapter 27
Civilisational Interfaces

"Yes, I'm afraid we're a few minutes late", said the Air Commodore. "But we were talking to your local laird".

"Local laird?" the Biffer repeated. "Who is *he* at all?"

"'Mr Waggett of Snorvig House".

"Laird!" the Biffer ejaculated indignantly. He's a fellow from London down in England".

"But he's been here a long time, hasn't he?"

"No time at all. Only just over twenty years. No time at all".

The party embarked in the *Kittiwake,* and soon she was chugging across the glassy Coolish in the warm May sunshine.

"You're even further from civilisation here than they are in Balmuir", Colonel Bullingham observed.

"Where's that?" the Biffer asked.

"Where's what?"

"Civilisation? Is that one of these new housing estates they have?"

"Civilisation is not a place," the Colonel said with an obviously determined effort to be patient. Surely you must know what civilisation is?"

"I know what civilisation is here in the Islands. But I never heard you had that kind of civilisation down in England".

The Colonel gave a glance at the Air Chief Marshal and shook his head. He hoped he was conveying to the higher peaks at 5 Whitehall Circus what a splendid job he was doing in trying to illuminate the darkness of these islanders' minds with the beams of official intelligence.

"So you don't think we're civilised down in London?" the Air Chief Marshal asked in that tone of indulgent condescension with which people in a position try to impress people not in a position with their keen sense of equality and fraternity without expecting any liberties to be taken as a result of such broad-mindedness.

"Och, its not your fault," said the Biffer. "You're all too busy getting on in the world. You don't have any time for meditation".

"I'm afraid we shouldn't get very far in this world if we all went in for too much meditation", said the Air Chief Marshal.

"No, I believe you wouldn't", the Biffer agreed. "But you might get a great deal further in the next world".

Never perhaps has the impact of one culture upon another been so tenderly and humorously described as in this passage from Compton Mackenzie's *Rockets Galore* (1957). Fraser Darling (1955) pointed out that the social life of Gaelic speakers in

Lewis, for example, is intense and hardly appreciated by outsiders whose presence cools the party often to the point of polite dullness. I once entered a bus in Skye unobserved and sat at the back. The bus was nearly full and the travellers, speaking Gaelic only, were humorous and happy. Everyone, it seemed, joined in. But at one stop an English couple came in. No more Gaelic was spoken and there was no more laughter or vivacity.

"One of the Highlander's mechanisms for protecting his civilisation is to hold the southerner at arm's length or further if he can. He extruded Lord Leverhulme; he resists many forms of exploitation; he often makes a fool of Government subsidies" (Robertson,1966).

The snag about such an interface, where a dominating class makes the rules, is that the main mass of the population have little say in the way their country is developed. "As David Lilienthal (1944) said, regional "development envisioned in its entirety could become a reality if and only if the people of the region did much of the planning, and participated in most of the decisions". I went on to say "these words will undoubtedly inspire the newly formed (1st November 1965) Highlands and Islands Development Board, but it is fair to point out that the whole of the Highlands (78 per cent of the area of Scotland) has even now no University or seat of higher learning or research, and the people themselves have little knowledge of their origins or how their culture might be strengthened to play an effective part in the changes which will soon take place".

In Chapter 13 I introduced the concept of the obduction of an older by a newer culture, and returned to it when considering the effect of centralised, metropolitan government upon native politics in Scotland in Chapter 24.

The effects of obduction are not always wholly malign. In Scottish cultural history we have seen how the punitive, indeed genocidal and memocidal legislation of 1746-47 led to the partial destruction of Highland culture as expressed in dress, music and the system of land ownership. Yet an élite class of outsiders can provide leadership which is badly needed when a culture is at or near a Dark Age.

There are instances of an obducting class of powerful but not artistic people sponsoring artwork from the conquered people and adopting the arts themselves. Perhaps George Bernard Shaw and WB Yates belong to this category in Ireland. In Scotland the essentially European phenomenon of the Enlightenment provoked the most intensive creative activity in Scotland. Most of the arts were involved, painting, literature, music, philosophy, architecture, all out of phase with the pattern of Scottish civilisation and all together. Creativeness had been thwarted by centuries of war and the threat of war. When the bottle was eventually opened the genie came out for all to see and enjoy, especially in the period 1770-1830.

The European peak of mechanics was marked by the design of the Forth Railway Bridge (Chapter 2). The designer was Benjamin Baker (1840-1907) who had worked with the Consulting Engineer John Fowler (1817-1898) on the London Railway Network. The phase difference was no disadvantage in bridge building since much of Scotland's released energy had gone into engineering in the late 19th century. William Arrol (1839-1913) born in Houston, Renfrewshire, was the contractor for the Forth

Railway Bridge, 1882-1890. He also built London's Tower Bridge (1886-1894) and the new rail bridge over the Tay, completed in 1897. His work-schedule for a while was incomparable (Sheila Mackay 1990).

In painting, the European tradition of Matisse and Picasso, in particular, continued during the years 1902 to 1914 and later. S J Peploe, J D Fergusson, F C B Cadell and G Leslie Hunter were followed by other Scottish painters, such as Anne Redpath, William Gillies, John Maxwell, William MacTaggart and others while English painters chose a distinctly different route. In this period of painting we are not considering the technical peak in the Petrie sense, but can see how the Scots character reacted to the European developments in the first half of the century. Roger Bilcliffe (1989) comments that "there seems to be in the Scottish character a sense of responsibility, caution and respect for convention that is balanced in almost equal amount by an element of irresponsibility, rebelliousness, even aggression. The latter qualities are all too often suppressed until they erupt, perhaps with uncontrolled vigour, this lack of control sometimes ensuring that little is achieved by the outburst. The Colourists were capable of harnessing this underlying aspect of their nature. Their achievements came from the expressions of emotions which - if the Kirk and the Establishment were to be believed - were uncontrollable once unleashed. Hunter, perhaps, overstepped the fine line between control and chaos too often, but in the other three painters the balance between order and disorder, aggression and convention, passion and Calvinist restraint was maintained sufficiently to allow them to achieve much that fellow-Scots aspired to and often failed to achieve and which many English painters, working on a less emotional plane, perhaps never experienced at all". In poetry the 'Caledonian anti-syzygy' is equally apparent; and in another part of the western margin of Europe, the 'Catalonian antisyzygy' is seen in architecture, which swings from commonsense to madness.

Chapter 28
How to manage a decline

If the pattern of history were to continue without a check, one could predict that the next European Period (IX) will be very long and very nasty. Hundreds of millions of people will suffer hunger, disease, violence and lack of civilised behaviour around them, though, as the peak of wealth in the present period VIII is likely to be about 2250 AD, we should begin to plan now to use the increasing wealth to identify and break the unknown forces which shape our history and to redirect them more acceptably - something which has never been achieved in all history. But if, as I argue later, civilisation itself may have already come to an end, forethought and careful planning are all the more vital.

We need not dwell on the dozens of predictions of the end of civilisation, from C Piazzi Smyth (1864), Astronomer Royal for Scotland, who was shunned and reviled for his attempt to prove that the dimensions of the Great Pyramid of 2623 BC had predictive value, to Peter Lemesurier (1976); with regard to Smyth's ideas which led to the British Israelite cult, Michell (1983) showed that from the more accurate measurements of Flinders Petrie (from 1880) and J H Cole (1925) that the Great Pyramid was a masterpiece of metrology, geometry and geodesy. It was built only two or three decades before the calendrical point of Period IV.

Before we can visualise what might be done to make 'A Better World' we need to know more about the mechanism behind the pattern of history. At the moment we simply do not know. Unwin (1940) was not optimistic: "by idealistic thinkers the changes in our political structure are supposed to have been made by reformers, but actually they have occurred in a state of nature, their character being controlled by the same necessity as controls the behaviour of any natural event. The reformers have merely been the mouthpieces of Time, saying and doing in due course the things that were due to be said and done".

Unwin continues (p 89) "Applying its mental energy to the phenomena around, the most energetic members of the Society discard the basis on which their old ideas rested. They cease to regard normal events as normal and abnormal events as the work of the gods; instead they entertain the conception of the 'natural'. Under the influence of mental energy they enquire into the structure of the 'natural' and begin to understand, or to think they understand, many things their fathers thought inexplicable. And so long as they retain their energy the area of the 'natural' continually expands into that which used to be occupied by the gods. The profane penetrates the sacred, and though some of the developed minds preserve a conception of godhead based on the yet unknown, in other minds the profane alone exists. Men begin to interpret the world for themselves. Wanting a universe to suit themselves, they proceed to construct it, and soon produce one that might satisfy them."...."Such a society is in the rationalistic condition. There is no particular merit in it, it is merely the way men behave when in a certain state of energy. Any metaphysical scheme is scientifically vulnerable. It is offered as a product of reason, but, as the psychologists have suggested, temperament plays the greater part in the construction".

Surviving a Dark Age or an Obduction is no easy matter. One reads of individuals who kept faith with their religion through appalling conditions of oppression; families who kept out of danger by frequently playing music together; those who published *samizdats*; many who took risks and lived dangerously to make a better future possible. Even in a world facing the milder forms of brainwashing and non-recognition by governments and quangos, groups of like-minded people can meet to discuss what can be done to 'improve the world'. There would be no funds to pay for such research. Sacrifice is called for and given. Yet in this humble world of private thinking the seeds of a desirable future may be sown. It was in this spirit that the Resource Use Institute was formed in December 1969 in Pitlochry, a small town in Pictish South Caledonia. And some ideas on how to manage a decline are summarised in chapter 38.

Chapter 29
How to recognise and manage an uprise

Close examination of the revised Petrie diagram shows that the Mediterranean, that is the Continental European and Egyptian, part of our civilisation appears to have begun about 4400 BC, at the same time as the Mesopotamian, Phoenician and Northwest European cultures. The last of these has continued to the present day uninterruptedly in Scotland, maybe because the population is much the same genetically as it was when it was founded eight to nine thousand years ago. In the Bronze Age, the Mediterranean culture seems to have escaped somehow from the normal long climb from Dark Ages about 1603 BC and 1085 BC to the beginning of high culture at the peak of sculpture.

What gave Periods V and VI, the Middle and Late Bronze Age, renewed vigour prematurely? The events of the 'First Intermediate Period' before the Middle Kingdom of Egypt, somehow caused the brilliant New Empire to begin 300 years too soon. Egyptian cultural life was certainly more disturbed by the Hyksos 'Shepherd Kings' than by the disturbances at the end of the Old Kingdom. The Hyksos invaders brought the horse and chariot, "tools of peace" and musical instruments, the lyre, the oboe and the tambourine. Unfortunately we do not know if these cultural gifts, which included copying the famous Rhind mathematical papyrus in the 33rd year of the reign of their king Apophis, had any profound effect on the behaviour and history of the Egyptian people or whether a few centuries of cultural and religious oppression led to "the spirited overthrow of the Hyksos" and eventually to "the glories in arms and arts which marked the New Empire".

If the pattern of history is more widely recognised, new questions may be asked. What are the forces which drive cultural history along its conical path? What are the best actions to be taken by people in a declining phase; and how can their neighbours in an uprise avoid being drawn into the decline of a larger, contiguous and unaware group of peoples? Since democracy characterises and motivates decline, how can it be modified so that it can become more creative than destructive? And more humane!

Petrie put it simply "when we know the cause of a cycle's death, we may be able to save our own from destruction", (*Nature*, 1.10.1938, p.620; Drower, p.428)

In this connection it is probably wise to make a list of desiderata (as in Fig.12) and to encourage people to think about them and to lobby for the most important of them. To those who wish to construct utopias the plans for reform in the French revolution are an Awful Warning. As an example "old festivals were overthrown and new ones were boldly conceived as a means of giving birth to a new culture and establishing new rites and traditions. They were not mere entertainment, then, but serious and high minded efforts". The famous 'Festival of Reason' celebrated the highest ideals of the Enlightment, proclaiming liberty and equality. Citizens were instructed as follows: "When the bells ring, all will leave their houses which will be entrusted to the protection of the law and Republican virtue. The populace will fill the streets and public squares, aflame with joy and fraternity". This was 'festival by decree'; it led to fear and proved self-defeating". Similarly May 1st became the day when the late Soviet Union displayed its awesome military power. The threat became absolute, commented Anthony Corones in his Essay on the idea of festivity (1990).

We must therefore exercise extreme caution in trying to find the way to a better future. There is no easy way forward. We may smile at the thought of the notice exposed in an American university - "This tradition will be inaugurated next Wednesday June 1st at 1400 hours".

Good ideas are often squashed rather than promoted. We may consider a few such disasters in the next essay called 'Parables'. Perhaps we can learn from the potato famine, the control of scurvy and the death of fish and forests how not to handle threatening phenomena facing mankind.

Parable 1 The potato blight

To find out what science could do to save the potato in 1845, Peel appointed as Scientific Commissioners Dr Lyon Playfair, "more successful as a courtier than as a chemist", it was said, and Dr John Lindley, editor of the *Gardeners Chronicle and Horticultural Gazette*, first professor of botany at the University of London and founder of Kew Gardens. They were at work in Ireland by 24 October,1845 (Woodham-Smith 1962, p.44). Yet in the summer of that year a scientific country parson in Northamptonshire, the Reverend M J Berkeley, "observed that whenever the new potato disease attacked the plants in his parish a tiny growth, a minute fungus, was invariably to be found on the blighted parts of leaves and tubers," (Id., p.95) He exchanged drawings and descriptions with Dr Montagne in Paris who described the new species of fungus on 30 August,1845: the claim was recognised and accepted. Berkeley published the cause of blight in January 1846 in the *Journal of the Horticultural Society* of London. In the vehement controversy which followed, Dr Lindley found that Mr Berkeley could not answer some difficult questions and the so-called 'fungal theory', though later proved to be correct, was universally rejected. So it came about that while the cause of the potato famine was known, no experiments were made to see if the fungus could be controlled by chemical treatment, even though Bordeaux Mixture's efficacy in controlling wine-fungus was known in France.

Even today some very promising ideas are not taken seriously; they may not become known to those who provide funds for investigation or, what is worse, they may be rejected by those who feel threatened by new ideas or practices, by the ignorant, the inexperienced and the prejudiced.

Parable 2 Scurvy

Lemons had been known as a cure for scurvy since about 1600 AD, but the first physician to make a thorough investigation of the disease and its cure was James Lind of Edinburgh, who confirmed in 1756 that lemon juice was the best specific. Admittedly it was nearly 40 years before the Lords of the Admiralty decided to introduce lemon juice in the Navy. If they had argued that they would not do this until the mechanism of the treatment was fully understood there would have been thousands of deaths from scurvy during the next 300 years.

Parable 3 Acid Rain

Delay in taking action can have catastrophic results. Hundreds of Scandinavian lakes now have no fish in them. The British government of course does not want to go to the expense of cleaning all the stack emissions from coal-fired power stations until it is absolutely sure that sulphur and nitrogen oxides (SOx and NOx) are really to blame. Meanwhile it has been shown that vast forests of conifers, planted to the water's edge, are also a major cause of the death of fish. Should the controversy be used as an excuse for indecision or inaction; or should the riparian sites around lochs (lakes) be planted with deciduous trees; or power station emissions be reduced for this and other reasons; such as the effect on global warming or ozone reduction?

WORK IN HAND

Resource Use Institute

Having followed the pattern of cultural history and listened to the warnings of many sages about the dangers of entering unknown territory, we shall now review some current lines of research which might help us to find our way towards a world in which east and west, north and south, would combine to share the sum of resources more fairly and sustainably. The aim must be to find a road to a new smooth curve and thus to avoid catastrophe.

My speciality has been the development of new products or processes in the field of *industrial mineralogy*, first in The Fullers' Earth Union Ltd. of Redhill, Surrey, and then, with S George Henderson in Resource Use Ltd. By 1969 I felt the need to know more about economics, finance, other natural resources and the social aspects of our work. I decided to "institutionalise" myself and founded the Resource Use Institute Limited, a company limited by guarantee and not having a share capital. The registered office of the Institute had to be in Scotland and the objects for which the institute was established were -

"to collect information concerning the development of natural resources and to maintain a special library for this purpose; to carry out feasibility studies on individual and regional natural resources; to select projects for detail study and assist in their development and innovation; to assist in general management, including the direction of research and development, during the innovative stages of new products and new industries in the Highlands or elsewhere; to teach the principles of raw materials development by the holding of seminars, publication of articles and other means; to offer facilities in the field of natural resource development, especially of mineral and organic industrial raw materials, to outside research workers; to maintain contacts with universities, technical colleges, research establishments and industry; to conduct the Institute in such a way that it could with only minor changes be assimilated into a university or pro-university set up in The Highlands; to provide as a service to established industry some functions of general management; to undertake, perform and carry on the various duties and kinds of business incidental thereto or connected therewith either gratuitously or otherwise".

Companies of this sort, which plough back their profits to further their aims are founded by well-wishers. Well known examples are Scottish Ballet, Scottish Opera and the Macaulay Land Use Research Institute. The ideas and proposals of 'RUI' were warmly supported by the Duke of Atholl, the Earl of Lauderdale, Lord Boyd Orr, Lord Ritchie Calder, Sir Robert Watson-Watt, Sir William Gammie Ogg and other distinguished people. It is managed by a Council of members, all of whom were resident in Highland Perthshire, among these were Alec W. Barbour, agriculturalist, and James Dow, banker.

Some of the members found that they could develop their 'extracurricular' ideas under the aegis and through the encouragement of the Institute. The spheres of interest within the institute have therefore been agglutinative. **Mathematical chemistry** is the most fundamental; **money and finance** need to be reformed to suit the world's needs today. Considering all matters of trade and industry in terms of **energy** instead of money requires a fundamental change of attitude; it could lead to simplification in a joint monetary system in Europe; and to the elimination of inflation since a joule is a joule and cannot vary or be manipulated. All **taxes** can be replaced by a popular excise duty on the energy content of goods and services; even the unpopular poll tax could be replaced at a very low cost of collection. Funds could be raised for welfare payments and for distribution as a basic income for all.

New concepts in **land use** are being actively worked on by biologist members. Accumulated knowledge shows that large areas of the Highlands can be restored; the ancient fauna and flora would mean a new Caledonian Forest. Repopulation will be possible. Estate management could be more profitable.

In a **language** division attention is being paid to the kind of English which could be taught to children in whose homes a 'minority' language is spoken. Thus Welsh, Gaelic or Scots could be the teaching language for the youngest children, and there would be graded introduction to English. At first a simplified form of English, based on Dr David Sharp's BEST (Basic English for Scientists and Technologists) could be taught. Students need never proceed beyond this because it can be as elegant and stylish as they may ever be called upon to write or speak. BEST would be better to read and understand than many PhD or MSc theses written in English universities today. Also, since the universal language used at conferences is bad English and Esperanto is beyond hope of acceptance, the promotion of BEST by the British Council and the publication of books for teaching English in this form as a second language worldwide is of the utmost importance - possibly even for World Peace. RUI has also produced a draft book of scientific word lists in Gaelic - *Facail Eòlais.* Its greatest value lies in suggesting Gaelic words for use in physics and chemistry, earth sciences, colours and zoology. Rules are given for making Gaelic words for hundreds of thousands of words used for chemicals. The present policy of relying on a data-base in Skye in inadequate.

Very little money in needed by such research groups to produce enormously important results. Reforms in the directions mentioned will not happen of their own accord. The following reports show the 'state of the art' in these various divisions.

Chapter 30
Raw material development, especially industrial minerals

My interest in the development of raw materials for use in industry was inspired by Sir William Bragg's Christmas Lectures in 1925 at the Royal Institution 'before a juvenile auditory', as Faraday put it: the subject was *Old Trades and New Knowledge* (Bragg 1926) and I am fairly certain that my lifelong interest in using science to create new products and industries thus began when I was 14. Four years later E A Hauser gave me a sample of bentonite after giving a lecture in London on thixotropy (1930). At Cambridge I enjoyed R H Rastall's lectures on economic geology but 'went down' at a time of economic depression (1933) with no idea of when I would ever find a job. No matter, I would seek adventure first. A R (Sandy) Glen had no vacancies on his projected visit to Spitsbergen, the Oxford University Arctic Expedition (1933), but I was so crestfallen that he made a place specially for me as 'hunter, handyman, assistant radio operator and geologist'. So it came about that I was up north when I was asked to attend interviews at the Burmah Oil Company Ltd and The Fullers' Earth Union Ltd and I replied via Longyearby's Norwegian radio station that I would see these firms on my return. I joined the F.E.U. in October that year.

I soon found that finding new uses for an old mineral was not a normally recognised profession. The Imperial Institute had long been active in this field, but there were no textbooks, government 'white papers' or university courses to guide me. Following Bragg, I read everything I could find about fuller's earth and had nearly every physical and chemical property of the mineral measured in the laboratory, which was already operating under F W Bird. The story is told in my history of the industry (1976).

The official view of how new industrial projects come to commercial life is that there is always an entrepreneur who has a bright idea, develops it himself, often taking a great financial risk, to a stage when further finance from banks or industry was fairly readily available.

This is still (1991) the official view even though it is hard to think of more than a few entrepreneurs who ran true to type. A good example is Graf Biro and his brother who invented and remained for long in charge of manufacture of their eponymous pens. Dr Salk still controls the manufacture of Salk vaccine. But this way of creating new industries is rare; by recognising only the entrepreneurial route the Department of Trade and Industry, the one-time Scottish Development Agency and the Highlands and Islands Development Board have all unnecessarily restricted the routes by which new industrial projects can be brought into a profitable state.

A conventional market survey of the uses of fuller's earth was of no avail since when we started work no new markets had been identified. The research programme, however, suggested possible outlets. We visited many factories and learned of their unsatisfied requirements. For example, how does one decolorise cod liver oil without removing too much of the vitamin content when using natural fuller's earth as an adsorbent? We found that Surrey fuller's earth was too adsorptive but Atherfield clay from Kent removed enough of the colour and only a little of the vitamins.,

Just before World War II we knew enough about fuller's earth to write a report on its probable new uses. The report was circulated by the Government to several research stations and in a short time our guesses were confirmed. How to make synthetic bentonite was discovered in 1937 by Dr Barbara Emödi now Neumann, and plant to make it installed in 1941. Foundry bonding clays were developed from the same year, and when S George Henderson joined the lab. in 1942 progress was rapid. He sold the FULBOND clays to all of the first 100 foundries which he visited, and 'tailor-made' varieties to suit all the different foundry practices he encountered. We used to discuss what we were doing during our joint selling tours and virtually laid the foundations of a new profession - that of raw material development. This was no theoretical exercise; it was an analysis of highly successful procedures. It is sad that no official recognition has yet been given to this methodology, though published accounts of it have been given in *The Advancement of Science* (1948), in *Natural Resources in Scotland* (1961) and in *Some general principles in the management of innovation* (1978).

By far the most important of the principles is **continuity of development** through the well-known stages of survey → analysis → laboratory-scale and pilot-plant research → production and sales, the whole being considered with respect to the size and purity of the mineral deposit, the human and financial resources available, environmental impact and the economic and political climate. In the second paper (1961) I developed the theme of **multiple utilisation** - finding the greatest number of uses for a product; **varietal utilisation** - making use of differences in composition or physical condition of a resource so as to satisfy different markets; **complex utilisation** - breaking down a raw material into constituent parts which then become separate raw materials on their own account; and **co-operative processing** - sharing plant, laboratories or management to treat more than one raw material.

The success of these methods has been measured in several ways. **Success ratio** measures the proportion of research projects which become commercially viable. In Resource Use Ltd, a company run by Henderson and Robertson, the ratio was above 85 per cent. In comparison, a very large chemical company said that they succeeded commercially with about one major project in 3 1/2 - a success ratio of about 30 per cent.

A more direct method of assessing our technique is to sum the ex works selling price of all goods which owed their origin to the use of the resource development methodology. In the 45 years 1934 to 1979 new goods amounting to about £0.9 billion (10^9) were thus produced as a result of the activities of roughly 1.5 people. This is equivalent to each person's generating output valued at £13 millions a year. One per cent of that turnover would have produced an income of £130,000 a year, which is not an excessive reward. As it was, through our inexperience, our income was about a fiftieth of this or 0.02 per cent!

When working out these guiding principles we paid too little regard to forces which work against the creation of new industry, though even before George died (18 December 1976) we were aware that, because of company mergers there were fewer scientifically-trained decision makers in industry, that chartered accountants expected one to prove the value of one's proposition and companies would no longer 'waste their time' looking at small or medium-sized projects, even though they appeared to have great promise of growth.

To these growing restraints on enterprise must be added some insidious and dangerous practices of the bureaucracy. Let us look at these a little more deeply.

Chapter 31
How bureaucracy can work against progress

Subconscious attitudes can sometimes be revealed in advertisements. The Scottish Council (Development and Industry) organised a symposium in 1960 on the natural resources of Scotland, yet their bookjacket for the published lectures showed a picture of the derelict Easdale slate quarry, which was flooded on the same wild night that a train fell into the River Tay. The Tay Bridge disaster of 28 December 1879 is remembered today as a monument of bad design and construction. A flooded pit can in no way represent the achievements of Scots in the field of resource development.

Another strange example was when the Highlands and Islands Development Board advertised in the leading British newspapers to say that creative people would be welcome to develop their ideas with the Board's financial help. The picture showed an ugly 'mad inventor' (a mythical type) of such unpleasant aspect that few self-respecting inventors would have been attracted northwards, nor would the legend 'people with an idea in their head and fire in their belly'.

In fact neither of these bodies had any intention of assisting in the actual development process. The Scottish *Development* Agency also gave a false impression of their abilities. This was shown when a company which had a unique record of success in helping new industries to be developed applied for a modest grant of funds. They were given eight 'reasons' why the SDA would never assist them. When the company explained that none of these 'reasons' could apply to them or to their proposals, two more spurious and irrelevant reasons were given in their reply. Here one can observe the method of intimidation described by Fanon (1967) and touched on under 'Memes' in Chapter 19. This cruel and misrepresentational technique may be classified as an 'Aunty Sally', a silly figure at fairs set up for the fun of knocking a pipe out of its mouth by throwing sticks or balls at it. It is also a cheap technique used by unscrupulous politicians at elections.

Architecture today

Whether we are living in the declining Period VIII or in the slowly upclimbing Period VIII´ we share the disadvantages of the widening cone of cultural history. The method of course does not highlight publicly acclaimed examples of sculpture or architecture, painting or literature or music which have occurred since their release from archaism because such acclaim is based on aesthetics rather than on typological excellence. And what can be done in a period of obvious decline worries H R H The Prince of Wales, who won the Body Shop's 'Best Architectural Social Invention Award' on 19 June 1990 because he stressed the need for a human scale in **architecture** and for a sense of privacy, such as by buildings around enclosed squares. His ten principles set out in *A Vision of Britain* are:
1. New buildings should blend with the landscape.
2. The size of buildings should be in relation to their public importance and key elements should be obvious.
3. Buildings should respond to a 'human scale'.

4. They should be in tune with neighbouring buildings (architectural good manners).
5. Architects need humility (as we all do).
6. The privacy and feeling of safety in squares, alms houses, universities and the Inns of Court should be studied.
7. Districts should compile inventories of local materials.
8. Buildings without decoration give no pleasure.
9. Traffic signs and lighting should be kept under control.
10. The users of buildings should be consulted more closely.

These rules should give ample scope for the design of new styles of building in appropriate places, the introduction of new materials of construction, the preservation of locally hallowed proportions of buildings, and the use or adaptation of old styles which do obey these rules. Architects today are faced with this difficult problem arising from the Pattern of History. Fortunately, the debate continues, usually in a civilised way!

Chapter 32
Modern science and technology

Modern science and technology can be plotted on the Period VIII time-line beginning about the time of the peak of literature 1594-1600 AD. No comparable development can be traced in previous periods. The remarkable phenomenon of the Enlightenment occurred about the time of the peak of music, 1794 or so. It is remarkable because, for only the second time in history , many art forms were flourishing at once and because cultural features of the Northwest European area were almost wholly replaced by those of the European continent.

In *The Chemical revolution and the enlightenment* Arthur L Donovan (1988) argues that "in the modern era science is a distinct mode of culture". It differs from art, architecture, music and literature not in the *products*, which appeal to the senses and the emotion, but resembles them in the *process* by which scientific work is done and in the fact that science is in the main part of high culture, which Donovan says is marked by three characteristics:

"(1) Its practitioners have through extensive and usually formal training mastered the central methods and techniques of their art;

(2) the meaning and significance of the 'goods' produced by high culture are accessible, at least in the first instance, only to initiates (in science such goods are general conceptions of nature and specific theories that order and explain natural phenomena; and

(3) high culture is intensively self-conscious, in the sense that its practitioners have a highly developed sense of what constitutes exemplary work in the field, how one should go about doing good work, and what criteria should be employed in appraising one's own work and the work of others".

Donovan makes a plea for clearer ideas of what science really is and advocates further study of scientific change. Towards this end he introduces the useful concept of 'traditions of interpretation', and states that "there is a move away from 'the age of disciplines' towards the use of 'intellectual resources of all sorts, whatever their origins', to the task of solving problems encountered in the study of nature".

The pattern of applied science differs from that of pure science because it is promoted by outside influences, which are too often of a military nature. There are those who look at the useful 'fall-out' from military research and development with approbation, but I am sure that many useful and needful developments are neglected because funds have been diverted to destruction.

Chapter 33
Mathematical chemistry

"Big Physics" is widely known; it costs hundreds of millions of pounds; its apparatus can be over a kilometer across; it leads not only to new knowledge about the structure of matter but solves cosmogenic problems and holds out promise of eventually making energy cleanly, safely and more or less indefinitely.

"Big Chemistry" by contrast has virtually no public recognition or international support, yet it is almost as fundamental and important. Still, these are early days when the theoretical contributors hold the stage; early products of this science, the new forms of carbon, the buckmasterfullerenes and their compounds, have fired the imagination of scientists and industrialists already.

Through the work of Dr Edward Cameron Kirby, the Resource Use Institute is known to those working on the interfaces between mathematics, chemistry and computer science.

Mathematical chemistry has to do with *connectivity*; the way in which things are put together. Unlike many constructs used in modern science, such as relativistic equations and quantum theory, the term is understandable at the level of common sense, yet its implications are surprisingly wide and deep. On the other hand to tease out these implications, one does have to use the somewhat obscure language of mathematical Graph Theory. It is deep in the sense that it seems to be dealing with fundamental properties of space and of the universe; there have been some suggestions (though they are still controversial) that it deals with certain aspects of reality more deeply than does Quantum Theory. There are applications in electrical engineering, sociology, geography, linguistics and of course, chemistry, to name but a few. Among long-term concrete and practical goals of interest to the Institute are the development of simple methods of ordering priorities for laboratory testing of some pollutants; the development of efficient codes for data handling; and in the design of drugs and conducting polymers. In truth though, one must also acknowledge that part of the motivation is aesthetic. The subject has a seductive and haunting beauty. As Yeats said of military flying there is a "lonely impulse of delight". (ECK's description).

This science is likely to escalate rapidly over the next decade or so and may yield substantial advantages in the reduction of research and development costs, yet at the moment there are comparatively few British workers. In Yugoslavia, Germany, the USA, China and Japan this kind of work is seen as having great potential. Dr Kirby has presented papers in most of these countries, as well as to the Scottish Quantum Group and the Royal Society of Chemistry Theoretical Section.

This contribution to culture has its roots in early Greek science and is part of a continuing attempt to understand the universe at a very simple yet profound level. For example, in Zagreb, a brief philosophical speculation about the nature of mathematical graphs to other objects in the universe was offered.

Another topic taken was the development and use of structural codes which can be used as topographical indices. An example is a code for hydrocarbons, consisting of a linear string of digits, obtained by counting connections in a particular way. This retains all the information needed for identification, and at the same time shows a simple relationship with some properties which are of interest to engineers, such as Motor Octane Number (the ease with which a fuel 'knocks' in an internal combustion engine), and the propensity of a hydrocarbon to deposit soot when burning (an important consideration in the design and maintenance of aircraft jet engines). So far, however, it has not proved easy to extend this treatment to fuels which contain cyclic structures. (ECK)

The contribution to this science by the Jugoslavians has been outstanding, especially at the two centres, in Zagreb (Croatia) and in Kragujevac (Serbia). Nowhere else in the world would you find as many as a hundred enthusiasts for this science meeting together. There are almost as many women as men, and most of these fine people were unable -at the end of 1991- to get to work. They have hidden their apparatus to protect it from destruction and pray for the end of a mindless war. These sad events make useful collaboration difficult.

In 1982 the only foreign scientist at their Annual Conference was from Scotland. A sympathetic letter from the Royal Society of Edinburgh was a rare boost to the morale of these war-shocked but brave people.

Chapter 34
Financial Reform

No one who tries to create new industry can fail to realise that money has to be found to pay for all stages of development from the idea to the finished project nor to discover that no joint stock bank, merchant bank or financial quango will finance anything which is not fully proved. They all bet on certainties. As many as 90 per cent of projects submitted for financing are turned down on the grounds that they are 'half-baked', but no names and addresses are given of specialist 'bakers' who could complete the process. They scarcely exist, and the economy suffers from their rarity. Resource Use Ltd and later the Resource Use Institute Ltd found during many years that the role of the banking system had been questioned by many serious authors and that the banks' uncreative role had been occasionally circumvented with success. There is room here to touch lightly on a few of these successful trials of 'alternative banking'.

Probably the best known monetary experiment began in Guernsey in 1815. The recent wars had allowed the roads, streets, houses, port area, public buildings, schools and other items of infrastructure to deteriorate so much that the States (Parliament) of Guernsey, knowing that loans would require unrepayable interest, decided to issue £4,000 in £1 notes, a capital sum which was increased to £40,000 and later to £200,000. The notes were issued free of interest. As a result Guernsey never suffered from the Great Depression of 1930; there were no unemployed and Income Tax was 10 pence in the pound. There was no Super Tax nor were there Death Duties. The reaction from London was to flood the market with £1 Bank of England notes, but these failed to kill this admirable example of self-help, so wisely controlled.

In 1903 Sir Daniel Hamilton, a Calcutta businessman, leased Gosaba and two other uninhabited islands from the Indian Government. He built dykes to keep out the sea at high water and installed a desalination plant. There were no bankers to interfere with him so he placed 1100 rupees in a safe in the Estate Office and issued another 1100 rupees in notes of his own design. What was written on them is recorded by Allhusen and Holloway (1959), p.86; but the important thing is that the labourers, brought from India, accepted these notes willingly as wages, and the island began to flourish. Eventually Gosaba had a population of 12000. Not bad for a desert island! Not a single rupee was owed to a moneylender.

Then, in 1931, the coal mine at Schwanenkirchen, Bavaria, closed down and caused a distressed area. A mining engineer called Hebecker bought the bankrupt mine, not with a normal bank loan because he objected to the 5 per cent interest charge he was asked for by the bank, but, as he was a disciple of Silvio Gesell, with an alternative source. Gesell was a monetary reformer whose followers formed an association (a Gesellschaft?) which issued their own money to be used among themselves. Hebecker borrowed from them 40,000 Wara as the private money was called. He then offered to employ any miner who was willing to accept his wages in them. At the same time he opened a shop in which they could buy their food and other necessities. Thus the Wara derived their value directly from the goods in his shop. He had to pay for these in Reichsmarks, but as his coal was also paid for in Reichsmarks this presented no difficulty. The other shopkeepers also accepted Wara, and they pressed their suppliers to accept them and confidence in this currency grew throughout Bavaria.

No longer was there unemployment; commodities were obtainable, debts were paid, prosperity had returned, and anxiety was soothed. But, in late 1931, the Wara was made illegal, the Reichsbank had won. One of the saddest consequences was that the Nazis were free to gain power without fear of such democratic experiments.

I shall tell the next story in Allhusen and Holloway's own words (p.88) "The sensational success of Wara made a deep impression on the Austrian side of the border, and in December (1931) another disciple of Silvio Gesell was elected mayor of Wörgl, a small town in the Austrian Tyrol. His name was Michael Unterguggenberger. He had to deal with high unemployment and general distress: the taxes were in arrears, and the streets and public buildings neglected. He therefore decided that the only thing to do was to follow the example of Schwanenkirchen. A committee consisting of himself, the priest, the Town Treasurer and the Commander of the garrison was formed to put the new money into circulation. This time it was known as Notgeld (Emergency Money). They began by raising the sum of 32,000 schillings which they deposited in the local bank as backing for their new money. They then started work on a new Town Hall and a bridge over the River Inn, both of which they paid for in Notgeld. The Treasurer agreed to accept it in payment of taxes and used it to pay the municipal creditors".

"At end of the first year the town was transformed, 100,000 schillings had been spent on public works, and there was even a new ski-run. In fact, everybody seemed to have been happy except the banks. The blow fell in January 1933 when the Austrian National Bank sued the Mayor and Corporation of Wörgl for infringing their right to be the sole issuers of bank notes. The Bank won and . . . the Notgeld was withdrawn".

These examples are worth volumes of theory. They show that there can be a new attitude towards money. Banking is still shrouded in mystery because there is still need to conceal the facts. In all four examples there was no place for mystery. There was no need for it. But confidence was needed and given. (What a pity Comhairle nan Eilean did not print Gaelic tokens to replace the £24 millions they lost by 'investing' in the crooked Bank of Credit and Commerce International).

In 1924 C H Douglas introduced *Social Credit* in the book of that name (1919). This and many others of his works are still in print and so is the journal *Social Crediter*, edited now in Edinburgh. His ideas of monetary reform met with the fiercest opposition in England, but his large following were well organised and informed. One Nobel prizewinner, Sir Frederick Soddy, FRS, the isotope man, wrote a book in support and was ostracised for his pains . A youth movement was founded in 1920 by John Hargrave; and the Green Shirt Movement in 1931. The question of a National Dividend was raised in the House of Lords on 4 July 1934.

Aberhart's Social Credit Party was victorious in Alberta on 24 August 1935; Douglas failed to act strongly enough in support; and the Federal Government of Canada made sure that the system would not work. See Douglas *The Alberta Experiment*. In the end the Albertan Government "lost the tread of the story" (Douglas, Social Crediter, 17 December 1949).

Independently C W Unwin wrote a book called *Hopousia* (1940), a made-up word meaning where or whither. The aim of the book was to construct a Utopia, a dangerous occupation; but the best thing to do is to read only Book II, that is his chapters V Wants, VI Currency, VII Money, VIII Four Methods of Commodity Exchange and IX The Four Follies, the last of which are worth quoting:

Folly Number One is the idea that no consumer is able to purchase a commodity till he has obtained, out of an existing supply, the money that expresses the exchange-value of that commodity.

Folly Number Two consists in the petrification of money and the granting to it of permanent existence.

Folly Number Three consists in the issue of money without the production of commodities.

Folly Number Four is the idea that Land is a Commodity.

The statement of these follies should inform our thinking. Here are some examples. (1) In the present system the amount of money available to help huge areas of the world is clearly inadequate. The 'existing supply' is finite, the world's needs are far greater than this. It is obvious that a new way of creating money to suit the needs of all parts of the world must be devised. (2) We are still paying in part for the Napoleonic wars. Is that rational or necessary? (3) I think this folly includes the disreputable profession of 'making money out of money', when nothing has been created. (4) The idea of the stewardship of land is slowly gaining ground.

The continuing interest in Douglas' Social Credit, especially in Canada, Australia and New Zealand, is partly due to its firm moral or one could say religious basis. In 1948 William Maclellan of Glasgow published Dr Thomas Robertson's *Human Ecology*. The author considered Administration, Sanctions, Politics, Education and Religion. (Sanctions, by the way, are the police force and the military). He upended the whole structure and wrote persuasively that the order should be **Religion, Education, Politics, Sanctions, Administration, Industry and Finance**. This was no idle ploy like the brilliant inversions of Oscar Wilde but a careful refocussing on the main mechanisms which operate in society by a mind steeped in philosophy (his Chapter 12). To him, history to be valid and to function at all must be Baconian - inductive or 'realistic' history as opposed to Hellenic - deductive or 'mythical' history. The former is truly scientific and the latter 'nescientic' or 'unrealistic'. I recommend anyone who talks about capitalism, value, unemployment, free competition, profit, money, debt, owner, bourgeoisie and so on to realise that "when words of this order are used to derive conclusions or general principles, the propositions so attained, being incapable of operational test, are valueless for control or understanding of the phenomena under consideration".

I am happy to say that the Department of Human Ecology at Edinburgh University does have a copy of this vital book. Robertson drew upon Indian and other oriental religions in his work and E F Schumacher in *Small is Beautiful: a Study of Economics as if People Mattered* (1973) even had a shot at devising Buddhist economics. The point to be taken is that religion is the concept being used and not a group of churches, which are all too often a part of the social structure of society we are beginning to see is so faulty.

The years 1976-7 when several works were written on this subject was astonishingly fruitful for reasons I fail to see. (I think Petrie was right; religion transcends the pattern of history and is not part of the mechanism). Anyway, in this year two books appeared with a similar message. Eugen Loebl had been Czechoslovakia's minister for foreign trade. The Soviet invaders imprisoned him for eleven years, the first five of which were in solitary confinement. He had time to think. He had been a good communist; admittedly he knew the West but did not approve of its financial power. So he wrote (in prison, like John Bunyon's *Pilgrim's Progress*) a book called *Humanomics*. He exposed the fallacies of orthodox economics and favoured democratic control of the economy for the benefit of consumers. He concluded that the printing of money should not be left in the hands of private banks but should be carried out by the state. He favoured no income tax but all revenues by indirect taxation. He recommended a social wage (a basic income) carefully graded to suit the needs of all. He foresaw low interest rates, no inflation, stable prices and full employment. He provided a reasoned philosophical and logical analysis of an alternative economy.

James Sacra Albus (1976), designer of electronic systems for over 15 spacecraft, had already published *A Theory of Cerebellar Functions* in 1971 but now turned his attention to the economic, social and political impact of superautomation. *Peoples' Capitalism* is his vision of how humankind could be liberated from poverty and oppression. I cannot do better than to quote his own summary:-

Peoples' Capitalism is a proposal which addresses all of these issues simultaneously. It offers a simple, straight-forward solution to each. Peoples' Capitalism could be instituted in the United States without any changes in our constitutional form of government. In fact, far from altering any of the fundamental principles upon which this country was founded, this plan would revitalize the free enterprise system, and realise the ideals of Jeffersonian Democracy in post-industrial America.

Three new institutions are proposed:

1. A semi-private investment corporation called the National Mutual Fund (NMF) would be established with borrowing authority from the Federal Reserve. The NMF would use the funds it borrowed to make stock purchases from private industry. The increased availability of investment capital would stimulate the economy and increase productivity. Profits from these investments would be paid to the general public in the form of dividends. By this means every adult citizen would become a capitalist in the sense of deriving a significant fraction of his or her income from dividends paid on invested capital. Estimates are that per capita income from the NMF would reach $6000 per annum in 1975 dollars within twenty-five years.

2. A Demand Regulation Policy (DRP) would be instituted in parallel with the NMF in order to provide sufficient savings to offset NMF investment spending. The DRP would temporarily withhold savings from consumers so as to prevent disposable income from rising prior to realisation of NMF stimulated productivity gains. DRP withholdings would be graduated so that low income people would be less affected.

Savings Bonds would earn interest in excess of current inflation and would be redeemable after five years.

3. A Cabinet-level Department of Science and Technology would be established in order to finance and direct long-term research into major productivity producing technologies.

Peoples' Capitalism is simple in concept yet its implications are truly breath-taking.

- It offers a solution to recession and inflation simultaneously.
  Increased availability of investment capital would get the economy moving again. Inflation would be controlled in the short run by DRP savings, and over the long run by increased productivity resulting from higher rates of investment.
- It resolves the fundamental conflict between economic growth and environmental preservation.
  NMF dividends to individuals would reduce the pressures for jobs and growth at any cost. Increased efficiency in production would reduce waste and provide the resources for improved pollution control and environmental conservation.
- It promises a degree of individual freedom based on personal financial independence which is unprecedented even among utopian proposals.
  Every adult citizen would possess a personal source of independent income. People would be economically free to live where they wished and to work at what they enjoyed.
- It offers a cure to poverty and old age insecurity without taxing the rich to give to the poor.
  NMF public dividends would be generated by wealth producing capital-investments. The NMF would be a profit-making, income-producing investment corporation, not a tax-consuming welfare program.
- It achieves economic equity without destroying incentives to individual excellence.
  The NMF would distribute the profits generated by high technology industry to everyone. Persons with ambition could afford to develop their talents, and society would be able, with clear conscience, to reward its high achievers.
- It opens up an entirely new road to economic development for emerging nations which completely by-passes the social dislocations of classical industrialization.
  In developing nations, Peoples' Capitalism could finance automated industries and robot factories which would pay dividends to farmers and villagers directly. Economic development would be achieved without converting the rural population into industrial workers or concentrating them in congested urban areas.

Even the most casual observer of what goes on in the average factory, office or construction project cannot help but notice that most of what is produced comes from machines and not human labour. Scholarly studies confirm this common sense observation, showing that the overwhelming percentage of productivity increases over the past two hundred years have resulted from technological progress, not from harder work or longer hours. Whether we like to admit it or not, most of what we have is produced by machines, not people.

Does it not then seem odd that more than two-thirds of our total output is distributed as compensation to labor? Might not such a large discrepancy between how wealth is created and how it is distributed distort the entire structure of the free market economy? Consider for example, that distributing the benefits of two centuries of productivity increases primarily through wages and salaries has raised labor costs so high that employers cannot afford to hire workers even when there are jobs which need doing.

Thus, we have massive unemployment even while
- Cities need rebuilding,
- New sources of energy need to be developed,
- Pollution control needs to be expanded,
- Better health care delivery needs to be provided,
- The environment needs to be protected and services of every kind need to be improved.

Yet no one can afford to hire people to do these jobs.

On the other hand the lack of any alternative to wages and salaries as a source of income creates such strong pressures for job security that
- Waste is encouraged,
- Featherbedding and restrictive work rules are commonplace,
- Pollution is condoned,
- Obsolescence is planned,
- Mass advertising of trivia is considered necessary,
- Unwise growth goes unchecked.

And much of what people get paid for doing everyday in offices and factories throughout this land could be eliminated without affecting the production of goods or services whatsoever.

Furthermore, even if make-work and waste could succeed in producing 'full employment' there would still be millions of Americans outside the wage and salary income distribution channels. The employable labor force makes up only about 40% of the population. Thus, even though practically every business in the country could easily expand production, and would gladly do so if markets were available, the lack of purchasing power of people without jobs makes such expansion impossible. *The result is that our enormous productive potential is never fully applied to our clear and urgent human needs.*

Rising Expectations vs Declining Resources

The two charts on page 139 show that long-term gains in productivity are closely correlated with investment. There is little reason to doubt that this correlation will continue into the future. In fact, recent technological developments in computers and manufacturing technology suggest that mankind may be on the threshold of a new industrial revolution. Within two decades it may be practical for computer-controlled factories and robots to produce virtually unlimited quantities of manufactured goods and to even reproduce themselves at continuously decreasing costs. Investments in such technology almost certainly will produce major productivity gains for many decades to come.

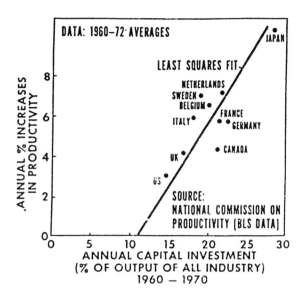

Fig. 32a

What causes a nation's productivity to grow? This chart shows that countries with a high rate of investment have high productivity growth, and vice-versa. This implies that productivity growth is not serendipitous or beyond human control. Instead, it is the direct result of economic policies which promote investments in new technology and in more efficient plants and equipment.

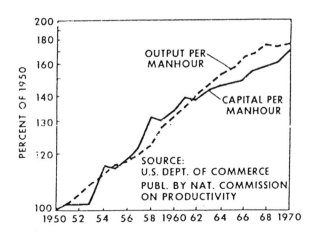

Fig. 32b

America's high standard of living is based on high productivity, i.e. high output per man-hour. This chart shows that productivity is closely correlated with the amount of sophisticated tools and capital equipment per worker.   *From J.S. Albus (1976)*

Unfortunately, the present mechanisms for increasing investment in high technology industries (such as tax credits for big business) serve to increase the already enormous concentration of wealth and power in the hands of a few *, while leaving the majority of the population just as dependent on wages and salaries as ever. Clearly robot factories will be a direct threat to the economic security of almost every American unless some alternate means of investment financing and income distribution can be found.

*A US Department of Commerce Survey of Current Business report on stock ownership in the United States dated November, 1974 states that one percent of the families in the US owns over 50 percent by value of all stock and that five percent of the families own 73.7 percent by value of all stock.

From J.S. Albus' Leaflet for Peoples' Capitalism.

Chapter 35
Taxation reform and the resource economics proposition

We have traced the history of financial reform from the Guernsey experiment to the theoretical treatments of Loebl and Albus. For interesting ideas about banking one may turn to Thomas Robertson's chapter on "The Myth of Money" (1948). A fuller history would have included the development of credit unions, producer's cooperatives, cooperative copartnerships and the Trustee Savings Bank, founded by the Rev Henry Duncan at Ruthwell, Dumfriesshire, in 1810 as the 'Penny Bank'. For many years credit unions were illegal in Britain, but a Model Constitution for a Credit Union by Elizabeth Orr was published by the Scottish Reconstruction Committee in 1946 and widely circulated in the Highlands. The mutual nature of the TSB was ended when it became another joint-stock bank, TSB plc.

The Government have always been able to keep new ideas at bay, though they did at one time have a small office in which submissions could be studied. Negative Income Tax, for example, was turned down by this office on the grounds that the Government (quite rightly) would examine only proposals which covered national and local taxation as well as welfare payments.

In the 70s and 80s demands for welfare support far exceeded the money brought in by the system, known as the 'Welfare State', which followed the Beveridge Report (1942). To be fair we should remember that Sir William (later Lord) Beveridge "had not hoped for what is called the 'Welfare State' and expressed the strongest dislike to having been dubbed its 'Father' (R B Mair, 1982) No political party has found a solution for the shortfall.

Progress was made, though, largely in Scotland, by the coming together of new lines of thinking and research. Fundamental to this significant advance was the observation that all commercial and manufacturing activities can be measured in terms of energy. Professor Malcolm Slesser had become an authority, known the world over for his researches, which measured all changes in state in gigajoules and no longer in national currencies. Here we can see that variable currency could give way to invariable units, the new 'numéraire'. Ecus could be linked to the expenditure of energy. Even in January 1941 Flinders Petrie wrote to Lord Stamp urging the adoption of an international currency (M S Drower, p. 428)

Slesser's computing team at Strathclyde turned their attention to writing an elaborate program called ECCO - Enhanced Carrying Capacity Options. Here for the first time we have a tool to show whether the choice of a dozen or more policy choices can lead to **sustainability**. They proved that no politician who does not have access to such a computer can think up policies which will have desirable results in 10, 20 or 30 years' time. Of course the Treasury have a computer for such calculations but ECCO accurately forecast the outcome of the UK economy 10 years ahead from 1974. ECCO now stands for Evolution of Capital Creation Options.

What a pity ECCO is not used in Britain,- though some work has recently (1991) been commissioned! On the other hand economists from Kenya, Peru, Mauritius,

Thailand and the Phillipines have been trained to use a simplified version of the program and RUI has copies of it for sale.

Farel Bradbury, an inventive engineer, of Ross-on-Wye, produced in 1986 *The delight of resource economics* introducing UNITAX, which John P.C. Dunlop, an accountant, has shown is really an excise duty collectable at very low cost at very few points. When these three began to cooperate, great progress was made. Many leading politicians have been sent copies of their proposals. Very shortly they are that: "The physical wealth of the country is created and maintained by the exploitation of energy. A minimum amount of energy is required for all persons to survive. Sensible people are coming to realise that this (minimum amount) should not be taxed. That is why RUI proposes that a minimum income should be available to all. Thereafter the surplus energy used to create extra incomes and disposable and capital wealth is available for taxation and our proposals for Energy Excise Duties are the only way which does not put a brake on that process. They do not inhibit or tax the individual's desire or ability to improve his share in the wealth creating process" (Dunlop 28 November 1991). See Table 8

Table 8

Some advantages of the Resource Economics Proposition and the resource tax UNITAX.

Less primary consumption. More durable products: sustainable growth.

Knock-on benefits on pollution, conservation of wild habitats.

Places a cash and environmental value on the rainforests.

The simplification of customs procedures.

True freemarket: no interventions, protections, quotas or subsidies.

The Common Agricultural Policy (CAP) can be discarded.

Curb intensive methods of (over) production.

Ends inflation.

No recessions.

Improved employment prospects; less drudgery.

No "black" economy of tax evasion.

Third World debt is eased.

Reduce cash crop and drugs orientation.

Reduces economic crime.

Less government, less bureaucracy.

Balanced budgets on current revenue.

Interest rates around 3%.

Simpler laws, less enforcement, fewer prisons, wider legal access.

Funds Basic Income for all
  (including pensions, child and disability allowances etc.).

Funds "no-fault" compensation: income and/or "lump sum"

Funds copyright income, intellectual property awards,peer grants, etc.

Environmental benefits in water, sea, land and air.

Solves "ageing population" pension riddle.

Releases adding-cost workers for adding-value employment.

More adding value, less adding cost, encourages "appropriate" technology.

Enhanced quality of life.

To this list, due to Bradbury, one may add

Recognition of women's work.

Easy replacement of Poll Tax or Council Tax.

No arguments about value of one's house.

No unfairness introduced by banding.

Flexibility for Government to decide which old taxes to abandon first,
  e.g. VAT, INCOME TAX, taxes on industry, and inheritance taxes.

Moreover, the Resource Economics Proposition has vital international importance. RUI has passed a Resolution, which is given here as Table 9.

Table 9

THAT WORLD GOVERNMENTS BE URGED INDIVIDUALLY TO EXAMINE THE RESOURCE ECONOMICS PROPOSITION (REP)

The REP is designed to operate at the nucleus of any separately defined economic system: it can be adopted by any single nation or group of nations. It entails a simple inversion of basic economic factors systematically located above party political operation but which factors affect all economic, social and political activity. The REP is victimless: it requires no tax targets, official redundancy or institutional reform. The REP instigates a process of change which is automatic, evolutionary and egalitarian with a natural tendency to promote a democratic free market: it is non-investigatory and is not dependent on general clerical literacy. It is self-stable and politically durable: it is easier and more visibly beneficial to adopt than to reverse. It self-optimises to worldwide sustainability.

The REP can have a positive influence on all of the broad issues confronting World leaders. These include social stresses, population pressures, resource depletion, air, sea and land environmental degradation, pollution and wastes, crime, punishment, drugs, wealth distribution, investment, interest rates, debt, exchange controls, trade balances, GATT, international economy, finance, health, education, defence, food, water, transport and communications, technology transfer, land use, housing, poverty, welfare benefits and taxation.

This comprehensive effect is no more and no less than is essential for a full-blown and radical economic reform commensurate with the problems confronted.

There are five main elements to the proposition.

1) The essence of the proposition is to value human economic activity in scientific terms of primary consumption. These scientific measures are related to money systems by linking with the revenue system of the operating national entity. In crude terms, the number of primary units of energy consumed in any given area carries a UNITAX duty which yields the public spending budget for that same area. The UNITAX is added once only at economic source without involving individual consumers and at a unified rate on all statutory defined primaries. In general terms, the higher the UNITAX rate, the more effective the resource economics.

2) The UNITAX duty replaces the revenue from another tax which is ideally then abolished completely. This has been described as "fiscal neutrality", but it should be noted that there is a skew to reduce labour-intensive and to increase "materials" - intensive costs. The first tax replaced is preferably a broad labour (added value) tax such as a general sales tax amounting to a small part (say 15% maximum) of total revenue. This first step establishes the system which can later be operated so as to increase the revenue yield. For example and initial EC UNITAX of 1 Ecu/GJ would abolish the 12 Member nations' value added tax contributions to Brussels. An early objective is to achieve a "balanced budget" so as to mitigate government borrowing (and government dependence on financial institutions) and to control the value of money, essentially (because of direct prices control) free of inflation. This leads to very reduced interest rates while maintaining a strong currency.

3) The operating nation, or nation group, is invariably a customs entity. The UNITAX is applied and rebated at the standard unified rate on all transactions crossing its frontiers.

4) The REP must be applied in controlled phases. This allows the evolution of durable product concepts, low depreciation activity, new employment patterns, multiple use, recycling, resource use economy, alternative life-style (with enhanced quality of life), the squeezing out of added-cost activity and the rationalisation of added-value activity. Government spending programmes can similarly be enhanced in phases, stripped of processing costs, and directed to the unrestricted but accountably visible funding of democratically approved public services, health and education by demand costing rather than budgetary supply limits.

5) A basic income is paid non-selectively to all citizens. This has five objectives. Firstly to compensate for higher base living (heating) costs as the UNITAX replaces more and more revenue systems. Secondly to allow labour mobility as work patterns change and subsidies and interventions etc. are scrapped. Thirdly to provide a means of wealth distribution to close the gap between rich and poor. Fourthly to remove and replace social security and welfare benefit "hand-outs". Fifthly to recycle 'first spend' money for economic damping (an end to recession).

28th October 1991

(Correspondence with RUI Ltd., PO Box 4, Ross-on-Wye, Herefordshire, England, HR9 6EB.)

The Resource Use Institute has always stressed that even further progress could be made if funds were made available for research and the management of the transfer of its accumulated knowledge. Contact with the Treasury and other permanent civil servants is urgently needed.

One question in particular has not been satisfactorily answered: *who judges what work is to be done?* There is little difficulty for the 2000 most progressive U.S. Corporations, according to Stuart Speiser (1986) , since they themselves could be allowed to decide how much new capital they would require year by year. The question becomes much more acute when medium and small companies and individuals require capital. Albus says that "the individual is the best judge of what constitutes his (or her) own betterment", but I am convinced that the banking system is ill-adapted to making judgments of the *potential* value of proposals made to them. This problem has not been resolved and all countries are the poorer for not having the answer. The following fifteen paragraphs may provoke thought on this critical subject.

1. What criteria are used by bankers or financiers of enterprise; what special training has been provided for those who judge what is to be financed or rejected?

2. No satisfactory answer is found in the books at our disposal. Albus' National Development Fund would have to judge the merit of projects but how would they do it?

3. Speiser relies on prosperity being created by the 2000 most progressive U.S. corporations. Yet the great international companies are not always wise in their handling of capital. Failures when they occur are on a huge scale and are damaging to the economy. Financial whizzkids and fraud are not unknown even in famous companies. Financing development out of profits sounds laudable but it increases prices and reduces competitiveness. Some chairmen of large companies have said that they do not mind where capital comes from as long as it is cheap and easy to come by.

4. The question of who judges is much more acute in the experience of medium - and small - sized companies and of individuals. After 50 years helping to get promising projects 'off the ground' I know that only a small proportion of these could have been financed by conventional financial sources.

5. One such institution accepted about 10 per cent of projects for financing. The remaining 90 per cent or so were judged to be unworthy of their support. The 'judges' played safe; some good projects had been ill-presented; many needed money to complete their development. Among the rejects of course are those of little merit because of overproduction, nationally or world wide (a saturated market). Some may be hopeless or plain dotty. The judges may think the proposals are on too small a scale.

6. We can see from this analysis - and there may be other categories - that the financial judges should also take into consideration the character of the proposer, not only his track-record in financial terms. (The Highland Fund lends on character, yet its failure rate was only about $2\,^1/_2$ per cent, when I last saw the figure. They had assessors in every Highland parish.

7. An extreme form of devolution in the financing world is the Credit Union - not well developed in the UK admittedly but by no means unimportant elsewhere. In this system a community pools its resources and decides on how best to spend their funds for personal and the community's good. A Credit Union would fit more naturally into a country where a minimum wage was provided, as in the Resource Economics Proposal, than into the present economy.

8. In the New Economics interest on loans need not exceed 1 per cent to cover the cost of the paperwork or not more than 3 per cent if technical advice is needed. Mortgages would be replaced by a simple contract to repay at an agreed (low) rate for an agreed number of years. J.D. Unwin's *Hopousia* is essential reading here. The cost of buying a £50,000 house would be £500 or rarely more; whereas the mortgage charges today can amount to £100,000 to £150,000, an unnecessary and discouraging burden, two or three hundred times as much as it need be.

9. In the present granting of mortgages the applicant's ability to pay is of great concern to the judges. In the Unwinian system the question of ability to pay is far less pressing.

10. In the same way the need for collateral would be lessened. Indeed at present, when a bank exercises its right to take the assets of a 'failed' borrower, it may make it impossible for the unfortunate entrepreneur later to succeed. The lending houses, still no doubt called 'banks', will concentrate not on maximising the bank's profits or on 'making money out of money' but will do their best to see that the best scientific, technical and financial services are available to and used by the applicant.

11. The national-banking systems would recruit specialists in helping people to run profitable enterprises and would not restrict their assistance to the 10 per cent of obviously suitable candidates.

12. Unemployment could be massively reduced, perhaps by a half, by providing funds to allow a high proportion of independent business to take on one additional worker, (*Innovation & Employment* by David Foster, 1980). This was the object of the Selective Employment Contribution of the last Labour Government.

13. Foster (1980, pp 75 et seq.) examines a number of measures which have been proposed for reducing unemployment, namely 13.1, more industrial production, 13.2 the siege economy and protectionism, 13.3 the innovation of new products, 13.4 growing all one's own food, 13.5 inviting the Japanese to manufacture in Britain, 13.6 expanding services, 13.7 backing small business, 13.8 sharing out the work, 13.9 supporting what he amusingly calls the natural growth areas such as crime and old age! Some merit can be seen in most of these ideas but only two are outstandingly promising:

13.3 The innovation of new products? YES... The sky is the limit for a nation which can innovate *wanted* products and beat the competitive market. There is no reason to suppose that civilisation has already innovated all that there is possible.

13.7 Back the small businesses? YES... This makes sense because small businesses have the natural expansive drive *now*. One does not have to invent an expansive principle because it already operates in the small businesses.

14. We know that obtaining capital even for promising-looking projects is extremely difficult at present and that many innovators are forced to give up in misery. I believe it is only under Resource Economics principles that the new style banks would say to an applicant for finance for a moderately-promising or partly-developed idea "yes, what you need is finance to complete the development to a commercial state in local workshops or by temporary visiting development specialists." No normal bank would or could do this.

15. Under the Resource Economics system money would be issued to support or provide for all needs for capital and the profits from these investments would, in whole or in part, be paid to everyone, as in The Universal Shareowning Plan (Speiser), except for a proportion temporarily held back in order to eliminate inflation. The body handling these funds would also pay for failures, having done its best to minimise them.

Chapter 36
Land Use Studies

I was introduced to land use when I joined The Fullers' Earth Union near Redhill, Surrey, in 1933. At that time huge cranes on railway tracks moved fitfully along the strike-lines and deposited the overburden to one side in long ridges. At one time these were planted with conifers but latterly were left as a source of calcium carbonate for neutralising the effluent from the acid-activation factory at Cockley. Yet in the 19th century "the outcrop in the Chartfield area was worked so carefully that all the overburden was replaced as a flat surface and it is difficult to tell that the area has ever been worked. The tidy operator was probably John Hynam" (Robertson,1986, chapter 36i). However, when the quarries had reached a depth of 45 metres in 1945, the FEU began to use draglines, bulldozers and enormous tractor-scrapers. At last they were able to engage in restoration and landscaping, so that neither scenery nor traditional land uses were spoilt.

Before WW II I walked with Sir Hugh Rankin, an estate manager, from Ardgour to Cape Wrath, 1033 km, during three summer holidays, usually within a mile of the sea, in order to study land use. At that time the geological survey of the Highlands had not been completed, but Dr L. Dudley Stamp, Director of the Land Utilisation Survey of Britain, lent me some six inch maps of the Parish of Rogart so that in August 1939 Dr Alex Muir, Soil Scientist of Aberdeen, Dr R Elfyn Hughes, agricultural botanist of Aberystwyth, Alexandrina Macleod of Kinlochbervie, secretary, and I could make what turned out to be the first land potentiality map - the second being made some years later in the USA. The unpublished work is preserved at the Macaulay Land Use Research Institute, Aberdeen.

Fifty years ago we saw the need for a cadastral survey, more accessible to the public than the Register of Sasines; we saw that the development and management of rural land could be better done if traditional estate boundaries were replaced by more rational, geographical limits drawn up to optimise land use; and ten years before that I had seen that Western Norway was a good model for Highland rural economy. In the British traditional way of doing things there were too many divisions and departments of responsibility. Is it helpful to consider hill sheep farming as a distinct and separate enterprise? Why should not more farmers grow trees? Can the Forestry Commission be improved? Can the Highlands, a sixth of the land area of mainland Britain develop without a university? Should not Sir John Myre's brilliant essay on Devastation (1943) be more widely circulated.?

In 1962 the Scottish Peat and Land Development Association proposed a national Land Development Board "to get food from the barren hills and glens". Their aim was to reclaim at least a third of the 11 million acres of unproductive hill and marginal areas in Scotland, (*Scotsman*, 25 May 1962, pages 1 and 6). Dr. R Maclagan Gorrie, famous for his work on the forests of the Punjab, was then vice-chairman of SPALDA and later joined the Resource Use Institute. In this plan of 30 years ago an initial expenditure of about £40 million was envisaged - roughly half the total paid out then in subsidies to Scottish farmers. This was to be spread over 10 years.

The ideas of land reclamation has never died but the emphasis has moved away from food production to the greening of inner cities and to bringing variety to the rural scene. Some land 'set aside' from food production has been converted by farmers to mini-nature reserves, now the home of birds and other wildlife. Central, regional and district government have all contributed towards the beautification of town and country. Tree-planting attracted individual enterprise as well as environmental groups. The Woodland Trust, founded in 1972 in Devon, now owns over 500 woods throughout Britain, in area nearly 7000 hectares; and is one of the most rapidly-expanding charities. It buys and manages woodlands to enhance natural conservation value, to increase its landscape value and to allow *informal* public access. It relies on fund raising from many sources. It recognises that the birch is an important tree ecologically. Alan Drever, after successful work in Buchan, founded in Aberfeldy the Scottish Community Woods Campaign in 1988; at its launch on 21st June 1988 we learnt of the first community-owned wood at Wooplaw Wood near Lauder, bought through the efforts of Tim Stead of Borders Community Woodlands; and the pioneer efforts in East Sussex of David Saunders. Alan had been inspired by the situation in Germany and Switzerland where woodlands are often under community control, as are the well managed fuel-coppices of Lorraine, France.

In October 1991 Alan Drever widened the scope of his activities. The new Scottish Native Woods Campaign (see reference under his name) works closely with landowners, advising on management and grants. Emphasis is given to the marketing of Scottish Hardwood products. "So much oak and birch that goes up in smoke as firewood could become parquet flooring... Such a product.... an example which greatly adds value, utilises short lengths of timber. We also currently import all our birch plywood from Finland! Birch in fact has the most potential. Fast growing and dominating 56 per cent of our native woodlands, it has a better overall age structure than any other species".

The community aspect is also growing in importance; over 70 Primary schools have become involved in "Growing Up With Trees", not only in Highland Perthshire, but in other areas, often in conjunction with involving the wider community. Growing Up with Trees is also 'taking root' in Highland Strathclyde, an enormous area, beginning with Argyll. Another initiative is the West Fife Native Woodland Project, sponsored by British Coal Opencast (Scotland) and covers 80 square miles. Activities centre on working with farmers, the first project of its kind in the UK. The Campaign grows in effectiveness and is now widely recognised and supported. Apart from its great commercial potential it is leading the way to a healthy woodland culture on the Scandinavian model.

A parallel development is the Loch Garry Tree Group, founded by Ron Greer and Derek Pretswell in 1986, (Roger Smith 1988). The immediate aim of these biologists is to revolutionise land use in the Highlands, managing both the fauna and the flora. Their Highland Wildland Project requires an experimental area of 20-28 thousand hectares (50-70 thousand acres).

Ron Greer as a laddie in Glasgow was fascinated by the colonisation of wasteland and pools of water on the site of what had been "Dickson's Blazes", an abandoned iron works. The words zoology and botany added nothing to what he actually observed, the gradual re-establishment of a flora and fauna in a scene of man-made dereliction. He 'discovered' the Highlands and knew that his future lay in that direction. He became a freshwater biologist at the Freshwater Fisheries laboratory in Pitlochry and an authority on subspecies of arctic charr and on the importance of broadleaved trees in the food-chain of these and other salmonids.

In his spare time he planted many species of such trees on the banks of Loch Garry, thanks to the generosity and forward-thinking of the owner and tenant. His early fencing, carried to the sites on his back, was not tall or strong enough to deter the deer from damaging his trees; but in the course of time he showed that many species would grow well at 1400 feet, or 425 metres; that is, above the generally accepted tree-line for such a place.

He has already had the satisfaction of recording the return of black grouse to the area, the sight of naturally regenerating willow and rowan within some of his enclosures and the healthy growth of oak and alder at this height above sea level. His Group has attracted awards and grants, which will greatly extend the scope of his research. Three of the four areas are strictly reserved for native species capable of living at this altitude. The fourth is an experimental area.

Wild lupins enrich and open up the soil, improve drainage, discourage heather, encourage worms and effect mineral cycling. Thus they promote tree-growth in acid soils and in gullies.These gullies remind one of how the topsoil can be lost. The Loch Garry Project is designed to find an optimal litter supply for the growth of broad-leaved trees, the leaves of which feed aquatic invertebrates. It is not an attempt to recreate any kind of replacement "Caledonian forest", though the requirements of the Native Pinewood Grant will be met where applicable. Ron can never forget that, through man's mismanagement or thoughtlessness, the area covered by trees in Scotland has declined from over 50 percent to about 1 $^1/_2$ per cent in the last 300 years. There is no room here to trace the changes which have occurred during the last 12000 years since the Ice Age; Ron has visited Iceland, which was once well afforested, but now has only a few demonstration woodlands,. The decline has been of the order of 40 down to 1 per-cent. Elsewhere the soil has all been washed away, thanks to the presence of too many sheep.

In the study of land use, Norway is a more promising land to turn to because:

1. Land is owned, typically and optimally, in vertical strips from road or fjord to mountain tops. The farmer-owners manage the land so that each horizon contributes in its own way and season to the economy of the farm. Most farmers have their own patch of timber for housebuilding and are members of a co-operative sawmill where the wood is cut and seasoned for their own use or for sale.

2. Sheep and cattle are in-wintered in buildings which might at first be mistaken for hotels. At one end the silage is stored *under* the roof. (No hideous blue silos there). The silage is automatically moved along to the animals.

3. The sheep spend months a year indoors. They are never allowed to be snowed under. The breeds and crosses are chosen to give fine wool, but more attention could be given to eating quality. In Scotland, though, in-wintering sheep is officially frowned upon even though the Best Farmer of the Year, voted this by other farmers one year, had converted his farm to this system. RUI has looked into the cost of converting existing buildings for this purpose.

4. Agricultural advisers live and work in every rural community. They far out-number those available in Scotland.

5. Family farms tend to be held in perpetuity. Even if the head of the family finds an important post in a city he has leave to attend to the farming in spring and autumn. They often provide for visitors. I stayed once with the Prime Minister, who welcomed me at breakfast.

Ron and Derek have made a study of the native wild animals of the Highlands; and recommend wildlife management as well as separate and limited divisions of agriculture forestry, fishing and so on. Moreover they see that the needs of man must be taken into account. To them (and to RUI) wilderness, if man-made, is anathema. A landscape brought back to life is more beautiful than such wilderness.

The Highland Wildland Project is based on the recognition that the primary resource is the **soil/vegetation complex**, which if carefully managed can provide occupations for a permanent population whose work would be in balance with nature.

More land would be found for reindeer, reconstituted aurochs could be brought from Lascaut and given a new home in Scotland. Beavers might be successful in a few places. Wolves would help to keep deer numbers down and improve their quality, but are not recommended because the public are not ready to welcome them and wolves could not be relied upon to stick to sickly deer! But muskox would provide a fibre cash crop of high value. Ron has had hands-on experience in muskox management in the north of Norway. Elk, wisent, and wild boar could one day be on the Scottish menu.

The Scottish Wildland Project would not only provide wealth to a new 'native' population - we are thinking of handknitting, research establishments, and tourism, but could show the wildlife to visitors in specially-designed, partially underground build-ings, where animals brought into view in telescopes could be seen without being disturbed.

Chapter 37
Languages

Scots Gaelic

The decline of Gaelic in Scotland has been a sorry story, which I need not recite here; but a revival has begun thanks to the devoted work of hundreds of individuals. Their combined efforts have been rewarded by political recognition of their cause and massive grants to save the culture of the Gaels.

Of course, not everything that is needed in this great enterprise can be done at once; there is a shortage of specially trained people. I remember when, fifty years ago, I was a guest at the Gaelic Society of London and learned that though every member spoke Gaelic very few of them could write it. They were, in fact, illiterate. The changes since then have been truly remarkable. Comhairle nan Eilean conducts its business in Gaelic and employs simultaneous translators; the Colaisde Fòghlam Ard Ire (College of Further Education), affectionately known as Sabhal Mòr Ostaig, in Sleat, Skye, trains people to carry out business, whether for local government or for commerce, and indeed for other roles in the life of the Gaelic world; the BBC has supplied news, plays, talks, and language lessons, which have attracted tens of thousands; An Comunn Gaedhealach's work has been extended by new organisations, which are truly indigenous, promoting the language, pre-school playgroups and other parts of the culture.

The intelligent outside observer of the Gaelic scene knows that some of the finest poetry ever written in the language has been published in the second half of the twentieth century; there are more fine players of the bagpipes and of the clarsach than ever before; and the unique contribution of Highland music is enjoyed the world over

The Scots Gaelic language in general, though, has one inherent disadvantage compared with Irish Gaelic. It has a limited vocabulary - limited to country pursuits, fishing, human relations, animal and plant life and so on. A glance at Dwelly's great *Illustrated Gaelic to English Dictionary* (1901-1911) makes the point. Professor Derick S Thomson's *The New English-Gaelic Dictionary* (1981) is playing a valuable role in the revival of Gaelic; but Dwelly has 1034 pages and Thomson only 210.

The question arises, now quite acutely, about the hundreds of thousands of scientific and technological words which do not have a Gaelic equivalent. All the major languages of the world have found a way of accommodating this enormous collection of words. In Ireland, for example, chemistry and other sciences are taught in Irish Gaelic in the University of Galway. In Catalonia some professors wanted all teaching to be done in Catalan; but the University of Barcelona voted against this. A university in the Highlands would probably not use Gaelic as a teaching medium for technical subjects, but would include research into Celtic languages and culture and would presumably teach in the Gaelic medium in that department all or some of the time.

The problem exists today of how to introduce without distortion such an army of words into a language. The official view is that the present needs of Gaelic are met by the operation of a computer database in Sabhal Mòr, Skye. A large number of words have been selected, many by a visiting Irish Gaelic scholar. Those who have contributed specialised word lists do not know which words have been selected and which have been rejected nor are they asked why they recommended any particular word.

Even the inclusion of a particular word in the database does not help an author who is searching for a new word. One cannot be expected to telephone Sabhal Mòr to find out the Gaelic name of an obscure element, mineral, physical effect or chemical. Even if a printout were published, there would be no guarantee that the word one wants to use is in the database. Keeping such a mega-database operative would be uneconomic.

Large numbers of computer users have made their own selection of words for their own use, but only a few specialists in other fields have done so. How can the general public join the process of deciding which words they accept and which they reject? There is no guarantee that the selectors of words for the database are great scholars either.

Translation or transliteration?

1. Scientists are obliged to use internationally accepted words; committees have been set up to regulate the nomenclature. One should therefore resist the temptation of inventing too many Gaelic words out of the native, vernacular word-stock. Thus *fos-foiricheachd* would be preferable to *teine-sionnachain*, *teine-ghealan* or *coinnle-Brianain Airgead-beò* gives way to *mearcur*, in chemistry at least.

2. In transliteration one must not assume that all words need to be given an English pronunciation. It is better to consider the origin of the word, and decide, for example, upon *computair* from Latin computare. The intrusive English i in compiutair is unnecessary and I'm pleased to see it has been dropped in a Gaelic headline in the *Scotsman* (1992).

3. We follow international practice in keeping people's names in elements and minerals unaltered, as in *einsteinium*, *fermium* or *nobèlium*, but favour the existing Gaelic forms of place names, as in *americium*, *bercèilium*, *fraingium*, *scaindium* and so on. We also like the root-form of such words as *bòr*, *clòr*, *cròm*, *fluor*, *iòd*, *seilèn* and *tiotàn*, because they form compound words without change.

4. Whenever possible we respect the vowel or 'quantity rule' of Gaelic, i.e. a consonant must be sandwiched between either a long vowel or a short vowel. However in compound words such as *heacsameitilèntetraimin* we do not invoke this rule on the grounds that hexa`methylene`tetr`amine is made up of four words stuck together by convention.

5. Accents. The grave accent in modern Gaelic usage is a mark of length; in ancient Greek accents denoted stress. As so many scientific words have a Greek origin, one has to choose between the historical pronunciation, the Scots Gael's tendency to stress the beginnings of words and the length of vowels.

6. Because many words are compound, in scientific Gaelic there may be more than one accent on a word, just as in the Book of Deer (Tocher,1910).

7. In chemistry, because one has to make a distinction between the final sound of words ending (in English) in -an, -ane, -en, -ene, -id, -ide, -il, -ile, -in, -ine, -ol, -ole, -on, -one, -yde, -yl and -yne. These should be accented when the vowel is long even though the syllable is at the end of the word.

8. We are pleased to note that Irish and Scots Gaelic will in this respect come closer. I am not suggesting that the very neat Irish plural, as in **hydrídí** (hydrides) should be brought into Scots Gaelic, which will have to say *hydrìdean* for the plural.

The need for a new dictionary. The printout from the Skye database has no accents and no genders. A new dictionary would have both. It should be inexpensive and ready to hand, but there are far more compelling reasons why a book is needed to complement the database.

1. The fish, birds and mammals are more convenient in a book, though the preferred Gaelic words would be taken into the database. In a book the local and disused names can be given.

2. A book would help people to become familiar with the international system ("S.I.") of units and would thus serve an adult educational purpose.

3. Only a book can lead to improvement in designation of colours. Gaelic, like Greek and Latin, has very few names of colours. We have kept the vernacular names like *beis, càirmin, marùn, ròs,* and *bhiolait* but have followed the system of the US Inter-Society Color Council - National Bureau of Standards which describes any colour according to its hue (tuar), value (luach) and chroma (chroma). As an example, greyish red purple becomes *dearg-chòrcair-car-glas.*

4. Another reform, which might be popular, is the replacement of the vigesimal by the decimal system of counting. Ronald Black of the Department of Celtic, Edinburgh University, has discussed this possibility (Scotsman, 28 April 1990). The idea could be given wider publicity if it were published in this new sort of dictionary. The Swiss have adopted septante, octante, nonante for 70,80,90; the French have not yet done so; Gaelic may not be the last European language to make this reform.

The name of the book written by Ailean Boyd and the present author is *Facail Eòlais (Scientific Words in Gaelic)*

The subjects covered by it are:

BITH-EOLAS	Na h-Eòin	BIOLOGY	Birds
	Na h- Eisg		Fish
	Na Mamailean		Mammals
CEIMIGEACHD &	Na h -Aonadan	CHEMISTRY	S.I. Units
FIOSACHD	Ceimigeachd	& PHYSICS	Chemistry
	Na Dathan		Colours
	Na h -Ealamaidean		Elements
TALAMH-EOLAS	Na Mèinnearan	EARTH	Minerals
	Na Seudan	SCIENCES	Gems
	Seud-eòlas		Gemmology

English as a second language

If Gaelic, or for that matter, any minority language, is to be as well taught in school as it deserves to be, the teaching of English or other major language could suffer because of the lack of time to do both languages justice. Where English is the second language the best solution of this problem would be to teach a simplified form of the language.

After years of research C K Ogden brought out his book *Basic English* (1930), a general introduction with rules and grammar. BASIC, which stands for British American Scientific International Commercial, fired the imagination of many enthusiasts but it had inherent weaknesses and interest in it died. Originally it had 600 words, but this was increased to 850, to which were added special vocabularies which were already in use. By the use of 'operators' such as *come, get, give, go, keep* etc. Ogden extended Basic's vocabulary five or ten fold, but had made the language far too idiomatic.

The next great step forward was when Dr David H Sharp, for many years the emminent Editor of Chemistry and Industry, remodelled Basic by restoring the verb, which Ogden managed to avoid. Sharp selected a framework of 850 word roots and wrote out paradigms of noun, verb, gerund or verbal noun, past participle, and performer, as in *drop, drop, dropping, dropped, & dropper.* Of all the -ing words in English only the gerund was retained. No homonyms were allowed; thus right is the opposite of left but the opposite of wrong is correct. The new language is known as 'BEST' (Basic English for Scientists and Technologists), but is, with a little change of emphasis, suitable for those whose native language is Gaelic, Scots or Welsh, because they would not only learn English more quickly but they could learn to speak and write English more stylishly than most native English speakers. Of course, those who wished to enter the literary or academic world in which an enormous vocabulary is an advantage will be able to acquire the wider skills in the last years at school and at university.

BEST as an international language

Esperanto has failed to attract enough speakers and writers to justify its further promotion. It cannot compete with the popularity of English all over the world. Mariners and airmen communicate in English; some of their exams are taken in English. Even when Morse Code was in use, the last words finishing an evening message were GNOM or 'Good Night Old Man' (this seems rather sexist now!). But most international scientific meetings, wherever they are held, are likely to be conducted in English - even in France.

Unfortunately when Chinese and Portuguese scientists discuss a point in one of these meetings the Hungarians often find it too hard to understand the Lingua Franca, which appears to be inconsistent and bad English.

Were BEST taught by the British Council's schools and Berlitz and other English-teaching schools did the same, communication everywhere in the world could become a lot easier.

Of course British, American, Australian, Canadian and other English-speaking people would have to learn BEST as well. Perhaps the minority language speakers of Britain would be the first to find work teaching and translating 'standard' English into BEST. The opportunities for Gaels, for example, will be enormous and some of this work could be done in their own homes, given a **Fax** machine to work with.

Education

One of the most exciting cultural developments is being pioneered at the Edradour School, Pitlochry, by the Headmaster Julian Romanes and his team. His work lies in finding new ways of transferring memes to children. The present way is 'teacher-directed'. The teacher's job is to 'transmit what he or she 'knows' to the students. The student's job is to 'take in' as much of this knowledge ... as possible. That is why it is important for students to 'be quiet' and pay attention in the classroom". "It is interesting to note that the teacher-directed process tacitly assumes that the students do not have much to contribute to each other's learning experience. Otherwise, they would not be arrayed in a physical arrangement in which they face the back of each other's heads". (Barry Richmond, 1990)

The learner-directed approach is founded on the assumption that "learning is a fundamentally *constructive*, rather than an *assimilative* process". This means that "to learn, the student must *reconstruct* what is being 'taken in'. Meaning and understanding are 'making' processes, not' imbibing' processes ...". "Because there are many strategies for 'making', learning can not be standardised. People construct in *different* ways, at *different* paces and in *different* sequences. Construction also is an active process. Being quiet and listening often can be antithetical to constructionist activity". The teacher's new role is to provide materials and alternative strategies for 'constructing' ... they play the role of project manager, keeping the process on track. Students are the construction workers. They design and then construct the knowledge edifice. They often accomplish more, reaping more enjoyment in the process by working in teams rather than alone.

The *thinking paradigm* or conceptual framework of this form of education is that when there are *many* causes of an effect (such as overpopulation, rioting) each of the 'causes' is linked in a circular *process* to both the 'effect' as well as to each of the other 'causes', in what are familiarly called 'feedback loops'. Some loops dominate at first, others 'take over' later. Thus *operational* models are built up so as to offer an explanation for how events happen.

The learning tool in this system is the *personal* computer provided with software supporting the thinking process. In this school all students are encouraged to use the principle of intelligent cooperation. Aggressive behaviour is not tolerated and the atmosphere of the school is vibrant and happy. As one eight-year old said 'This school is the best school in the world.'

Desiderata

Ending this book on such a hopeful note, I give in Table 10 a list of what seem to me to be among the world's most desirable developments - the things I think most people would like to see brought about by logical thought, science and religion combined, and by research development. The seeds of these wishes have been sown. Will they die of inanition or will they be cultivated by adequate funding? The future lies in our own hands.

Table 10

Eight important desiderata

1. Population reduction and self-control of procreation.
2. Search for the replacement of the pattern of cultural history - the route from catastrophe to sustainability.
3. True democracy in control of faceless bureaucracy and government.
4. Small nations not imperial giants.
   Many languages but one *linga franca* (e.g. BEST)
5. Education by learners discovering how to think and discover by themselves and in groups, using computers and aided by 'facilitators'.
6. No taxes on enterprise or hard work, only on consumption and related to energy content. Distribution of wealth to replace unworkable welfare system.
7. Almost unlimited energy from nuclear fusion and other 'clean' sources.
8. Massive funds to support wealth creation, including university teaching and research, and technological development.

Chapter 38
Where we stand in history

Continental Europe and what is called the West is moving inexorably towards the peak of wealth due in 2240 AD and towards a rapid decline to a lengthy and unimaginably horrible Dark Age, or else its civilisation has prematurely ended. The most important area for careful thought and action is to find ways of founding a new civilisation not only for the West but also for all areas living in different periods of civilisation. A concerted effort should be made by a combination of interests, left and right, rich and poor, clever and less gifted, to understand how history has worked in the past and to think of how it can be replaced. The change will have to be 'more radical than radical' since the word radical as used at present usually means following the stale teachings of the last century.

We have seen that Continental Europe is surrounded by countries which still show signs of the culture of the earliest inhabitants - the crust of the 'flan of Europe'; and that the European 'filling' of the flan is thin in parts. Those who are to a large extent descendants of the oldest inhabitants of Europe are recovering from a Dark Age centred on 1720 AD. They are in grave danger of being dragged down into the declining European mode.

Democracy

Democracy in the West is a symptom of the decline of period VIII of European civilisation. The European fringe now at the beginning of period VIII´ is usually kept in order by the traditional forces of law and order belonging to period VIII culture. This is one of many benign effects of a civilisational interface. Scotland has benefitted in some respects from this close relationship with England. Northern Ireland has suffered grievously from it. England, in its decline, has become insufferable, and its government is seen, even in Scotland as showing signs of dictatorship. The assumptions of both right and left, the very symbols of catastrophic and 'unstoppable' decline, is that unionism, that is the conquest of the north by the south and the eradication of its culture, industry and possessions, must overcome all notions of 'separation' or 'nationalism' which could lead to a 'breakdown of the United Kingdom'.

These words are all heavily coloured. Independence which is felt by the majority of Scots (1982) to be desirable is dubbed 'separation' by their opponents in Westminster. Separation is a pejorative term and should be abandoned in this sense. Nationalism, seen all over Europe as a desirable and creative force, is used in Westminster and most newspapers in Britain in the sense of 'imperialism'. This foolish mistake may indicate the subconscious feelings of those who use the word as a weapon. The Danes, Norwegians, Scots, and Swiss, for example, have no thoughts of making war on their neighbours and should be listened to.

Can the word 'democracy' survive its misuse in the phrase 'Soviet Democratic Republic'? I doubt it. What the resurgent nations want is social justice.

Social justice however demands that individuals have a right to equal voting power in a democracy; that is one person one vote. Equal opportunities for all regardless of colour, creed or nationality are demanded by all, but the fairer distribution of wealth has hardly begun to be considered by the political parties, much less the distribution of power. This last is the essence of new ideas about where sovereignty should lie. Nationalists tend to believe that the people are sovereign; on the other hand the Westminster parliament is held by unionists to be the source of sovereignty, a view which nationalists have rejected.

Positive aims in a new civilisation

If we assume that it is possible to break the course of history we may consider (a) symptoms of decay, (b) elaboration of these in terms of period VIII-thinking, (c) some positive aims in an entirely new civilisation. The symptoms, descriptions and cures in Table 10 are arranged in no particular order; some are more important than others.

With regard to (b) how we react to the symptoms of decay at present, we must add a note here on a characteristically British (or rather, English) way of conducting important business, which is hallowed by the name of muddling through. The idea that one does what seems best when action is called for without deep study, learning or much consultation. The practitioners of this pernicious art were and are often from English public schools, but they have been joined by state-educated people who are suspicious of both the humanities and science. Continentals and many Scots are often horrified at this phenomenon. Mr Ian Lang, Secretary of State for Scotland, gave a textbook example of muddling through in his embarrassingly unintellectual speeches to the Great Debate on Constitutional Reform organised by *The Scotsman*, at the Usher Hall, Edinburgh, 18 January 1992.

Yet one has to admit that many social and political problems which have to be solved are beyond the wit of anyone to solve without knowledge, experience or research. Until the public are better informed there would be no point in having referenda; but the Great Debate should be widened in scope and more people should be free to contribute towards building an escape route to the 'new smooth curve' which could be the logo of a new, fair, prosperous and enjoyable New Civilisation.

Table 11

Symptoms of decay and their cure as a route towards a new civilisation

a Symptoms of decay	b Relationship with old civilisation	c Positive aims in new civilisation
1 Haves and have-nots	Catastrophic	Distribution of national dividend. New attitudes to work.
2 Capitalists v socialists	Catastrophic	Emphasis on creativity and sharing in success. Cooperatives.
3 Adversarial habit of mind	Muddling through in politics and in industry	Higher intellectual content in decision-making. Vote on merits of case, not party line.

4	Bureaucratic growth	Endemic	Reduced by decentralisation, financial help to voluntary organisations.
5	Alienation	Endemic	Policies should unite and inspire people, and aim at satisfaction for all individuals.
6	Neo-nomadism	Destroys social cohesion locally	Experience through travel. Communities survive if more clever ones remain.
7	Resistance to new ideas	Unintellectual leaders. 'Not invented here'	Finance should stimulate development and pay for its management.
8	Rich getting richer though fewer	Equal percent rises maintain the difference	With no inflation, pay should reflect skill, ability, quality of work etc.
9	Sexual freedom	300-year cycle, self-correcting	Prevented from getting out of control by sound and not exaggerated principles.
10	Increase in diseases	Iatrogenic diseases through 'pill-taking'	Emphasis on health, diet, exercise and satisfaction. WHO's role widened.
11	Increase in crime	Burglary, car-theft, arson	National dividend would remove poverty. Better ways of earning. ND requires settled address.
12	Increase in suicide		Less if bankruptcy and 'unemployment' are reduced. See also 5.
13	'Unemployment'	A function of monetarist economics	Large investment should mop it up, with new work ethic the word would lose its stigma.
14	Impotence of parliament	Permanent civil service too important	Decentralisation. Home Rule for Scotland and Wales. More democratic control.
15	Centralisation	Virtually London-control	Decentralisation not of individual departments but whole apparatus of government.
16	Stock exchange and banking system	Banks founded 1694-5. See Unwin's Follies 1-3	People's Capitalism developed. Banks a service only, not PLCs.
17	High interest rates	A blunt weapon and sign of failure	Nil or not more than1% for loans (not more than4% ever). No need for this, but no ban on private loans.
18	Churches' weakening	Declining membership	Churches could play a vital role in the new social/psychological climate.
19	Powerful groups under no control	Former trade union and employer's policies	Under Peoples' Capitalism, the catastrophic element is removed.
20	Education's limited scope	A class phenomenon, conservative	Should help to build the new civilisation; better social attitudes. Education for all ages.
21	Company mergers	To maximise profit for the few	Reduce to optimal size; share services; emphasis on creativity and servicing needs.

22	Flocking to towns	World wide problem	Move work places to rural areas. Education to achieve this, and housing.
23	Decay of town centres	World wide problem	Rebuild to provide national and regional cultural services.
24	Population increase	World wide problem	Knowledge of carrying capacity of land, more research and education.
25	Alcohol abuse	Genetic connection (R Lynn))	Those who profit by these abuses should pay for measures found to be (a) curative and (b) preventive.
26	Drug abuse	Genetic connection)	
27	Solvent abuse	Genetic connection)	
28	Inflation	Endemic, tolerated	Could be eliminated, eg by UNITAX.
29	Land ownership	Suggested reforms have never appealed	Custodianship. Emphasis on land use and rights of farmers, cf Norway.
30	Capital from an existing supply	Universally accepted dogma	Credit to be created strictly in proportion to needs of society.
31	AIDS	Pandemic	WHO and UN given authority to work towards elimination.
32	Pop music	Deeply decadent if unmusical & too loud	Financial assistance to folk music.
33	Ailing leaders	A world problem	New mechanism for groups within nations to seek redress from tyranny. See Appendix 8
34	Waste of energy	Pandemic	See last paragraph of this book.

ND = National Dividend
PLC = Private Limited Company
UN = United Nations
WHO = World Health Organisation

Regarding 3, 4, 9, 14, 19, 21, 24-27, 31 and 34 see Appendix 9 on Addictions.

Human Progress, Petrie's View

Has the course of history, undulating through millenia, shown benefits for mankind? Petrie was emphatic that it had. He plotted the gains and losses in a table of the Highest and Lowest Conditions (p. 162).

"The comparison of the successive periods may usefully be made by defining the greatest feature of each period in Egypt or Europe, and the nature of the collapse at the close of each period in Europe by conquest.

We can thus see the widening of the outlook in the summer of each period, and the amelioration of the collapse in the winter. This is the real nature of human progress".

Before discussing this table I would make one small correction. The cataloguing of Nature was originally a Greek occupation. Pliny acknowledges this in his *Natural History:* most of his sources of information were Greek.

GREATEST FEATURE		COLLAPSE IN EUROPE
IV	Power of construction (IV dynasty)	Extermination of the conquered (?)
V	Foreign connections (XII dynasty)	Destruction of the males only (?)
VI	Utilising of natural products (XVIII dynasty)	Slavery (Dorians)
VII	Cataloguing of Nature (Roman) (North races)	Taking share of property
VIII	Utilising natural forces (Modern)	

Human Progress, a Present Review

When I first pondered over the dropping of the two nuclear bombs in the light of Petrie's analysis, I thought that Period VIII must have ended prematurely on the 7th and 9th of August 1945. The destruction of Hiroshima and Nagasaki seemed then to be a Dark Age phenomenon. This was before I had discovered the 'Mindless Wars' which look like a widening split on the Pattern of History. The bombing was followed by 45 years of anxiety as thousands more nuclear bombs were made by the USA and the USSR - 'enough to kill everyone in the world several times over'. See Fig 34, p.185.

I thought that the split of the Mindless Wars between 1914 and 1949 would heal once the Vietnam war was over and that the course of cultural history would move on smoothly towards a peak of wealth about 2250 AD before plunging to the abyss of a Dark Age about 2400 AD; but no! I am now convinced that the delicate Pattern of History came to an end in 1991. The Eastern nations of Europe declared their independence in this fateful year and then the Union of Soviet Socialist Republics began to fall into pieces and, finally, Yugoslavia broke messily into constituent parts. By early 1992 more than 50 per cent of Scots were shown by an opinion poll to favour independence and only 29 per cent wanted devolution - a form of government we have seen in Chapter 24 is in a metastable part of the catastrophe curve.

Essentially what has happened in Europe and western Eurasia is that millions of people had become fed up to breaking point with centralised, bureaucratic, inefficient government. Both communist and unionist leaders were dubbed 'conservative'; their patronising belief in their own superiority contributed to their rejection. Perhaps it is no coincidence that this epoque-making series of events occurred at Kondratieff's Trough of Secondary Depression (Fig 26).

The picture that is emerging is a world made-up of small nations. Nationalism of a benign kind will be the unit for what David Lilienthal (1944) called 'areas of manageable proportions'. Some adjustments may still have to be made in the size of nations; the new Russia, for example, seems to be ungovernably big and too diverse. Bavaria is larger than some nations in the European Community. Newspapers and other commentators should not confuse nationalism, which is the philosophy of small nations, with imperialism, which has disgraced the name of large countries of all ideological persuasions. Victor Hugo said "there is no such thing as a little nation. The greatness of a people is no more determined by their number than the greatness of a man is determined by his height."

If we recognise and concede that 'catastrophe' has already occurred we can understand why the US and Russian Presidents at last talk to each other in a rational and friendly manner. They must move towards complete disarmament, because in a post-catastrophic *civilisation* there is no need to use threats. Arms will be needed only to keep the peace.

The people of the late communist empire are rediscovering religion but are confused when their newly gained freedom brings higher prices and hunger. Ex-communists think that western capitalists have the answers to their problems. True, the 'West' can give some immediate help in food, advice on running industry and other vital short-term issues, but in the long run the recipients will be disappointed because their former adversaries will themselves have to make major reforms. At present the leaders in the West are ill-prepared to help the East. The North is ill-prepared to help the South.

Since the world will be a jigsaw of smaller units and the laboratory dedicated to concocting a glue to hold them together is the United Nations, the voice of smaller nations should be listened to now. The importance of the Scottish nation in the rebuilding of a new civilisation is obvious. Westminster cannot fairly discuss a world of small nations; besides, as Rose Macaulay said "England is slow but sure - slow to act and sure to be too late".

To create a new civilisation to replace the last one which ran for 64 centuries or roughly 250 generations is an essential and urgent task. If this book sets people thinking constructively about how to move in the right direction and how to build a new world, it will have served a good purpose. We should all remember that the decaying civilisation we are not lamenting was finally brought to a halt by the combined efforts of millions of people guided by little more than their instincts and their consciences. We hope that what George Davie (1961) called *The Democratic Intellect* in Scotland will be allowed to play a creative role in European and World Affairs.

Appendix 1
Calendrical Reforms

So often in this book we have found that familiar arts such as music and dancing are much older than we had supposed. Now we read (*Scotsman*, 10 June 1991) that the European calendar dates from as early as 12000 years ago - in the Upper Palaeolithic. We have got used to the idea that Palaeolithic cave paintings may have been made as instructions for methods of hunting. The earlier paintings show how deer could be driven in hordes to places where they could be ambushed and slaughtered. When their numbers began to fluctuate through over-hunting, the pictures showed how bison and horses would have to be chased as a new source of food.

The American scholar Alexander Marshack has published a summary of his work on the engraved rib bone, 88mm long, found by two young archaeologists in the Grotte du Taî in southwest France in 1969. Over a thousand incisions on this piece of bone, dated to 10,000 BC, had been made to indicate a 365-day solar year alongside a sequence of lunar months. Even older lunar calendars have been found elsewhere, but the indication of solstices was a great leap forward in the calendrical science. Marshack points out in the first issue of the *Cambridge Archaeological Journal* that the Taî calendar is positional rather than arithmetical as in our modern version.; "we read the position of a day within a seven-day week, the position of a day within the named month, the position of the month within the twelve-month year, and the position of the year within the decade, century or era ... This may seem simple, yet it is a profoundly complex form of integrative imaging and thought. In contemporary society the symbol systems involved and the frame itself, learned with apparent ease, are the result of thousands of years of calendrical development".

In Fig 9 the calendrical line does not pass through the year 3550 BC where all the other arts converge but through the point at 4400 BC and, now we know, far further back in time than that. Later reforms of the calendar are now considered.

The Jewish calendar, for example, is dated from the year 3760 BC, about the sculpture peak of period I.

Whether the Egyptian calendar was introduced in 4241 BC or 2781 BC has been a matter of controversy, though the latter seems the more probable if our diagram is a guide. The first fixed in the British Isles for setting the date when cereals should be planted was at Newgrange in Ireland in 3150 BC (Ray 1989). This is about two-thirds along the upward part of period III, where one would expect it to be, since a people cannot move towards its cultural peaks without knowing when to plant food crops.

A similar position in period IV (=IV′) would have been at 2600 BC: Babylonian barley planting was first set by calendar in the 27th century BC. In Chapter 29 we noted the age of the Great Pyramid, 2623 BC: this is close to the calendrical line. Silbury Hill, the largest man-made earth-hill in Europe may have been made about the same time and to have had the same significance.

The earliest Chinese 60-day system was invented in 2357 BC, and dating of events began in 2277 BC, only 80 years afterwards.

The magnificent and awe-inspiring monument of Stonehenge was constructed in several stages, formerly known as I, II and III. The late-Neolithic Stonehenge I was an open-air circular sanctuary, surrounded by a ditch with a bank outside. Within this earthwork was a circle of 56 pits or Aubrey holes, four feet deep and six feet wide, filled with chalk, soil and ashes soon after excavation. A hundred feet outside this circle was erected the Hele (or Heel) and other stones used in making observations. Dating of this and later phases of building Stonehenge is notoriously difficult to measure. I shall assume that the dates given by Julian Richards (1991) are the most reliable because they are the latest. See Table 12.

Table 12

Stonehenge

I	NEOLITHIC	The circular ditch and bank were made ca 2800 BC as a sanctuary, but were abandoned soon afterwards, though the area was used as a cemetery for several hundred years.	This was in the Dark Age beginning Period IV=IV'. Instability shown by its abandonment. (Silbury was made at the calendrical point of this Period).
		The 56 Aubrey Holes were prepared ca 2200 BC. Lunar eclipses could be predicted.	This is the end of Period IV=IV' and is obviously 'under new management'.
II	BRONZE AGE	The 'axis of symmetry' was established, making possible the observation and marking of the midsummer sunrise/ midwinter sunset. The 'paired' Heel stones are also suggested as belonging to this phase about 2000 BC. The construction of the huge sarsen stone structures may have been done ca 1900 BC. The horseshoe was probably set up at the same time.	This phase is just before the calendrical point on V'. This is exactly on the calendrical point of V'.
III		About 1500 BC the Y and Z holes were dug to hold bluestones, which came from the Preseli Mountains in Wales, thus completing Stonehenge as we see it.	The completion of the complex corresponds with the wealth line of period V'.

From J. Richards (1991.)

165

The dates Richards quotes are from Atkinson (1979-1984). They belong to the time-span of Periods IV' and V' and do not agree with the European (or Mediterranean) phase. Stonehenge I is an early example of a henge construction, within the same date bracket as Balfarg in Fife, Llandegai in Gwnedd and Stenness in Orkney, rather than within the later Wessex Group, typefied in this area by Woodhenge and Durrington Wells (Richards, p.88)

Many a star-gazer may have wondered when the 600 or so brightest stars were grouped, rather unconvincingly, into an array of constellations. Archie Roy, former professor of astronomy at Glasgow University, provided some answers in 1984 (see Hughes, in the same year). Apparently Hipparchus (ca.125 BC), Eudoxus (409-356 BC) and Aratus (315-250 BC) all mention these constellations, but Roy's re-analysis of Aratus' poem led him to date the descriptions to 2000+ 200 BC. "Neither Aratus nor Eudoxus bothered to check that their poetic picture agreed with the Greek sky" in their times. "Hipparchus did check and the discrepancies probably led him to discover polar precession". True enough the Sumero-Akkadian people of Mesopotamia were great believers in astrology, and the movement of planets through the Zodiac was used for calendrical and religious purposes. As far back as 2100 BC they were using a system of constellations essentially similar to that given in Aratus' poem. However, their sea traffic was closer to the equator than the 'observer's latitude' derived from Eudoxus. Roy therefore concludes that it was the Minoans who borrowed and developed early Babylonian ideas and transformed them into a complete celestial sphere of constellations for navigational purposes. But why was the Eudoxian sky 1600 years out of date? Roy suggests that with the complete destruction of the Minoan civilisation by the volcanic explosion of Thera (Santorini), their astronomical ideas and constellations were frozen in time.

The archaic phase of the development of the Greek calendar began in the 8th century BC or even earlier. The third part of Hesiod's famous didactic poem *Works and Days* (§765 to the end) forms a sort of Euboean shepherd's calendar, a religious calendar of the months, with remarks on the days most unlucky or the contrary for rural or nautical employments. The peak of attainment was reached when Thales of Athens correctly estimated the total solar eclipse of 28 May 585 BC, exactly when the diagram (Fig 9) indicates in Period VII. His feat could have inspired the calendar devised in 538 BC in Iran. Meton of Athens proposed a new version in 432 BC, near to the sculpture peak of the same period.

In *The Celtic Empire* (1990) Peter Berresford Ellis writes: "The earliest known surviving Celtic calendar, dated from the first century BC, is the Coligny Calendar, now in the Palais des Arts, Lyons, France. It is far more elaborate than the rudimentary Julian calendar and has a highly sophisticated five-year synchronization of lunation with the solar year. It consists of a huge bronze plate which is engraved with a calendar of sixty two consecutive lunar months. The language is Gaulish but the lettering and numerals are Latin. Place-names, personal names and inscriptions testify to a certain degree of literacy in the Celtic language. Caesar explains: 'They count periods of time not by the number of days but by the number of nights', and in reckoning birthdays and the new moon and new year, their unit of reckoning is the night followed by the day", (pp.17,18). Coligny, by the way, is only 58 km WNW of Geneva, Mâcon 102 km and Cluny 120 km WNW of Geneva).

"The Coligny Calendar and the recently discovered Larzac inscription on a lead tablet give us our longest known Gaulish texts to date" (page 67). "The Coligny calendar is a masterpiece of calendrical computation, which also confirms many remarks made by Greek observers about the skill of the druids in astronomical observation" (p.175). It may not be a coincidence that Coligny and Larzac are prehistoric names Examples of -igny and -ac place names are given in Appendixes 6 and 3e.

According to Baigent and Leigh (1991) the Qumran community, near where the Dead Sea Scrolls were found, used a solar calendar, in contrast to the lunar calendar used by the priesthood of the Temple - for the Judaic calendar was lunar. In each calendar, the Passover fell on a different date, and Jesus, it is clear, was using the same calendar as that of the Qumran community. Cardinal Jean Danielou refers to "the last supper [being calculated] on the eve of Easter according to the Essene calendar".

"The Celts had a 28-day lunar calendar, but this would not have helped them to work out the quarter days, since these depend on the sun's position at the solstices and equinoxes. Hence it is only by *counting* days , not moons, that one can arrive at the correct answer" wrote Anthony Jackson (1984). The Pictish calendar, indicated by the Ogham inscriptions of the 8th and 9th centuries AD was in use in the 'high summer', of their culture from the time of the Book of Kells towards their totally frustrated peak of literature. Calendar-making for agriculturists, which one would have expected to be revised ca 400 AD was probably not undertaken then because of the disturbed times after the Roman withdrawal from Britain, but later.

The Pictish Calendar, as reconstructed by Jackson, consisted of four quarters of (3+4+3+3) weeks = 91 days requiring the intercalation of only ca $1^1/_4$ days a year to keep it accurate. It has affinities with the 13 week quarters used by British Retirement Pensions, for example.

The last calendrical reforms were introduced by Julius Caesar in 46 BC after a long era of arbitrary adjustments. The new feature was the division of the year into months of 28 (or 29), 30 and 31 days. In 1582 Pope Gregory XIII dealt with the accumulated error of 11 minutes a day by dropping 10 days between October 4 and 15 of that year. The system was adopted in Germany in 1700, Great Britain in 1752, Russia in 1918, and Greece in 1923!

The Pictish calendar fared better than the Julian in one way. Jackson holds that "the Oghams are calendrical markers intended for the highly important task of working out the annual Pictish calendar ritual. Like other Celts (for I hold that the Picts were in fact P-Celts) they wished to know when to celebrate the beginning of Spring, Summer, Autumn and Winter - or to give these quarter days their common (current) names, the time for the fire-festivals of Bride, Beltane, Lammas and Hallowmass. Today these feast days are fixed on February 1, May 1, August 1 and November 1, the Celtic New Year's Day". Even if we adopt for business purposes a calendar of 13 months and 5 holidays, plus Leap Year holidays, we could still have our quarter days. I'm quite content to have my Retirement Pension paid every lunar month; and would not object to the fixing of the date for Easter. We can surely do better than the Synod of Whitby where in 664 AD

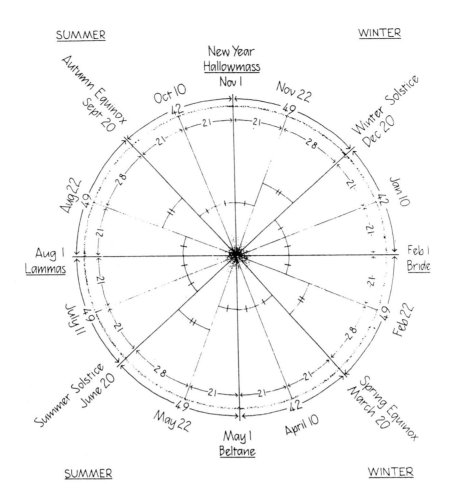

Fig. 33a
The Pictish Calendar.
From A. Jackson (1984)

the complicated way of calculating Easter in the Roman Church was adopted. The church of Moulin, the parish my family belong to, is dedicated to Bishop Colman of Lindisfarne, who retired to Iona with some monks and thence to Ireland, the whole of which accepted the Roman Easter in the 680s.

As we have seen in other parts of this book, the Picts were not p-Celts; they were the descendants of Stone Age people who recolonised Scotland after the end of the Ice Age. Some of the names in the prehistoric section of the Pictish king lists are very odd, having suffered changes in the course of time or invention by the first-millenial scribe. *Canatulachama,* if Gaelic, could mean 'singer for the (sacred) knoll season'; *Usconbuts* has a Ligurian look about it, but to a Gael it might convey the meaning of 'a jewel of a fat man' (usar - jewel, put - a bulging one); but *Bliesblituth* is, as de Beer said, very outlandish. Perhaps self-described 'celticists' should mind their ps and qs and look for signs of more ancient tongues in the names of the early Pictish kings!

Event	Date	Interval		
Hallowmass	November 1			
	November 22	49 { 21 days		
		{ 28		
Winter solstice	December 20		} 91 days	
		21		
	January 10	42 {		
		21		

Bride	February 1			
	February 22	49 { 21		
		{ 28		
Spring equinox	March 20		} 91 days	
		21		
	April 10	42 {		
		21		

Beltane	May 1			
	May 22	49 { 21		
		{ 28		
Summer solstice	June 20		} 91 days	
		21		
	July 11	42 {		
		21		

Lammas	August 1			
	August 22	49 { 21		
		{ 28		
Autumn equinox	September 20		} 91 days	
		21		
	October 10	42 {		
		21		
Hallowmass	November 1			

Fig. 33b

The important calendrical events

Where ogham inscriptions are found today, in both north and south Pictland, place names are usually Gaelic. The *pit* names are said to have the Gaulish word *pit* from late-Latin *petium*, a parcel of land, in them; what follows is often Gaelic as in Pitlochry. For nearly a hundred years scholars have tried to translate the oghams. Sir John Rhŷs, professor of celtic languages at Oxford University, suggested in 1892 that they might be in Basque but retracted this view in 1898.

Nevertheless this idea was revived in 1968 by Professor Henri Guiter of the University of Perpignan, a native Basque scholar who was able to read all 25 oghams at his disposal. No copy of his article on *La Langue des Pictes* is to be found in the British Library though a few copies are now held in private libraries. The critics were merciless: his translations were 'ridiculous' or 'virtually meaningless'. Certainly many of them are banal or pointless - to <u>us</u>. How can this have come about? These people were highly intelligent and ought not to have written rubbish.

The first thing to do was to ask a number of Basque-speakers what they made of the transliterations. All four of them said almost immediately "But this is in Basque, it's astonishing. Eight or ninth century you say. That may account for the odd spelling, but this is older than any Basque text from the home country". Sadly, none of these people provided me with a considered translation of all of the inscriptions. All I can say is that native Basques recognise in them a number of words in their own language. Further properly organised research is needed.

Yet I think Jackson is right. The oghams are numerical and calendrical - primarily; and letters were used as a sort of mnemonic. The ogham script was easy to carve on a stick; but the letters need not have had very learned meaning. After all not all the sentences thought up when sacred phrases were made up as equivalents of magic numbers are meaningful to us. One has to think only of St John's Book of Revelation, Chapter 13, where 666, the sacred number of the Chaldeans, was rendered "the Beast". Gematria, as this word-number puzzle was called, was done in cabalistic circles in Hebrew and Greek (Michell, 1973, ch.13). The ogham writers had a simpler task; their sentences had to be arranged only in multiples of 7 (Jackson, p.191). In gematria each letter represented a number, and the numbers were added together to make the sacred number desired (±1 to make it easier!)

We now have to explain why the inscriptions appear to be in Basque, partly or wholly. I would suggest that the inscribers were holy men who either knew Basque having visited that country and used these strange looking sentences as part of their magic. On the other hand the calendrical department of the druids may have employed Basques to do the work. Whoever made the inscriptions they were not good craftsmen; the oghams are more crudely inscribed than the Pictish symbols.

Appendix 2
Sea Journeys

The great sea journeys of the world may have begun two and a half millenia before Columbus sailed westwards. Professor Cyrus H Gordon (Helm, 1975, p. 137) of Brandeis University in Boston has recorded the belief of the Melungeons, a light-skinned tribe in East Tennessee, that they came from Phoenicia about 995 BC. This would have been exactly on the line of calendrical reform and astronomical advance in period VI´. Professor Gordon wrote (26 Oct 1990) that "the few remaining descendants of this tribe have been so transformed in the American 'melting pot' that they look like normal southeast US folk. All we have is their traditions which are far from consistent. The only reference I can give you is a book of 125 pages entitled: *The Melungeons: Yesterday and Today* by Jean Patterson Bible (1975). The fact that is central is that the original British settlers found the Melungeons already settled in parts of Tennessee and regarded them as non-Indian". Gordon (1990) prefers to use the term "Phoenician" in the way Herodotus did, as people from Canaan and not solely as people from Cyprus, Sidon, Tyre, Gath and Ekron. The Phoenicians always referred to their land as Canaan. They required no interpreter when speaking to their fellow Semites the Hebrews. They were however culturally distinct; they were not circumcised, and they were great artisans and traders.

When the Phoenicians rounded the Cape of Good Hope (ca. 600 BC) and returned safely through the Gates of Herakles into the Mediterranean, the Middle East was enjoying a time of high civilisation. Ashurbanipal's great reforms took place when the literature line cuts the line of Period VI´.

"The *Ora Maritima* (the sea-coast), written by Festus Avienus in the middle of the fourth century AD, is recognised as containing elements of an early Greek exploratory voyage dating, from internal evidence, to around the sixth century BC, and it contains references to Celtic tribes on the North Sea as well as in France and Spain at that time. This puts the existence of Celtic tribes on the continent back into the Hallstatt period" wrote Peter Harbison in "Pre-Christian Ireland" (1989). This journey would be somewhat later than the line of calendrical reform in Period VII.

Pytheas, the Greek Massiliot, on the other hand, sailed round the Bretannic Isles at the merchant city's peak of wealth, VI´, in 325 BC. He had noticed the effect of the moon on tides, made estimates of latitude by shadow-sticks and of time by a water-clock. He used equinoctial hours of 60 minutes each. His itinerary was annotated by place-names, such as Kantion (Kent, meaning angle), Thule (meaning an offering, so possibly Iceland's Mt Hekla), and Ierne (Ireland), but also by commodities for trade or revictualling, such as Belerion (Cornwall, shiny metal = tin, wool), Orcas (Orkney, boar) and Haimodaia (Shetland, blood merchandise = salami and black puddings).

Amphorae, probably Roman, and thought to date from 100 ± 50 BC, were found beside a submerged volcanic rock 15 miles from Rio de Janeiro. If they are genuine they were lost in a ship which foundered there not long after the literature point of Period VIII (Rex Cowan, *Scotsman Magazine* (1985)) 5/12,19)

In Period VII′ the voyage to Vinland in North America by Leif Eriksson, son of Erik the Red, who established a settlement in Greenland in 986 AD, was close to the literature peak of Northwest Europe. His story was told by Snorre Sturlason (English edition 1931).

In 1398 Prince Henry Sinclair, Lord of Rosslyn and the First Sinclair Earl of Orkney and the Premier Earl of Norway, continued this tradition by taking 12 ships from Bressay to the Faroes, Iceland, Greenland and then on to Newfoundland and 'Estotiland' or Nova Scotia where they overwintered with the Micmac Indians; next year they explored Massuchusetts and Rhode Island. One of his knights, possibly his cousin Sir James Gunn of Clyth, died climbing Prospect Hill in Massachusetts. He was identified by his shield carved on a rock face. At Rosslyn Chapel are 14th century carvings of the aloë cactus and Indian corn, drawn 94 years before Columbus was born. Seven ships returned. This story has been documented in a film The Sword and the Grail, by Niven Sinclair (Scotsman 29 Aug. 1992). The expedition, funded by the Knights Templar, was undertaken roughly a century before the peak of wealth of Period VII′.

The journeys of Christopher Columbus, 1492-1504, coincided with the forced conversion of Jews to Christianity. A number of historians believe that Columbus was of Jewish origin - possibly a marrano or 'secret Jew'. Five of his crew, as well as his interpreter, were known to be Jews". (Josephine Bacon 1990). His journeys, as well as those of Vasco de Gama, 1497-1524, and the circumnavigation of the world by Ferdinand Magellan, 1519-1521, occurred near the peak of Wealth of the ancient people on the fringe of Europe in Period VII′. As these journeys occurred between the peaks of Art and Literature in Period VIII, the Kings of Portugal and Spain were in a mood for supporting expeditions which held promise of bringing home spices and gold and of extending their lands by conquest.

Sir Francis Drake's great sea journeys began in 1565 and lasted until his death in the West Indies in 1595. He and his kinsman Sir John Hawkins operated in the reign and with the patronage of Queen Elizabeth I of England, at the time of Shakespeare's peak of literature, which we take as 1594 AD, in period VIII.

Great sea journeys require navigational instruments. Their invention seems to precede the peaks of literature. The planispheric astrolabe is believed to have been a Greek instrument for the taking of altitudes of heavenly bodies, from which time and latitude are deducible. Hipparchus (150 BC) or even Apollonius of Perga (ca. 240 BC) have been claimed as the inventors in Period VII. A much improved astrolabe, such as Humphrey Cole's, 1574, allowed ships at sea to find their latitude and time of day. This too is just before the literature peak of Period VIII.

Appendix 3a

Sc Names in Switzerland

-asca names in Ticino
(1) inhabited places.

Albinasca	Ciavasco	Prugiasco
Alnasca	Cugniasco	Remaglasco
Barnasco	Cumiasca	Remiasco
Biasca *	Frasco	Tendrasca
Brugnasco	Giubiasco	Vegnasca
Camprovasco	Maiasco	Vercasca
Carpogniasca	Morasco	Davesco (Lugano)
	Predasca	Juliesco Tesso

* not Brasca as in de Jubainville

(2) Names of mountains.

Alzasca	Bolsasca	Lughezasca
Piaciasca	Piencascia	
Torrasco	Pizzo Brunescio	

(3) Names of rivers.

Gribiasca	Verzasca

To these names we may add Ascona, Bosco and Gnosco

(4) Names of valleys.

Bondasca	Calancasca	Capriasca

-asca names in Vaud

Cubizasca (1228-1242) near Lausanne
Veviscus now Vevey

-asca name in Appenzell
Urnasca now Urnäsch

-asca names in Grisons

Perlusco	Poschiavo	Campascio	Lughesasca
Privilasco also in Vol.Poschiano		Mt.Caschauna	

Appendix 3b

sc, sg, sk - PLACE NAMES IN SCOTLAND—SKYE

Ascrib Islands
Bornesketaig
Coruisk, Loch
Fiskavaig
Grasco, Ben and Glen
Harsco, Loch
Marsco, & Loch
Oisgill Bay

Roskill
Sca, Ben
Scalpay
Scavaig, Loch
Sconser
Screapadale
Sculamus

Skeabost
Skinidin
Skraig, Ben
Skudiburgh
Talisker
Tarskavaig
Totescore

sc,sg,sk - PLACE NAMES IN OTHER SCOTTISH ISLANDS

Ardskenish, Colonsay
Asknernish, S Uist
Askival, Rum
Askog, Bute
Auskerry, Orkney
Bhlanisgaidh
Easkadale
Erisgeir, Leac, W of Mull
Eriska, Lismore
Eriskay, N of Barra
Eskernish, Eigg
Esknish, Islay
Gasker Is., Harris
Harskeir, Lewis
Hascoway, Yell, Shetland
Haskeir Islands
Heisker or Monarch Is.
Heiskers, N.of Mingulay
Isgill, Lewis
Luskentyre, Harris

Oskaig, Raasay
Oskamull, Mull
Pliasgaig, Rum
Scadabay, S Harris
Scadaway, L. N Uist
Scaladale, S Harris
Scalloway, Shetland
Scalpay Is.
Scaratovore, S Harris
Scaravat, L. na, N Harris
Scarista Airport, Shet.
Scarista House, S Harris
Scarp Is., N Harris
Scatsta, Shetland
Score Head, Bressay
Scorrodale, Arran
Scotusay Is.
Scousburgh, Shet.
Scresort, L. Rum
Scridain, L. Mull

Scrienon, Ben
Scurrival, Barra
Skaill, Orkney
Skara Brae, Orkney
Skaw Taing, Shet.
Skeld, Easter, Shet.
Skerries, (many)
Skeultar, N Uist
Skigersta, N Lewis
Skiport, L. Benbecula
Skolpaig, N Uist
Toscuid, Dun
Uskavagh, Benbecula
Vatisker Point, Lewis
Scolpaig, N. Uist and
Skibinish, N. Uist
Noiskinish, L. Maddy
Dunskellar, N Uist
Skealtraval Bay, N. Uist
Scaravay, N. Uist

sc,sg,sk - PLACE NAMES IN THE MAINLAND OF SCOTLAND

Askaig, Suth
Arngask pa. S of Pths
Baleskie, Fife
Buttergask in Ardoch par.
Danskine, Had.
Deskry burn, Abdn.
Dask, Edzell
Duisky, Upper L Eil
Dunaskin PO, Ayrs.
Dunloskin, Dunoon
Dunscore, Nithsdale
Dunscriben, Glenmoriston
Dunskeig hill, Argyll
Dunskey, Cas. Portpatrick
Dusk/Dhuisg, S Carrick

Esk, L. Angus
Esk, R. Dumfr.
Esk, R. Midl.
Eskadale, Inverness
Eskdale, Dumfr.
Eskielawn, Angus
Eskin, R. Inverness
Fascadale, Argyll

Faskally, Pitlochry
Faskine, Lan.
Fasque, nr Banchory
Fingask, Cas, nr Errol
Fingask est, Daviot
Fingask, L. S of Blairgowrie
Finiskaig, L. Nevis
Flisk, nr Cupar
Garscube, Glasgow
Gask or Findo Gask,
    Strathearn
Gask Hill, Collessie
Gask House, Turriff, Suth.
Gorgask, Laggan
Hoscote Ho. nr Hawick
    Inveresk,
Kingask est. St Andrews
Kylesku, Assynt
Lathrisk Ho. nr Falkland
Luscar Ho, Carosk par Fife
Moneymusk, Abdn
Muiresk, Turriff
Rescobie, L. Forfar
Risca Is., L. Sunart

Risga, Moss, nr Flanders Moss
Ruskie Is., Pt Menteith
Rusko Cas. Anworth
Scar nr Kirkcolm
Scarsburgh, Jedburgh
Scone, Perth
Scoonie, Fife
Scourie,
Scullamie, Kyle of Tongue, Suth.
Skelmorie, Ayrs.
Skerrow L. Galloway
Skiach, L. Little Dunkeld
Skinnet, L. Halkirk,
Skirling, nr Biggar
Throsk, Alloa
Toscaig, Applecross
Toskerton, Stoneykirk
Trinity Gask

Deskie chapel, Glenlivet

Appendix 3c

-SC PLACE NAMES IN THE AMERICAS

The -sc cluster is remarkably common in the Americas, often localised. The Northwest American Indian group includes Alaska, Iskut River (Yukon), Athabasca (Alberta), Saskatoon (Saskatchewan) Wetaskwim (Alberta), Lake Itasca (N.Dakota). Wisconsin, Winisk River and place (Ontario), Attawapiskat River, Escanaba (Wisconsin), Kapiskau River (Ontario), Kapuskasing (Ontario), Lake Timiskaming (Ontario), (Quebec), L. Baskatong (New York), Kaniapiskau Lake (Quebec), Kegaska (Quebec), Tuscola (Illinois), Kaskaskia River (Illinois), Petoskey (Michigan), Kalkaskia (Michigan), Muskegon R. (Michigan), Biscotasing (Ontario), Oscoda (Michigan), Sandusky (Michigan), Scugoy (Ontario), Megiscane (Quebec), Baskatong Lake (Quebec), Madawaska River (Quebec), Susquehanna (New York), in the Mid-West Nebraska.

In Mexico we find Escinapa (Nayarit), Mascota (Jalisco), and Tasco, the silver town near Acapulco. Also Tabasco, a state west of Yucatan.

In Peru Pisco is on the coast opposite Chilco Island which produced guano. Cuzco (or Cusco), the old Inca capital of the Aztecs. From here many long straight tracks run. The most famous example is in the area around Nazca in another part of Peru, though the most spectacular linked the sacred places of the Aymara Indians in Bolivia (Michell, 1969; Morrison, 1978). Ascope also occurs in Peru.

Sicani, which might be an sc place name (like Sicily), is southeast of Cuzco; and there is also a Mount Cuzco in Bolivia. Ascotan is in North Chile, and Iscuande in Colombia.

The Inuit were formerly called Eskimo.

The **-ac** names are not rare among American Indians, e.g. the Micmacs, Toltecs and Aztecs: as well as the Potomac River and Frontenac. Inca, another ancient form, is also found as a place name in the Balearics.

Appendix 3d

-ac, -ec, -ic, -oc, -uc NAMES IN WESTERN EUROPE

-ac place names are commoner in the west of France than anywhere else in Europe. Here is a mouth-watering selection from Bordeaux (Bx) and elsewhere.

Armagnac, s.w. France
Ch.d'Agassac, Bx.
Ch. Arsac , Bx.
Aurillac, Corrèze
Barsac, Bx.
Bergerac, Dordogne
Boussac, Indre
Camensac, Bx
Cantenac, Bx
Carnac
Cissac, Bx.
Cognac
Cubzac,St.André-de-
Cussac, Bx.
Dauzac
Figeac, Lot
Figeac, Ch., Bx
Florac, Lozère
Fronsac, Bx
Gaillac, SW France
Jonzac, Charente
Larzac, south of Massif Central

Lirac, Bx
Loupiac, Bx
Lussac, Vienne
Listrac, Bx
Lussac, St Emilion, Bx
Martillac, Bx
Médoc, Bx
Meymac, Creuze
Monbazillac, Dordogne
Naireac, Bx
Néac, Bx
Nérac, Lot & Garonne
Pauillac, Bx
Potensac, Chat. Bx
Puy-Razac, Chat. Bx
Ribérac, Dord.
Ruffec, Charente
Sénéjac, Chat. Bx
Souillac, Lot
Toutigeac, Dom.e,Bx
Volvic, Puy-de-Dôme

Corsock near Castle Douglas
Marnock as in Kilmarnock
Botallack near St Just, Cornwall
Ben Aslac, East of Skye
Ettrick
Morthec, a chief who died of grief on St Kentigern's
   death 612 AD
Cadoc, the Welsh patron of Cambuslang
Senlac, the site of the battle of Hastings,
   near the Forest of Anderida

Appendix 3e

SC and AC NAMES IN HISTORY

Casca, the first to knife Julius Caesar: was he a Ligurian malcontent?

Judas Iscariot may be derived from the Sicaru, the Zealots' terrorist cadre of a militant, nationalistic, revolutionary, xenophobic and messianic movement (Baigent p.206)

Ossian's son was Oscar.

Asclepius, god of medicine

Ascra in Boeotia was Hesiod's birthplace.

Scarphia is in Boeotia.

Tasciovanus, prince of the Catuvellani, father of Cunobelin, (Cymbeline).

Lis iscla d'Or (Les isles d'Or), the name of Mistral's famous book in *Provençal*.

Pablo Escobar, billionaire drug baron in Colombia, surrendered to the authorities 19 June 1991.

Karnák village which gave its name to Egyptian temples of Thebes N of Nile. Luxor being on the S.

Kaski, N. of the Hittite Empire. S of Black Sea.

Oescus, place & river whch flows N into the Danube.

The Ordessus or Ardiscus River, (Argisch R) map 10 of Samuel Butler, joins Danube from the North.

Transmarisca South of Danube.

The Osci were a people between Campania and the country of the Volsci; (They assisted Turnus against Aeneas; and are the same as the Opici.

The Rugusci lived between L.Como and L.Maggiori.

Adrian Goskar, proprietor of a china clay company in Cornwall, held that his Phoenician appearance was no coincidence.

Tosca. Verdi's librettist, may have had an Etruscan type of woman in mind when he chose the name. Scarpia was the villainous head of police.

Aeneas' son Ascanius.

Huascar, one of the Inca emperor's sons in 1532 (near Cuzco)

Scipio: his family came from Campania.

Bethoc, the wife of Crinan, was the Pictish ancestress of Scottish kings, the earls and dukes of Atholl and Clan Donnachaidh.

Hossack, Cromarty, a surname, may be an -ac name.

ascia, a fire-setter's mining tool, possible a mattock rather than an axe (used in Iberia said Pliny).

Ask (English) is a 'you to me' communication-word.

Boadicia from Boudic (ca), a possible -ac . . . name.

Appendix 4

CIRCUMLEMANNIC PLACE NAMES from Bossard and Chavan

Every tenth -az name is given by way of example:

Arbalaz
Aubaz Terraz
Binnaz
Bourlaz
Chandellaz
Chavonnaz
Chivraz
Corbettaz
Crosettaz
Derbonnaz
Donzallaz

Epetaudaz
Favaz
Frachiaz
Grattaz Leyvraz
Lageltaz
La Liaz
Méleriaz
Mounaz
Palaz
Perreyvuaz
Planta(z)

Praz, La
Prilaz
Rétaz
Rouvenaz
Saùtaz
Soresevaz
Tornettaz
Veudalaz
Zorettaz

Every third -ez name is given:

Delez
Ecorchevez

Paudez
Pourriez

Renolliez
Trez

Every fourth -oz name is given:

Coudoz
Dérupoz
Etrablioz
Frenoz

Grebloz
Meyjoz
Planoz
Rimbloz

Seingloz
Trembloz
Vuargnoz

Of -uz the following were noted:

Claruz
Orjuz
Pierrafuz

Roubatauz
Ruz, val de
Vératruz

Appendix 5

SWISS DISYLLABIC PLACE NAMES ENDING IN -Y : Lac Léman

FRENCH EXAMPLES FROM NORTH SAVOIE marked F

Ally
Anthy F
Atry
Audzy
Bally
Barry
Bossy
Bougy
Brotty
Bussy
Chailly
Chamby
Champy
Chauchy
Chaussy
Cheory
Claudy, Pré
Cindry
Closy
Corsy
Creusy
Crosy
Cubly, Mt
Cugy
Cully
Dailly
Dully
Fêchy
Fessy F
Feuilly
Filly F
Flaugy
Folly
Fouly
Fully
Gilly
Glary
Grésy
Grilly F

Jussy F
Lally
Lancy
Larry
Latry
Lully
Lussy
Lutry
Luy
Milly F
Mivy
Motty
Mussy Mt F
Ouchy
Pailly
Parchy
Paully
Peuty
Plany
Pomy
Praly
Prilly
Pully
Rachy
Rosy
Sassy
Saugy
Scauly
Sorvy
Sotty
Souvy
Telly
Tilly
Torry
Traisy
Trésy
Trossy F
Veigy F
Vitry

Vorzy
Vouvry F
Vurzy
Vusy

see also names ending
in -gny

179

Appendix 6

SWISS TRISYLLABIC PLACENAMES ENDING IN -Y LacLéman

FRENCH EXAMPLES FROM NORTH SAVOIE MARKED F

Arzilly	Donery	Montossy
Azilly	Echemy	Morenny
Araby	Epity	Pacoty
Bélossy	Eschelly	Perbosy
Boutzeny	Esserpy	Renaly
Bovery	Esserty	Renolly
Buchilly	Laraby	Rosaly
Chambesy	Lavanchy	Saverny
Chésery	Lévanchy	Solavy
Chevrery	Lovaty	Sulavy
Colondy	Malatry	Tillery
Confrary	Milavy	Vaugendry
Darbally	Montbarry	Vaugueny
	Montelly	Vauterry

SWISS PLACENAMES ENDING IN -gny

FRENCH EXAMPLES FROM NORTH SAVOIE MARKED F

Disallabic	Trisyllabic	
Dugny F	Bretigny (and F)	Montagny
Jongny	Bussigny	Montmagny
Magny F	Celigny	Tutegny F
Pregny	Cigogny	Pitagny F
Ségny	Commugny	Vuargny
Signy	Lavigny	
Vegny	Lentigny	
Vigny	Martigny	

SWISS PLACENAMES ENDING IN -i

Aï	Battendi	Buqui
Agni	Batzi	Champi
Arbi	Borni	Censui

SWISS PLACENAMES ENDING IN -ie

Bâtie	Clergie	Fleurie
Boiterie	Clie	Gollie
Bouverie	Confrérerie	Mollie
Boverie	Corraterie	Pachissie
Cernie	Ecofferie	Saunerie
Chevrerie	Essangie	

Appendix 7

SCOTTISH DISYALLBIC SURNAMES ENDING IN -ie

a		e		i	o		u, y	
Addie	Archie	Beagrie	Benvie	Ainslie	Bodie	Broadie	Bluie	
Adie		Beakie	Bertie	Airdie	Bogie	Brackie	Brydie	
Baikie	Barrie	Beedie	Berrie	Airlie	Borrie	Brodie	Buie	
Bailie	Blackie	Bennie	Bertie	Aithie	Bousie	Brodlie	Burnie	
Baldie	Bradie			Binnie	Bowie	Brownie		
Baigrie					(Bridie)	Brownlie		
Baptie	Brandie							
Barklie		Clemie		Christie	Collie	Corsie	Cluckie	
Carie	Caskie				Comrie	Coutie	Clunie	
Carnie	Craigie				Conchie	Cowie	Cubie	Currie
Darmie	Darrip			Dickie	Cormie		Dumphie	
Dandie	Davie			Dinnie	Dobbic	Dorsie	Durie	
Dargie				Dippie	Dobie	Dowie	Duthie	
Eadie	Edie							
Eddie	Eggie							
Fachie	Emslie	Fechlie	Fernie	Filshie	Foggie		Fyvie	
Fairlie	Fargie	Fergie	Ferrie	Finnie				
Gaddie	Garyie	Gearie	Geikie		Goldie	Gourdie	Guthrie	
Gambie	Gauldie	Geddie	Gerrie		Gorie	Gowrie		
Gammie	Gracie	Geekie	Glennie		Gorrie			
Garrie	Grassie							
Hardie		Heatlie	Hendrie	Hinnie	Hosie		Huie	
Harvie		Heggie	Hennie		Howie		Hurrie	
Hastie				Imrie	Ionie			
Jamie		Keanie	Kelbie	Kiltie				
		Keddie	Kelvie					
		Kedslie	Keppie	Lillie	Lochtie	Lourie	Lundie	
Lackie	Laurie	Leckie	Leslie	Lindie	Lockie	Lovie		
Lannie	Lawrie	Lennie	Lesslie		Logie	Lownie		
					Lonie	Lowrie		
Mackie	Marnie	Meikie		Michie	Lornie		Mudie	
Manzie	Massie	Mekie		Oddie	Mochrie	Monie	Mulvie	
Markie	Mathie	Mennie		Opie	Moggie	Moonie	Muncie	
Naughtie	Pattie	Peatie	Perrie	Pirie	Poustie	Powrie	Murdie	
		Peddie	Petrie	Pithie			Murchie	
		Peggie	Pettie				Murie	
Rannie	Rathie	Reddie	Rennie	Ritchie	Robbie	Rosie	Purdie	
		Reckie	Rettie		Robie	Rothnie	Ruckbie	Rudie
		Reggie	Revie		Rogie	Rougvie	Ruickbie	
					Rorie		Runcie	
							Ryrie	
Sandie	Stadie	Selbie	Speedie	Shimmie	Scobbie	Sorbie	Suttie	
Shankie	Swankie	Smellie	Sweenie	Simmie	Scobie	Sorlie	Sydie	
Spankie				Smillie	Scorbie	Stobbie		
					Scorgie	Stobie		
					Scroggie	Storrie		
					Sloggie			
Tassie		Tweedie			Tolmie	Torrie	Turpie	
							Tyrie	
Waldie	Wattie			Wilkie			Urie	
				Willie			Wylie	
							Wyllie	

Appendix 8
AILING LEADERS

In the course of history men in power have often managed to conceal illnesses which clouded their judgement, or caused them to act in a cruel, tyrannical and unstoppable manner. Pierre Accoce and Dr. Pierre Rentchnick were the first to write a book about this appalling problem *Ces malades qui nous gouvernent* (1976). They examined the deteriorating medical condition of Franklin D Roosevelt, Thomas Woodrow Wilson, Warren Harding, Dwight Eisenhower, John Fitzgerald Kennedy, Lyndon Johnson, Richard Nixon, Adolf Hitler, Benito Mussolini, Neville Chamberlain, Edouard Daladier, General Maurice Gamelin, Winston Churchill, Antonio Salazar, Francisco Franco, Konrad Adenauer, Charles de Gaulle, Georges Pompidou, Giuseppe Motta, Pope Pius XII, Lenin, Stalin, Nikita Kruschchov, Leonid Brezhnev, Anthony Eden, Gamal Abdel Nasser, Chou En-lai, and Mao Tse-tung. And showed how nations and the world suffered because there was no mechanism for giving power to the doctors to say "No, Mr President, you are no longer in a fit state to govern". Admittedly the British wartime cabinet appointed Lord Moran to do his best to keep Churchill in good working order, and Eden resigned when he felt unable to cope, but democracy needs to be protected from the arbitrary and despotic powers of the aged and the sick. In 1990-91 the Iraqi citizens suffered appallingly from the unsoundness of their leader, Saddam Hussein. So did Germans under Hitler, who developed the technique of making a whole nation madly loyal to him. One should be suspicious of blind loyalty to a political party or leader.

Appendix 9
ADDICTIONS

Finally, we may learn from John Spencer's description of the energy dependence syndrome (1990) since we are hooked on energy as if it were a drug or alcohol. Seven elements of the dependence syndrome are recognised for drugs and alcohol, 1. Tolerance, 2. Withdrawal symptoms, 3. Relief of withdrawal symptoms by use of the substance, 4. Compulsion, 5. Narrowing of the behavioural repertoire, 6. Salience, and 7. Reinstatement of use after abstinence. Of these perhaps number 6 needs explanation. Salience describes the individual giving increased priority to maintaining alcohol usage despite the obvious unpleasant consequences. The spouse's distressed scolding - once effective - is later rationalised by the drinker as evidence of her (or his) lack of understanding.

A similar parallel can be drawn between misuse of power in politics and the misuse of drugs. For example, for many years after the Union of 1707 Scotland was not overgoverned by the British parliament; but after the rail connection about 1845 government became more centralised and tolerated by the Scots. Elements 2 and 3 did not closely apply at first, but the Scots' feelings were mollified to some extent by service in defence of Britain, in service overseas - in Empire building and in numerous wars. 4. The phenomenon of compulsion is known as the 'cringeing' Scot with his begging bowl. 5. Scots Tories can barely speak to those who seek freedom. They tend to dress and speak differently. 6. Tories faced with dreadful opinion poll ratings often say their policies are best for Scotland but the voters don't understand them.

In a world of smaller units, the European Commission and the United Nations should provide legal facilities for judging complaints against arbitrary and despotic power, waiving their present excuse that they cannot interfere with the internal affairs of a member state.

People with addictive behaviour often do not change until there is a crisis, writes John Spencer, (4/2/1992). A succession of crises is wearing and demoralising. Government of areas of manageable proportions should make fewer mistakes and should be able to encourage creativity. The Union of 1707 relieved us of the fear of war; a return of nationhood will relieve us of ignorant and half-hearted government and of a feeling of dependence. With freedom in Scotland there will be a great resurgence comparable perhaps with the Scottish Enlightenment. Mutual respect will be strengthened in the British Isles and the Scots in Europe will strengthen not weaken England's role in European affairs.

The addiction to procreation

I have written in Chapters 22 and 25 that if 'everything goes according to plan' there will be in the West or European civilisation a peak of wealth in 2250 AD and a Dark Age about 2450 AD; and in Chapter 38 I suggested that the breakup of the USSR and Yugoslavia, and the unrest in Northern Ireland and Scotland all suggest that a Dark Age has begun centuries before it might have been expected. The immediate cause is the widening split known as the 'Mindless Wars'. The old civilisation itself is falling apart. You may think that the evidence is not enough to force one to think more, but you would be wrong because civilised living on this planet will cease before the wealth peak has been reached. Professor J P Duguid reminds us (*Scotsman*, 9 May 1992) that the United Nations Population Fund calculates that the world population will grow from the present 5.5 billion to 10 billion by the year 2050 AD, and possibly to 28 billion by 2150 AD. The wealth peak will never be reached because the population would either have risen to 70 billion or death by famine would have brought the numbers down to a level no amount of accumulated wealth could make tolerable. In Duguid's view Britain's population should be brought down to between 30 to 40 million (*Scotsman*, 27 April 1992).

If politicians cannot face this, the world's most important issue, there's something wrong with politicians and the political system. The public must be warned to cut their procreation in half. Worldwide the Catholic Church should tell its adherents that it is sinful to produce more children than the number for which they can properly care and provide - the principle of sustainability.

FINALE

Don't

continue to caulk a cracked cornucopia

but

build a bridge to a better base.

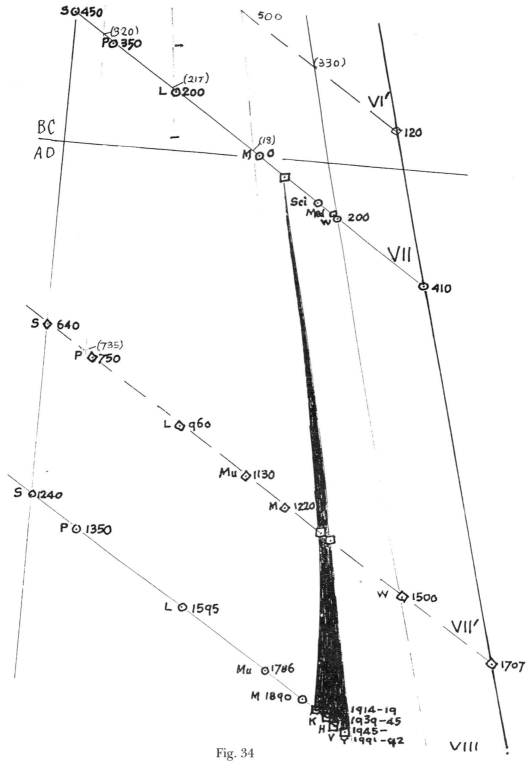

Fig. 34
The Cracked Cornucopia.

References

Accoce, Pierre and Rentchnick, Pierre
  (1976) Ces malades qui nous gouvernent. Editions Stock
Albus, J S
  1971 A Theory of Cerebellar Functions. *Mathematical Biosciences,* **10**, 25-61.
Albus, James S.
  1976 Peoples' Capitalism. New World Books, 4515 Saul Road, Kensington, Maryland,
  20795
Allhusen, Desmond and Holloway, Edward
  1959 Money:The Decisive Factor. Christopher Johnson:London
Allen, D Elliston
  (1968) British Tastes. Hutchinson & Co.(Publishers) Ltd:London. p.180
Alexander, Pat
  The Lion Concise Bible Encyclopedia, Lion Publishing, Icknield Way, Tring, Herts,
  England.
Arensburg, Baruch and Tillier, Anne-Marie
  (1991) Speech and the Neanderthals, *Endeavour, New Series,* **15**/1.26-28
Atkinson, R J C
  1979 Stonehange. London and later publications cited in J Richards.

Bacon, Josephine
  1990 The Illustrated Atlas of Jewish civilization, with an introduction by Martin Gilbert.
  André Deutsch:London
Bain, George
  1951,1977. Celtic Art:The Methods of Construction, William Maclellan, Glasgow.
Baigent, Michael and Richard Leigh
  1991 The Dead Sea Scrolls Deceptions. Jonathon Cape, London p.136
Barrow G W S
  1981 Kingship and Unity. Edward Arnold: London pp.70, 79-81.
Beer, Sir Gavin de
  1965 Genetics and Prehistory. The Rede Lecture. Cambridge at the University Press
Beckman, Robert C
  1983 The Downwave. Pan Books:London and Sydney
Bertram, Colin
  1963 Man pressure, *Onyx* **7**, 97-101
Beveridge, Craig and Turnbull, Ronald
  1989 The Eclipse of Scottish Culture. Polygon, 22 George Sq., Edinburgh (esp. p.5)
Beveridge, Sir William,
  Nov.1942 Social Insurance and Allied Services, Report, Cmd 6404, HMSO (p.117)
Bible, Jean Patterson
  1975 The Melungeons:Yesterday and Today, East Tennessee Printing
  Company:Rogersville, Tennessee, Library of Congress Catalog Card No.75-41654.
Billcliffe, Roger
  1989 The Scottish Colourists, John Murray (Publishers) Ltd. London
Bragg, Sir William
  1926 Old Trades and New Knowledge. Bell's:London
Bradbury, Farel
  1986 The delight of resource economics. PO Box 4, Ross-on-Wye, Herefordshire. HR9
  6EB
Bonfante, Larissa
  1990 Reading the Past:Etruscan, British Museum Publications Ltd, 46 Bloomsbury St.,
  London WC1B 3QQ

Bory, Jean-René
1965 The Swiss at The Foreign Service and their Museum. Nyon, éditions du "Courrier de La Côte" S.A. (in French, German and English)
Bory, Jean-René
1978 La Suisse á la rencontre de l'Europe, David Perret, Lausanne.
Bossard, Maurice and Chavan, Jean-Pierre
(1990) Nos lieux-dits. Typonymie Romande. Editions Payot Lausanne.

Carlyle, Thomas
(1833-34) *Sartor Resartus,* and Ian Campbell's review of Fred Kaplan's biography, Cornell/Cambridge
Cavalli-Sforza, L L
(1983) The Genetics of Human Races, Scientific Publications Department, Carolina Biological Supply Company, Burlington, North Carolina 27215.
Cavour, Ernesto
(no date) La Quena, Columbians Ltda, La Paz, Bolivia
Chambers, Sir Edmund K
1929 Shakespeare *Encyclopaedia Britannica,* 14th ed., Vol **20**, p. 446.
Charles, Prince of Wales, (1948-)
A Vision of Britain, Doubleday, London W5 5SA
Chartered Institute of Public Finance and Accountancy
(1990) Public Library Statistics.
Clark, Kenneth
1969-1976 Civilisation. British Broadcasting Corporation and John Murray:50 Albemarle St., London
Clement, A G and Robertson, R H S
1961 Scotland's Scientific Heritage. Oliver & Boyd:Edinburgh and London, Introduction and Chapter 8, previously in *The Eugenics Review.*
Cole, J H
1925 Determination of the Exact Size of the Great Pyramid of Giza, Cairo:Government Press
Coleman, R G
1971 *Journal of Geophysical Research,* **76**, 1212-1222
Collinson, Francis
1966 The Traditional and National Music of Scotland, London, and Nashville, USA.
Colpi, Terri
1991 The Italian Factor and Italians Forward. Mainstream Publishing Co.Ltd. 7 Albany St., Edinburgh EH1 3VG
Colinvaux, Paul
1980 The Fates of Nations: A Biological Theory. Simon and Schuster. Review by W H McNeill.
Collingwood, R G
1926   The Theory of Historical Cycles and Progress. *Antiquity* , **2**,435
Corones, A., Pont, G., and Santich, B
1990 Festivity Food, 4th Symposium of Australian gastronomy, Sydney (1989) p. 104
Cowan, Rex
March 1985. The Romans in Rio. *Scotsman Magazine,* **5**(12), p.19
Crawford, O G S
1931 Historical Cycles. *Antiquity,* V, 5.
Curwen, E. Cecil
1940 The Significance of the pentatonic scale in Scottish song. *Antiquity* , **14** (56), 347-362

D'Arbois de Jubainville, H.
    1894 Les premiers Habitants de l'Europe. Vol 2. 2nd ed., Paris:Thorin & Fils, Editeurs., Libraires du Collége de France, De l'Ecole Normale Supérieure, Des Ecoles Françaises d' Athénes et de Rome, de la Société des Etudes Historique.
Dawkins, Richard.
    1976 Memes and the evolution of culture. *New Scientist,* 28 October.
Davie, George E
    1961 The Democratic Intellect, Scotland and her Universities in the Nineteenth Century
    1982 ed Edinburgh at the University Press
Devoto, G.
    1962 Origini indoeuropee. Sansoni:Firenze
Dickson, M G
    1989 The Voyage of Pytheas to Britain, ca. 325 BC. MG Dickson, 1 Hauteville Court Gardens, Stamford Brook Avenue, London W6.
Dickson, M G
    1989 Tales from Herodotus. The Book Guild:Lewes, Sussex
Dillon, Myles and Chadwick, Nora K.
    1967 The Celtic Realms. London: Weidenfeld & Nicolson.
Douglas, C H
    Economic Democracy 1919. Social Credit 1924. The Development of World Dominion 1961 (postumous quotations, edited by Bryan W Monahan). Bloomfield Books, 26 Meadow Lane, Sudbury, Suffolk, England. CO10 6TD
Douglas, C H
    17 Dec.1949 (The end of the Albertan experiment), Social Crediter and in *The Development of World Dominion.* K R P Publications Ltd:London, page 99 (1969)
Drever, Alan
    Tree Planters Guide to the Galaxy, No.6, 31-32 Scottish Native Woods Campaign, 3 Kenmore.St., Aberfeldy, Perthshire, PH15 2AW (Tel. 0887 820392).
Drower, Margaret S
    1985. *Flinders Petrie* London:Gollancz Ltd.
Dronamraju, Krishna R
    1985 The life and work of J B S Haldane. Aberdeen University Press

Ellis, Peter Berresford
    (1990) The Celtic Empire, The First Millenium of Celtic History, 1000 BC - 51 AD, Guild Publishing/Constable and Co.Ltd

Foster, David
    1980 Innovation and Employment.. Pergamon Press, Oxford etc.

Gibbon, Edward
    1770 The Decline and Fall of the Roman Empire, a one-volume abridgment by D M Low. London:Book Club Associates, 1960, reprinted 1981.
Gimbutas, Marija
    1974, The Goddesses and Gods of Old Europe, Myths and Cult Images. Thames and Hudson:London.
Giraldus Cambrensis,
    1188 (probably) The Topography of Ireland
Gordon, Cyrus H.
    [Phoenicians] *in* Symposium on the 12 century BC, at Brown University (16-19 May 1990)
Graham-Campbell, James and Kidd, Dafydd
    1980 The Vikings. Book Club Associates by arrangement with British Museum Publication Ltd.
Guiter, Henri
    1968 La langue des Pictes. *Boletin de la Real Sociedad Vascongada de los Amigos del Pais*, San Sebastian, **24** (3 & 4), 281-321

Harding, Rosalind M and Sokal, R R
    1988 Clasification of the European language families by genetic distance. *Proc. Natl. Acad. Sci.* USA, **85**, 9370-9372

Han Suyin
    (1952) A Many Splendoured Thing. Jonathan Cape (especially pp.274-206,284,298,304,311)

Harrois-Monin, Françoise
    9 Nov. 1990 Les grands anciens du nouveau monde. *L'Express International,* pp.48-50

Harrison, Jane
    1961, Prolegomena to the study of Greek religion, 3rd ed., Cambridge

Harbison, Peter
    1989 Pre-Christian Ireland. Guild Publishing:London

Henderson, Isabel
    1967 The Picts. London: Thames & Hudson

Herm, Gerhard
    1975 The Phoenicians, translated by Caroline Hillier. V.Gollancz and Book Club Associates.

Hesiod, Theogony, 79; *Anth.Pal.*, ix, 504,1.

Hodges, Richard
    1987 Dark-age cities discovered. *Nature,* (22 October 1987), **329,** 673

Hughes, David W
    1984 Draughtsmen of the constellations, *Nature,* (20/27 December 1984), **312**, 697

Hugo, Victor quoted on page v of Frank Waters, q.v.

Hume Brown, P (ed)
    (1891) Early Travellers in Scotland (1295 to 1689). Edinburgh:David Douglas

Hutton, Ronald
    1991 The Pagan Religions of the Ancient British Isles, BCA:London, New York, Sydney, Toronto.

Jackson, Anthony
    1984 The Symbol Stones of Scotland. The Orkney Press Ltd., Victoria St., Stromness, Orkney.

Jones, J S
    A tale of three cities, *Nature* (18.5.1989) **339,**176

Keith, Arthur
    1928 Concerning Man's Origin. New York: G P Putnam's Sons

Langaney, André
    22 June1990. Les fausses couleurs du racisme, *L'Express international,* 31 cours des Juilliottes, 94713 Maisons-Alfort Cedex, France, pp.58-65

Laski, Marghanita
    1961 Ecstasy, a Study of some Secular and Religious Experiences. London: The Cresset Press

Lawrence, John
    1990. Lawrence of Lucknow. Hodder and Stoughton

Lawrence, P D
    1971 The Gregory family, PhD Thesis, Aberdeen university.

Lawrence, P D
    1980 James Gregorie, (1674-1733) his life and his books. Royal Society of Edinburgh, occasional papers No.1.

Lemesurier, Peter
    1976. Great Pyramid Decoded. London:Compton Russell

Lenihan, J M A and MacNeill, S
    1960, The Scale of the Highland Bagpipe, *Piping Times,* **13,** nos. 2-7.

Liebermann, Philip
        1991 Uniquely Human: the Evolution of Speech, Thought and Selfless Behaviour, Harvard University Press. Review by Paul Fletcher, *Nature* (11 April 1991), **350**
Lilienthal, David E.
        (1944) TVA : Democracy on the March, Penguin Books:Harmondsworth.
Livy, Titus
        Ab arbe condita. Ca. 27 BC I. 1.3
Loebl, Eugen
        1976 Humanomics. New York: Random House
Lynn, R
        1979 The social ecology of intelligence in the British Isles. *Journal of Social and Clinical Psychology*, **18**, 1-12.

MacFadyen, Dr Alastair
        1992 Dancing Dynasty, *The Scots Magazine*, March number, p.560
Macgregor, Forbes
        (1984) Famous Scots: the Pride of a Small Nation, Gordon Wright.
Mackay, Sheila
        1990 The Forth Bridge, A Picture History. Mowbray House Publishing:Edinburgh.
Mackenzie, Compton
        (1957) Rockets Galore, Chatto & Windus, pp.84,85
MacNeill, Seumas
        1968 Piobaireachd, Classical Music of the Highland Bagpipe. British Broadcasting Corporation, Edinburgh.
MacNeill, Seumas and Richardson, Frank
        1987 Piobaireachd and its Interpretation. John Donald, Edinburgh.
McNeill, William H
        1981 Trap for the unwary, *Nature*, (23 April 1981) **290**, 642-3
Mair, Philip Beveridge
        1982 Shared Enthusiasm, Ascent Books Ltd., Surrey, England
Martin, Jacques
        1986 and other dates. Personal communications.
Maxwell, James Clerk: Scotland's uncelebrated Genius
        The James Clerk Maxwell Foundation, 249 West George Street, Glasgow, G2 4RB. (Tel: 041-221 7090)
Mees, C E Kenneth
        1946 The Path of Science. New York: John Wiley & Sons, Inc.; London: Chapman & Hall Ltd.
Megaw, Ruth and Vincent
        1989 Celtic art, Thames and Hudson.
Menozzi, P, Piazza A., and Cavalli-Sforza, L.
        (1978) Synthetic Maps of Human Gene Frequencies in Europe, *Science*, **201**,786-792
Merle, René
        (1991) Une Naissance Suspendue S.E.H.T.D., c.p. 206, Lausanne 6:reviewed by Luc Weibel, *J de Genéve & Gaz de Lausanne*, 14,15 Sept 1991: "Suisse Romande, Le patois, langue oubliée".
Meyer, Niels I., Petersen, Helveg & Sorensen, Villy, 1981. Revolt from the centre. London: Marion Boyars.
Meylan, Henri
        1973 L'Histoire Vaudoise, published under his direction as Volume 4 of Encyclopédie Illustrée du Pays de Vaud. 24 Heures, Lausanne and Payot S A Lausanne, distributors.
Michell, John
        1983 The New View over Atlantis. Revised Edition Thames and Hudson:London pp.100-103
Michell, John
        1973 City of Revelation . Abacus: London, pp.7,15.

Milne, W P
    1942 Scholarship in the North-East. Transactions of the Buchan Club, Aberdeen:The University Press, 47-97.
Morgan, David
    (1986) The Mongols, The Peoples of Europe. Basil Blackwell, Oxford
Morell, Virginia
    (1990) Confusion in Earliest America. *Research News* (27 April), 439-441
Morris, Desmond
    (1984) The Book of Ages
Morrison, Tony
    1978 Pathways to the Gods, Salisbury, Wiltshire:Michael Russell
Mourant, A E & Watkin, I Morgan
    1952 Blood groups; anthropology and language in Wales and western counties, *Heredity*, **6,** 13-26
Mourant, A E
    1954 The Distribution of the Human Blood Groups, Blackwell:Oxford
Mourgues, Marcelle
    1983 Les danses de Provence, Jeanne Laffitte, Marseille
Myres, Sir John
    1943 Devastation. Journal Royal Anthropological Institute, **73**, 17-26
    1981 Revolt from the Centre. London: Marion Boyars

Oman, C W C
    (1913) A History of Greece. Longmans, Green & Co.:London (first printed 1900)

Paget, Richard
    1930 Human Speech, Kegan Paul, Trench, Trubner & Co.Ltd:London
Paget, Richard
    1935 This English. Kegan Paul etc.
Parsons, Denys
    1975 The Directory of Tunes and Musical Themes, Spencer Brown, Cambridge, and *New Scientist* 24 March 1977
Pendell, Elmer
    1977 Why Civilisations Self-destruct.
     Howard Allen Enterprises: Cape Canaveral
Petrie, W M Flinders
    1911 The Revolutions of Civilisation. London & New York: Harper & Brothers, 136pp
Piazza, A., Cappello, N., Olivetti E. & Rendine S.
    1988 A genetic history of Italy. *Ann.Hum.Genet.*, **52,**203-213
Piggott, Stuart
    1968 The Druids. Thames and Hudson:London, p.186
Pont, Graham
    17 August,1990. The Circle and the Cross
Pont, Graham and Nevile Jennie
    1990 Geography and human song, *New Scientist,* 20 January 56-59.
Potts, W T W
    1991 Who are the British? (in the Press)
Pulgram, E.
    1958 The Tongues of Italy. Harvard University Press:Cambridge, Mass.
Purser, John
    1992 Scotland's Music. A History of the Traditional and Classical music of Scotland from Earlier Times to the Present Day. Mainstream Publishing:Edinburgh & London in conjunction with BBC Scotland.

Ray, T P
    1989 The winter solstice phenomenon at Newgrange, Ireland, accident or design? *Nature,* (26/1/89) **337,** 343.

Renfrew, Colin
        1977 Ancient Europe is older than we thought. *National Geographical Magazine* **152** (No.5), 615-623.
Revel, Jean François
        (1985) How democracies perish, translated by William Byron:Weidenfeld and Nicholson. Review by Geoffrey Finlayson, *Scotsman,* 30 March 1985
Richards, Julian
        1991 Stonehenge. BCA London, New York, Sydney, Toronto
Richmond, Barry
        1990 "Systems Thinking: a critical set of Thinking Skills for the 90s and beyond". International System Dynamics Conference, 1990. quoted in *the Edradour School Newsletter,* autumn 1991, 1 (19), 11. Pitlochry, PH16 5JW; 0796 473868
Roberts, Richard G., Jones, Rhys and Smith, M A
        (1990) Thermoluminescence dating of a 50,000 year old human occupation site in northern Australia, *Nature* (10th May) **345**, 153-150.
Robertson, John Mackinnon
        1929 Shakespeare, *Encyclopedia Britannica,* 14th ed., **20,** 446.
Robertson, Robert H S
        1984 Music a clue to bright ancestors, *The Scorpion,* Issue No 6, Winter/Spring, pp.17-18
Robertson R H S
        1948 Some principles of raw material development. *The Advancement of Science,* **5** (17), 20-23. (Lecture to British Assocn., Section C, 1 Sept 1947, Dundee)
Robertson, R H S
        1961 Utilisation of minerals; research and development techniques in "Natural Resources in Scotland", Scottish Council (Development & Industry):Edinburgh
Robertson, Robert H S,
        1962 Some notes on the acceptability of mineral group names, *ClayMin, Bull,* **5**,41-43
Robertson, Robert H S
        1966 The Scottish Pre-Celtic Heritage, *Mankind Quarterly,* **7** (No. 1), 3-12
Robertson, Robert H S
        1976 Isonymy and genius. *Q,* (a short-lived journal). January,p15
Robertson, R H S
        (1978) Some general principles in the management of innovation, Discussion Paper 8, The Fraser of Allander Institute, University of Strathclyde.
Robertson, R H S
        1982 Petrie unpetrified: a re-examination of "Revolutions of Civilisation", *National Democrat,* Issue No. 2, Spring/Summer, p6
Robertson, Thomas
        1948 Human Ecology. Glasgow:William McLellan
Roy, Archie
        1984 (on the constellations) *Vistas in Astronomy,* **27,** 171
[Royal] Scottish Country Dance Society
        1930. The Scottish Country Dance Book No.2, dance 12: The Eightsome Reel. Patersons Publications Ltd:London,Edinburgh,New York.
Ross, Anna and Robins, Don
        1989 The Life and Death of a Druid Prince. Century Hutchinson Ltd and Guild Publishing: London

Sage, Donald, Memorabilia Domestica, 1650-1860.
Sauter, Marc-R
        (1977) Suisse Préhistorique, des origines aux Helvétes. Editions de la Baconnière, Neuchâtel-Suisse adapted from
        (1976) Switzerland from Earliest Times to the Roman Conquest Vol. 86 in the series *Ancient Peoples and Places* General editor: Professor Glyn Daniel
Schove, DJ
        1967 Sunspot Cycles *in* the Encyclopaedia of Atmospheric Sciences and Astrogeology, Encyclopaedia of Earth Sciences Series, Vol. II, edited by Rhodes W Fairbridge, Reinhold Publishing Corpn., New York, Amsterdam, London.

Sharp, David H
  1984 The contribution of the learned societies to international goodwill [BEST]. *Chemistry and Industry* (16 April) 282-85.
Schumacher, E F
  1973, Small is Beautiful, Blond & Briggs. Abacus edition 1988.
Shetelig, H and Brøgger, A, The Viking Ships, Dreyers Forlag, Norway
Smith, Roger
  1988 Transforming the Highlands Environment Now
Speiser, Stuart M
  1984a How to achieve peace and justice in our time. Council on International and Public Affairs, 777 United Nations Plaza, New York, NY10017.
Speiser, Stuart M
  1984b How to end the nuclear nightmare. North River Press Inc., Croton-on-Hudson, New York.
Speiser, Stuart M
  1986 The USOP Handbook. Council on International and Public Affairs. N.Y.
Spencer, John
  1990 The energy dependence syndrome. *Drug and Alcohol Review*, 9, 173-176
Spengler, Oswald
  1919 The Decline of the West
Stewart, Agnes Grainger
  1901 The Academic Gregories, Famous Scots Series, published by Oliphant Anderson and Ferrier, Edinburgh & London.
Sturlason, Snorre
  1931 Heimskringla or The Lives of the Norse Kings. Edited by Erling Monsen and translated with the assistance of A H Smith. Heffer:Cambridge

Tacitus ca 55 - ca 118 AD. Agricola, 11
Thom, Alexander
  1971 Megalithic Lunar Observatories. Oxford:Clarendon Press.
Thom, René
  1976 in reply to Dr James Croll's Is catastrophe theory dangerous? *New Scientist,* (17 June 1976) p.632
Thom, René
  1983 Mathematical Models of Morphogenesis. Ellis Horwood Halsted. Pp305. Reviewed by Brian Goodwin, *Nature* (1 May 1984), 309,93.
Thomson, D and Grimble, I
  1968, The Future of the Highlands, London:Routledge & Kegan Paul
Thompson, E A
  1975 The Icelandic Admixture Problem. *Ann. Human Genetics,* **37**, 69-80

Unwin, J D
  1940 Hopousia or The Sexual and Economic Foundations of a New Society. London: George Allen & Unwin

von Beckerath, Jürgen
  1971 Abriss der Geschichte des Alten Agypten, Verlag R Oldenbourg:München-Wien, pp.63-66.
Vogt, E
  (1948) Die Gliederung der schweizerischen Frühbronzezeit, *Festschrift O Tschumi,* Frauenfeld

Walker, Michael E
  Editor of *The Scorpion*, Schnellwelerstr. 50 5000 Köln, Germany.
Waters, Frank
  1963 Book of the Hopi. Ballantine Books a division of Random House Inc., New York. Twelfth printing August 1978.

Watson, William J
    1926 The history of the Celtic place-names of Scotland. William Blackwood: Edinburgh & London

Weibel, Luc
    1991 Suisse romande; Le patois, lanque aubilée, Journal de Genève et Gazette de Lausanne (14,15 Sept 1991) review of

Weyl, Nathianel
    1966 The Creative Elite in America, Public Affairs Press, Washington.

Weyl, Nathaniel
    1966 The Creative Elite of America, Public Affairs Press, Washington D.C., pp 22 and 25.

Wood, Ian
    1985 In search of the Trojan war. British Broadcasting Corporation and Bookclub Associates.

Woodcock, A., & Davis, M
    1978 Catastrophe Theory. Harmondsworth:Pelican, p.122

Woodham-Smith, Cecil
    (1962) The Great Hunger, 1845-9, Hamish Hamilton Ltd:London

Wormald, Jenny
    1981 Court, Kirk and Community, Edward Arnold: London

Youngs, Susan (ed)
    1989 'The Work of Angels', masterpieces of Celtic metalwork, 6th to 9th centuries, AD. British Museums Publications Ltd., London.

Zimmer, Heinrich
    1898 Matriarchy among the Picts. Translation by George Henderson in *Leabhar nan Gleann*, Edinburgh:Norman Macleod, The Mound

INDEX